Christophe
LIVING AND
IN PA.........

A guide to inexpensive living, retirement and making money in Central America's most overlooked country

Written by
CHRISTOPHER HOWARD

Christopher Howard's
LIVING AND INVESTING IN PANAMA

First Edition

First Edition, published in Costa Rica

© 2004-2006 Editora de Turismo Nacional, S.A.

ISBN 1-881233-12-X

Costa Rica Books
Suite 1 SJO 981
P.O. Box 025216
Miami, FL 33102-5216
www.costaricabooks.com
www.liveinpanama.com
www.amazon.com

"A fascinating place full of the most beautiful people and glorious landscapes..."

John Boorman, Director of the "Tailor of Panama"

ACKNOWLEDGEMENTS

This edition would not have become a reality without the invaluable help of many people.

I would first like to thank my graphic designer, William "El Mago" Morales, for his hard work and patience.

I am also very grateful to Mary De Waal and Pam at Blue JewelTravel.

A special thanks to the following local writers and Costa Rican residents for their contributions to this edition: Bruce Silverman, Les Nuñez , Paul Karns, Roger Gallo, Roberto Guardia, Kathleen Peddicord and so many others.

I would like to acknowledge all of the help I have received from the Publishers Marketing Association's and Amazon.com's programs for independent publishers. A special thanks to my Costa Rican distributor, 7th Street Books.

Finally, I would like to express my eternal gratitude to members of my family, especially my late mother, for their constant support when I needed it the most.

Christopher Howard
San José, Costa Rica

MORE ABOUT THE AUTHOR

Christopher Howard has resided in Costa Rica for twenty years and is a Costa Rican citizen.

During this time he has had the opportunity to gather a plethora of first-hand information about living, investing and retiring in Costa Rica, Nicaragua and Panama. It is not surprising that he has first-hand knowledge and insight into all aspects of CentralAmerica's culture and its people. Due to his expertise he is a frequent lecturer at numerous investment seminars.

Mr. Howard has an extensive foreign language background, having earned a B.A. in Latin American studies and a Master's degree in Spanish from the University of California, Berkeley. He also has credentials to teach Spanish at all levels from California State University, San Francisco.

The author in front of his home in Lagunilla de Heredia.

Howard was the recipient of scholarships for graduate study at the University of the Americas in Puebla, Mexico and the Jesuit University of Guadalajara, Mexico in conjunction with the University of San Diego, California. He has written three foreign language books including the best-selling *Costa Rican Spanish Survival Course* and, in 1985, founded a successful language institute in San José, Costa Rica.

At present, Chris Howard has been busy leading monthly relocation tours for people thinking of moving to Costa Rica; working as a paid consultant for *National Geographic Magazine*; putting the finishing touches on a book about Costa Rican idioms; publishing articles for various newsletter about living abroad and working on a feature action movie script to be filmed in Central America.

Christopher Howard's most successful title to date has been the number-one best-selling *"The New Golden Door to Retirement and Living in Costa Rica."* In 1999 Mr. Howard published the visionary guidebook, *"Living and Investing in the "New Cuba."* In 2001 he published the one-of-a-kind *"Living and Investing in the New Nicaragua."*

Finally, Mr. Howard serves as an officer on the Board of Directors of the Residents Association of Costa Rica.

CONTENTS

CHAPTER IV

CHAPTER V

(HAPTER VI

(HAPTER VII

(HAPTER VIII

CHAPTER IX

CHAPTER X

FOREWORD

WHY LIVE IN PANAMA?

More than 15,000 Americans currently live in Panama. This figure is not surprising since the Panama Canal Zone was under U.S. control until the year 2000. When the U.S. bases were operating there were around 60,000Americans living in and around Panama City. During this time the country had strong American presence and became very Americanized. In fact, in some ways the country is more like a U.S. colony than an independent nation. Most of the first-world infrastructure the U.S. put in place is still standing. As a result Panamanians learned to provide many services which are up to U.S. standards. Even neighboring Costa Rica, with all of its advances, cannot compare to Panama because of the deeply embedded U.S. influence.

Although Panama's official language is Spanish; English is widely spoken in the Panama City area.

International Living's annual Quality of Life Index ranks Panama as the 27th best country in the world for living.

Another reason for living in Panama is country's near-perfect climate. If you're tired of cold weather you will be happy to know Panama is hot and sometimes humid in the lowlands. Cooler year-round spring-like temperatures may be found in mountain areas like Boquete. In 2001 *Modern Maturity Magazine* (AARP) considered Boquete the fourth most desirable place in the world for retirement living partially due to its great climate.

Panama City is one of the most vibrant modern and prosperous cities in Latin America with over one million people. The city's array of tall skyscrapers are reminiscent of

Miami. It boasts incredible shopping, where almost any product from the U.S. may be easily found. At the same time, Panama has a very low population density with respect to its total area so you never feel crowded.

Panama is considered one of the safest counties in Latin America and has the highest rating for tourist safety from the Pinkerton Intelligence Agency. Because of the Panama Canal the country is still under the real protection and watchful eye of the United States.

The country fits the bill for anyone sick of the hustle and bustle, seeking a more laid-back way of life. It will also appeal to people of all ages seeking to move to a new and exotic land. The energetic entrepreneur, the burned-out baby boomer, those sick of long rush-hour commutes and anyone seeking an alternative way of life, will find Panama the ideal place to live.

Panama's beautiful, smiling people will make you feel welcome.

But Isn't It Expensive?

You will find Panama a place where you can maintain your current lifestyle for less money. Panama offers the world's best incentive program for retires. Residents pay NO local taxes on their foreign earned income.

Retires can bring in a new car and furniture every couple of years. On top of that, they receive substantial discounts ranging from 10% to 50% on a wide variety of local products and services.

What you really spend depends on your lifestyle. If you must have a luxurious home, drive a late model car and buy imported goods, you could spend as much or more than you would in the States. But if you live more like the locals, take advantage of all of the perks, and watch your spending, you will spend considerably less.

Many Americans living below the poverty line in the United States can live in moderate luxury on a modest retirement or investment income in Panama. The country lends itself perfectly to living and retiring overseas, something that was once reserved for a few wealthy individuals.

You will not have to worry about an unfavorable exchange rate since the U.S. dollar is the official currency. The cost of food, utilities and entertainment are all substantially lower than in the United States.

Panama's affordable medical care is among the best anywhere. The quality of health care is comparable to North America but the prices are one half or less! A local Panamanian Insurance Company can provide full medical insurance for under $50 per month per person. Even if you have to pay out of your own pocket, medical costs are still affordable.

Panama has an over all life-expectancy rate of 75.68, which is almost as high as — (72.94 for men and 78.53 for women)— the United States (76 for men, 79.8 for women).

Hired help is a bargain when compared to prices up north. A full-time maid can be hired for under $200 per month.

In Panama any legal resident may buy and own property. Retires do not have to pay property taxes until they sell their homes. On new homes there is a 20-year exoneration from taxes. Property prices are very reasonable when compared to what you will pay in the U.S., Canada or Europe. A decent apartment may be rented for as little as $200 per month. A luxury apartment in the best area of Panama City can range from $500 to $800 monthly. A new home may be purchased for under $50,000.

What gets people excited about Panama, however, is that it offers some of the best real estate on the planet at affordable prices. The price will eventually go up as the rest of the world catches on. There is only so much beautiful beachfront and prime real estate left in the world. When one considers that almost every bit of the coastline in the U.S. is becoming overcrowded and overpriced, Panama seems like a bargain.

An excellent transportation and communication network, the highest per capita income in Central America, a well-developed economic infrastructure, every imaginable activity to stay busy and happy, a government which goes to great lengths to make retirement and living as easy as possible, contribute to Panama's appeal and make it one of the world's top retirement and expatriate havens.

A Place to Invest

Word is getting out about Panama as an investment and banking haven. And that's why now is such a good time to invest.

The U.S. dollar is Panama's currency, which makes investing in the country easy. Panama offers some of the very best banking and communication services in Latin America.

Panama has a wealth of business opportunities awaiting creative hard-working entrepreneurs. You can run a global business by using Internet access, fax machines and cell phones. A business may be started for far less than in the United States. Wages are very low when compared to U.S. standards. Furthermore, tax incentives and a government which encourages investment contribute to a propitious business climate. As more and more foreigners move to Panama and tourism grows there will be an increasing need for travel related business and American products.

If you are foreign -born resident you will pay little or no taxes to your home country or Panama.

With the new millennium upon us, a shrinking world due to better communication, a burgeoning global economy— possibilities are unlimited for doing business in Central and South America. Trade pacts between Central America, U.S., Mexico and South America will be a reality by 2005. These trade agreements promise to link all of the nations in the hemisphere in to one trading block. Panama is sure to be an excellent base of operations.

Panama offers one of the world's best offshore tax havens and banking systems. The country is a time-proven business and tax haven with most of the country's 130 banks offer a high degree of secrecy. They also offer attractive CD's. There is NO tax on interest earned from bank accounts for locals or foreigners. Furthermore, there are NO corporate of personal taxes on offshore activity.

The Adventure of Starting Over

Some move to Panama to start over and seek adventure in an exotic land. They are tired of dead-end jobs or the rat race and want new challenges, a chance to pursue their dreams and achieve greater personal growth. As an expatriate, you have the challenge of immersing yourself in a new culture and, if you choose, the rewards of learning a foreign language.

Newcomers will make friends easily because foreigners gravitate towards one another. One Florida transplant told us he had lived in Florida for 20 years and hardly ever had contact with his neighbors. He claims not to be the most sociable person in the world, nevertheless he has made over a hundred friends in Central America. He proudly says, "Everywhere I go, I bump into people I know."

Adjusting and Keeping Busy

Adjustment to a new way of life can take many months. However, an open mind, a positive attitude and a willingness to seek out new experiences can make the transition relatively painless.

Central America, especially Panama and Costa Rica, has come a long way in the last decade. Satellite and Direct TV, private mail service and the Internet make it easier to stay in touch with family and friends in the United States and keep up with what is going on all over the world. If you do not own a computer, you can go to an *Internet café*.

Panama's modern technology has made life easy for foreign residents. In most areas of the country you can get cash at a local ATM, manage your investments online, and read almost any major newspaper in the world the day it comes out.

You will never be bored here unless you choose to be. Panama has something for everyone. This little known country offers a real paradise for the nature lover with its uncrowded beaches and mountains, the fishing enthusiast and water sports fanatic as well as the retiree. You can find hundreds of interesting activities such as movies in English, support groups, computer and bridge clubs. You name it, and Panama has it.

Seven Reasons Why Panama is The World's Top Retirement Haven
By Kathleen Peddicord, International Living

Panama City is a complete surprise, especially the first time you see it. A skyline of skyscrapers, modern office buildings and hotels, all glass and steel, facing out over the water. Just like New York. Just like Miami.

That's the impression as you drive in from the airport. As you get closer, you notice upscale restaurants and shops on many streets, a bank on nearly every corner (there are more than 80 international banks in Panama and all are physically present, as brass plate banking is not permitted) and then you realize that the roads you're traveling on are well-paved and pothole-free, and that the people walking along are well-dressed.

If you spend time here, you will realize that the city is virtually crime-free and that there's no violent crime here whatsoever.

In Panama City, you can avail of any service or convenience you take for granted back home. Every major franchise and most major retailers are here And the infrastructure (yes, largely thanks to the extended U.S. presence) is First World, even if the country technically isn't.

Panama has switched successfully from military (a common denominator for typical Banana Republics) to elected rule. And it is stable not only politically, but also economically, thanks largely to the U.S. dollar, which it uses as its currency and to its geographic position, at the 'crossroads of the Americas.'

Historically, Panama has been recognized as a bridge literally and figuratively and today this country is the largest trading zone in the Western Hemisphere and the second-largest in the world. Panama is the world's largest shipping registry. And the Colon free trade zone is the largest in the Americas, second in the world only to Hong Kong.

In short, Panama is on its way to becoming the world's top retirement haven. It will become the next San Miguel de Allende, Lake Chapala, or San Jose, Costa Rica. Here's why.

First, Panama offers advantages over every other Central and South American destination. Tax advantages. Privacy advantages. Indeed, it is one of the world's best jurisdictions for offshore asset protection and banking. If you're looking for a private, offshore bank account, a tax-free corporation, a trust, or other offshore structures, Panama is one of the few places in the world worth considering right now.

Second, this country offers near-perfect weather, especially in the interior (mountainous) Chiriqui region.

Third, Panama offers what we consider to be the world's best incentive program for retires, offering substantial savings on everything from mortgage rates to utility bills.

Fourth, Panama is a very affordable place to live. A full-time, live-in maid costs $120 a month...first-run movies cost $1.50. Groceries cost 20% to 30% less than in the United States.

Fifth, Panama is the safest place in Central or South America (the Pinkerton Global Intelligence Agency recently gave Panama its highest rating for tourist safety), boasting stable political and economic situations.

Sixth, it's the most developed country south of the United States, home to some of the top companies in the world (including 80 of the world's biggest banks, and other giants such as Federal Express, DHL, Sears, Price Costco, and Bell South) and many top-drawer restaurants and hotels. You could even call Panama City 'sophisticated.' And, as I've mentioned, you'd certainly have to call its infrastructure First World.

Seventh, Panama uses the U.S. dollar as its currency and has virtually no inflation. By the way, here it's not a case of 'dollarization' as a recent experiment as elsewhere in Latin America; the U.S. dollar has been Panama's official paper currency since 1904.

As The Economist recently reported, in Central America, 'Panama has stood apart, sustained by its Canal, its banks, and its free-trade zone.'

In short, Panama has its act together. Yet few foreigners, particularly Americans, consider Panama as a travel destination...and even fewer think of it as a 'retirement haven.'

In 1998, the most recent year for which the World Tourism Organization has tourist figures, the country's total overnight visitor count was 431,000...100,000 of whom came from the United States. To put this in perspective: Panama gets about as many American tourists in a year as Disneyland sees in three days.

In other words, there's plenty of room for you.

*Courtesy of International Living. For more information about International Living see: **www.internationalliving.com**

Things to Think About Before Moving to A New Country or Making Foreign Investments.

☐ What is required to become a legal resident? Can I meet these requirements? What is the cost? How often does residency have to be renewed, what are the conditions of renewal and what is the cost?

☐ What is required to visit, or stay while I'm waiting for residency?

☐ What is the political situation? How stable is the country?

☐ Weather (Will I like the weather year-round?)

☐ Income taxes (Will I be taxed on income brought into the country?) (Am I allowed to earn income in the country?) If yes, (How is it taxed?)

☐ Other taxes? (Sales tax, import duties, exit taxes, vehicle taxes, etc.)

☐ How much will it cost in fees, duties, import taxes to bring my personal possessions into the country? (Cars, boats, appliances, electronic equipment, etc.)

☐ Rental property - How much? Availability?

☐ Purchase property - Property taxes, restrictions on foreign ownership of property, expropriation laws, building regulations, squatters rights, etc. Is there a capital gains tax?

☐ Communications - Are there reliable phone and fax lines, cellular phones, beepers, connections to Internet and other computer communication service? Is there good mail service between the country and the rest of the world? Are there private express mail services like DHL, UPS and FEDEX? Are there local newspapers, radio and TV in a language I will understand? Is there cable or satellite TV available?

☐ Transportation - How are the roads? Are flights available to places I will want to go? How are the buses and taxis ? How costly is it to travel to and from other international destinations?

☐ Is it difficult for friends and family to visit?

☐ Shopping - Are replacement parts available for the items you have brought from home? If so, what are the costs? If not, how much will it cost to import what I need?

☐ Are the types of food I am accustomed to readily available in both markets and restaurants?

☐ If I have hobbies, are clubs, supplies and assistance available?

☐ What cultural activities are available? (Art, music, theatre, museums, etc.)

☐ What entertainment is available? (Sports, movies, nightclubs, dancing, etc.)

- [ ] What recreational facilities are available? (Golf courses, tennis, health clubs, recreational centers, parks, etc.)
- [ ] If I like the beach, are good beaches available? Can they be reached easily? What is the year round temperature of the water?
- [ ] What is the violent crime rate? Minor crime (theft, car and house break-ins)? What support can be expected from the police department? Are the police helpful to foreign residents?
- [ ] How do local residents treat foreign visitors and residents?
- [ ] What are the local investment opportunities? Is there any consumer or protective legislation for investors? What return can I expect from my investments?
- [ ] Is the banking system safe and reliable? Can they transfer funds and convert foreign currency, checks, drafts, and transfers? Are checking, savings and other accounts available to foreigners? Is there banking confidentiality? Is there a favorable rate of exchange with the U.S. dollar?
- [ ] Are good lawyers, accountants, investment advisors and other professionals available?
- [ ] How difficult is it to start a business? What kinds of opportunities are there?
- [ ] How is the health care system? Is it affordable? Do they honor U.S. and Canadian health insurance? Are there any diseases which are dangerous to foreigners, and if so does the local health care system address the problem? What is the quality of hospitals, clinics, doctors and dentists? What is the availability of good specialists?
- [ ] How is the sanitation? Can I drink the water? Do the restaurants have good sanitation standards? Are pasteurized milk and other dairy products available? Do meat, fish, and vegetable markets have satisfactory sanitary standards?
- [ ] If I am interested in domestic staff, what is the cost of cooks, housekeepers and gardeners, etc.? Is the local help reliable? What regulations are involved in hiring employees? What are the employers' responsibilities to the workers?
- [ ] What legislation is there to protect foreign residents? What rights do foreign residents have in comparison to citizens?
- [ ] What natural disasters are there? (Hurricanes, tornadoes, typhoons, earthquakes, droughts, floods.)
- [ ] Can pets be brought into the country?
- [ ] Is there religious freedom?

*Courtesy of the Costa Rican Residents Association

PANAMA'S LAND, HISTORY AND PEOPLE

The Lay of the Land

Panama is the southernmost country in Central America. It occupies an area of about 30,000 square miles which is about the size of South Carolina. Bordered by Costa Rica to the west and Colombia to the east, it is a long narrow country in the shape of a horizontal S. The country is between 50 and 120 miles wide and is bounded on each side by 477 miles of Caribbean and 767 miles of Pacific coastline. Thus, the country has almost endless coastline on both sides for beach lovers. The isthmus of Panama is the narrowest land mass between the Atlantic and the Pacific Oceans. The narrowest point being about 35 miles wide. The Panama Canal which is about 60 miles long and divides the country into eastern and western regions.

A mountain chain stretches almost the entire length of the country. The highest peaks of this range are in the west. Volcán Barú in western Chiriquí Province is the highest point in the country. The country also has around 500 rivers which empty into the Caribbean and Pacific.

PANAMA GENERAL INFORMATION

Capital	Panama City
Population	2,800,000
Size	30,420 square miles
Quality of Life	Excellent,(good weather, friendly people, affordable)
Official Language	Spanish (English is widely spoken)
Political System	Democracy
Currency	US dollar $1.00 = 1 Balboa
Annual per capita income	$3,000
Investment Climate	Good-many opportunities
Official Religion	85% are Roman Catholic
Foreign Population *(U.S., Canadian and European)*	Around 20,000
Longevity	75.68 is almost as high the U.S.
Literacy	90.8%
Time	Eastern Standard (U.S.)

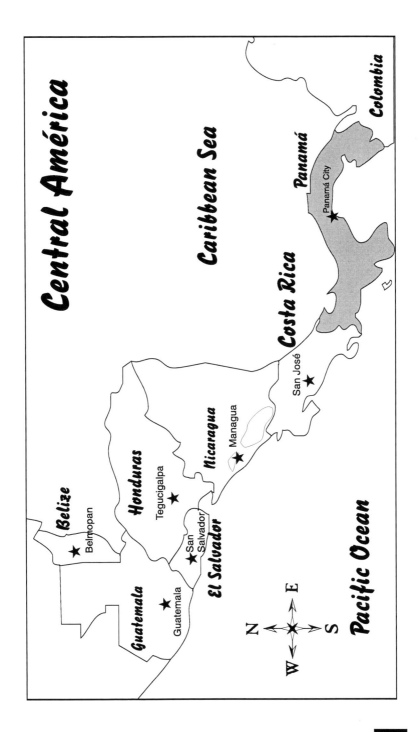

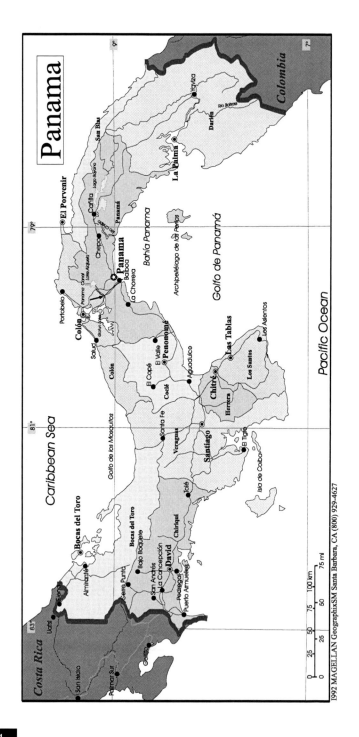

1992 MAGELLAN GeographixSM Santa Barbara, CA (800) 929-4627

Panama also has a large number of islands scattered on both sides of the isthmus. The two main island groups, both on the Caribbean side, are the Bocas del Toro and San Blás Archipelagos.

Due to its climate Panama has a wide variety of animal and plant life. Panama's lush verdant forests contain the greatest number of species of all the new world's countries north of Colombia. Thirty percent of the country's total land is set aside for conservation.

Politically Panama is divided into nine provinces two Indian territories (*Comarcas*): Bocas del Toro, Coclé, Chiriquí, Darién, Herrera, Los Santos, Panama, Veraguas and the Comarcas of Kuna Yala and Emberá.

Weather

Panama has a tropical climate since it lies so near the equator. Its weather is pleasant year round with temperatures remaining constant. So, most of the time you'll be able to dress in lightweight clothing . A jacket may be needed at some of the higher elevations. Don't forget your umbrella for the rainy season. U.S. style rain gear is too warm and cumbersome for the tropics.

Temperatures vary little from season to season and fluctuate with altitude. Weather can also vary due to location. The higher you go, the colder it gets, and the lower you go the warmer it is. The sea-level temperature is around 80 to 85 degrees F. (27 degrees C.) most of the year. The Atlantic side tends to receive more rain. The weather on the Pacific side of the country is to be drier both on the coast and in the mountains.

Like the rest of Central America, Panama only has two seasons. The summer or *verano* is generally from late December to mid-April with March and April being the warmest months of the year. The rainy season or *invierno*, runs from mid-April to December. However, there is plenty of sunny weather during the rainy season.

During the wet season, many mornings are sunny and clear with only a few hours of rain in the afternoons. Since the temperature varies little, the wet months are usually as warm as the dry months. It is unusual to have two or three days of continuous rainy weather in most areas of the country. October is usually the rainiest month of the year.

Foreigners should not let the rain get them down since there are a variety of indoor activities available. Panama City has many museums, theaters, malls, casinos, roller skating rinks, Internet Cafés and other indoor activities that will more than keep you busy when it rains.

Where to Live in Panama

Panama City is the country's capital and definitely place for those who like the stimulation of living in a modern cosmopolitan metropolis. It is home to more than half of the country's population and a bustling center of international banking and commerce. The original city was founded the the Spaniard Pedro Arias Dávila in 1519.

Panama City runs about 7 miles along the Pacific Coast, with Panama Bay (*La Bahía de Panamá*) on the south, the Panama Canal on the west and the ruins of Panamá la Vieja to the east. Most avenues run parallel to the coast with streets running perpendicularly.

Modern day Panama City boasts a wide range of architecture, from stately 16th century homes in Casco Viejo, the oldest part of the city, to the city's imposing Miami-like string of high-rise buildings. Prestigious neighborhoods like Alto de Golf, Dos Mares abound with greenery and flowers. Other areas as Obarrio, Campo Alegre, Paitilla and El Cangrejo teem with interesting buildings and designs.

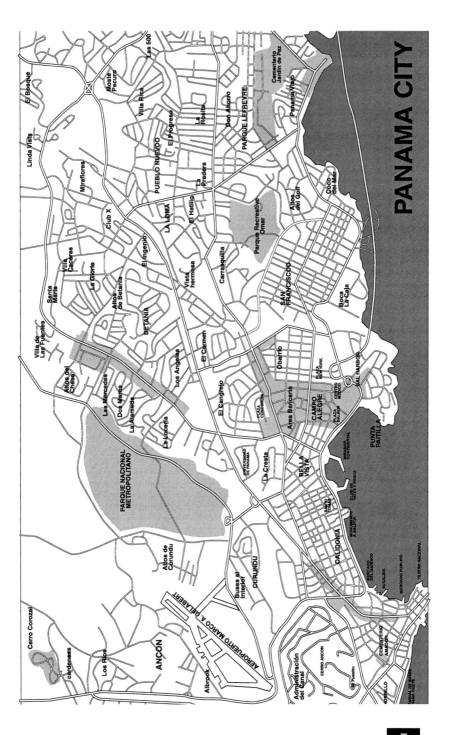

PANAMA CITY

The city's other treasures include a palm-lined *Malecón* (waterfront promenade) the historic ruins of Panama la Vieja and much more. There is even a rainforest reserve within the city limits at Parque Metropolitano.

Panama City has perhaps the best shopping in Central America. Therefore it attracts visitors from neighboring countries. Due to a long-time U.S. presence in the country, American products are easily found. Prices are similar to what they are in the States. Foreign residents can find many products from their home town. There are dozens of shopping centers to meet your needs. The stores that dot the *Avenida Central* pedestrian mall and Vía España offer first-class shopping. Thanks to low import duties, shoppers can find incredible bargains.

There is no shortage of urban amenities in Panama City. Panamanians love nightlife and there are numerous establishments where you can always find some action. In addition, the city offers more than 300 international restaurants,

Panama City's imposing skyline

modern supermarkets, theaters, movie theaters, discos, bars, cabarets, casinos and more.

Familiar spots like TGI Fridays can even be found here. Entertainment costs about half the price you would pay in any U.S. city. Visitors remark that the city reminds them of Miami but prices are much more reasonable.

For sports enthusiasts there is an American-style golf and country club located near the city. Nature lovers will find rainforests and beaches nearby.

The city's infrastructure is excellent. This is primarily due to the long U.S. presence in the area. Most streets in the city are paved with concrete instead of asphalt. The downtown area has a real first-world ambience. Tocumen International Airport is located about 20 miles from downtown Panama City. It is easy to get around the city by using taxis and public transportation.

Here are some of the areas where you might want to consider living, taking different tastes and budgets into consideration. A three bedroom apartment in Panama City can be purchased for under $100,000; a home on a former military base may cost $70,000 to $150,000; and a new condo in a high rise in **Punta Paitilla** will go for around $150,000 to $175,000. Land in the countryside or a small town is much less expensive.

Panama City is divided into a series of neighborhoods. The city's old section, *Casco Viejo* or 'old city", was founded in 1673 as a fort. It is the historic center of today's capital. Casco is a quite charming district of narrow streets overlooked by balconies of two and three storied houses. The facades of many of the buildings, with their wrought-iron balconies appear to be frozen in time. This area has cobblestone streets and rich ethnic diversity. At its tip lies French Park, the lovely French Embassy, a monument to the French builders who began the Panama Canal, . The area has three basic styles of architecture: Spanish, Italian and French. The latter style reminds many , including the author of New Orlean's French Quarter.

There has been some gentrification in this area with many of the old buildings restored to their former splendor. Enterprising entrepreneurs are beginning to realize this area's potential and are renovating homes. Many homes have been converted into trendy restaurants. **Las Bóvedas**, a prime example of the restoration process, is a French restaurant located in a former colonial jail in Casco Viejo.

The government is even offering incentives to encourage investment in *Casco Viejo*. As a whole this area has a long way to go but is worth considering due to its unique ambiance and many possibilities. Rubén Blades, Panama's most famous singer and actor, has a beautifully restored three-story home

Casco Viejo is reminiscent of New Orleans' French Quarter.

looking out over the bay facing Panama City. It is an excellent example of what one can do to restore one of the many old homes found in this charming area.

Balboa is the area of once called the "Canal Zone." At one time it was the center of U.S. military activity in Panama. Balboa looks like a microcosm of the U.S. with its wide palm-tree lined boulevards and streets and American-style homes. Many good housing bargains can be found since the U.S. pullout. There are a number of single-family homes and duplexes in this area as well as the other former bases. The old Officers homes and facilities are more sumptuous than the homes for enlisted men. The latter are usually made of wood and not as big, however the cost is lower. Many of the homes have two stories. Amador, Albrook, Ft. Clayton and Ancon are other former military bases which offer good housing.

An upscale Panamanian home

Marbella is an area of exclusive high-rise living. Due to its convenient central location, many excellent services are found around this neighborhood. There are luxury apartments for rent and sale here.

Punta Paitilla is another affluent part of town and very popular with foreigners. Housing here has all the amenities of the U.S., Canada or Europe. There are numerous high-rise apartment complexes with apartments for rent or sale. They all have swimming pools and indoor parking. Do not be discouraged by the high prices. If you look hard bargains can be found. Good shopping, including a new megamall, can be found nearby.

The **El Dorado** neighborhood is more middle class than the areas just mentioned. It was once very popular among foreigners and military families. Malls and shopping centers are found there. There is affordable housing in the area.

San Francisco is a predominately middle-class Panamanian neighborhood. Affordable single family homes are for rent and sale in this area. It is less densely populated than some of the other sections which makes it suitable for living. Excellent shopping is also found there.

The **Obarrio** area is found near the banking district. Single homes are plentiful and there is a foreign population living in this part of town. At present, there is a great deal of construction going on there.

El Cangrejo is a pleasant hilly neighborhood with both single family homes, high-rise buildings and other housing options. Restaurants, good shopping and other services are available. The financial area is located within this area.

El Carmen and **Coco Bay** are other areas you might want to consider for living in Panama City. Major services are found nearby.

If you don't like the hustle and bustle and heat of Panama City there are mountain areas from which to choose.

About an hour's drive northeast of Panama City is **Cerro Azul**. A housing development nearby with the same name. The elevation is about 2,500 to 2,800 feet and the climate is much cooler than Panama City's. Prices start at about $80,000 for a three-bedroom home. **Altos de María** is another development 60 miles west of Panama City in a mountain area about 10 miles (as the crow flies) from **El Valle de Antón**. Due to its higher elevation, the area enjoys year-round spring-like weather with temperatures ranging between 60 to 70 degrees. This place is perfect for anyone who wants to "get away from it all" and still enjoy quality lifestyle. **Chorrera**, the quickest growing city in the area, is less than an hour away and offers good infrastructure including supermarkets, restaurants, shopping centers, movies and more. Beaches are accessible from this there.

The picturesque town of **El Valle de Antón** is another area to consider. This resort is located about 2 hours west of Panama City in a crater of an extinct volcano. Hence it gets its name *"El Valle"* which means valley in Spanish. If you like a cool year-round climate this spot might be the place you're looking for. The abundant vegetation makes this area ideal for ecotourism. The town has become a week-end retreat for many of the people who live in Panama City with many wealthy Panamanians have their country homes there. The most salient feature of this town is its local zoo. There are some basic services found there. Market day is every Sunday with residents of neighboring towns selling their handicrafts.

Located west of Panama City along the Pan-American Highway are Panama's Central Provinces: Coclé, Veraguas, Herrera and Los Santos.

Coclé Province is located right in the center of the Panamanian Isthmus and famous for its rich culture heritage. It is also known as the birthplace of the largest number of Panamanian presidents. The city of **Penonomé** is the capital of this province. Santa Clara and Farallón are two white-sand beaches.

Veraguas is the only province in Panama with coasts on both oceans. This province is rich in natural wonders including rivers, lakes, waterfalls, beaches and incredible mountain scenery. From its capital, **Santiago**, one can explore the **Golfo de Montijo**, famous for its world class sportfishing. **Playa Santa Catalina** is a world-famous surfing area in this province.

The Province of **Chiriquí** is considered to be the most beautiful region of the country. **Boquete** is a tranquil town in the heart of Chiriquí province. It lies in a verdant valley surrounded by mountains. *Boquete* means "gap" in Spanish, which appropriately describes the town's setting. Its spring-like weather, rich flora and fauna combine to make it one of the country's top retirement areas in the world. The Caldera River runs right through the center of town. Boquete is tucked into a fertile landscape of coffee plantations and orange groves where you can escape the heat of the lowlands (temperatures in the valley average 80 to 90 degrees year round). A variety of outdoor activities like bird watching and hiking may be practiced in the area surrounding Boquete.

Trout fishing is also excellent. Hot springs can be found in the town of Caldera near Boquete.

A local attraction is the nearby **Volcán Barú** (11,450 feet). It lies directly west of the city and is the most dominant geographic feature in the area. If you are in good shape you can take an all-day hike to summit of the Barú Volcano—the

Altos Del Maria
Live in a Garden in The Mountains of Panama
by Roger Gallo

The temperature is 75 degrees, there is no humidity, I can see for hundreds of miles, out over the oceans, both oceans, the Atlantic and the Pacific, there are flowers and trees everywhere, two rivers, hiking trails, dozens of creeks, beautiful houses, excellent neighbors, paved roads, electricity, telephone, internet connections, Direct TV, pine trees, waterfalls, a heliport, and I'm 20 minutes by car from the beach and 20 minutes from a golf course.

The building lots average a half acre in size, they range in price from $20,000 to $70,000, you can get in for ten percent down with low interest financing, building costs are under $35 a square foot and the construction is terrific.

You are one hour from Panama City. You can own horses, the area is a garden paradise with more species of birds than almost anywhere on earth, there are no earthquakes, no floods, no crime, no hurricanes, no tornados, and no taxes.

Over 3,800 acres in size, Altos is the most ambitious real estate development in Panama. What it has that most other developments don't have is proximity to Panama City, cool temperatures in a 24/7/364 mountain-top guarded and gated community. Altos has views that are breath-taking, perfect year round temperatures, crystal clear mineral water, a flawless infrastructure, plus roads, flowers, trees, and garden-like landscaping within its vast common area that is lovingly maintained 364 days a year by a crew of very dedicated groundskeeper.

Altos sets a very high standard for gated communities worldwide, especially in such an affordable price range. There is over 42 Kilometers of paved roads, roads which are maintained daily by the Altos' maintenance crew. Consisting of over 3,800 acres of land that is rich with indigenous trees, plants and flowers, Altos consists of several distinct sections, four of which are already up and running. The first four sections consist of 680 lots, 350 of which have already been sold. The project consists of wide 'green areas' upon which there will be no construction. There are 25 Kilometers of natural trails in the area, five kilometers of which have been improved with the addition of suspension bridges, stairways, walkways and buttresses. Yes, you can own horses and you can ride for miles without ever crossing a public road.

The temperature is another great attraction. Panama lowlands can be hot and humid at certain times of the year. Altos has perfect year round temperatures, with averages in the high and low seventies depending on the elevation of your house. [I am told it gets down into the sixties, but I haven't been up there in the evening yet so I cannot verify that statement.] I understand that it gets cool enough at night that many residents have fireplaces, a rarity in Panama, though they are more for pleasure than necessity; neither air conditioning nor heating is a requirement in Altos — one of the reasons the area was chosen for the project. Many houses have pools which can be used year round, although you are only 20 minutes from several beaches, so one has the choice of pool or beach any day of the year.

There is excellent grocery shopping in the beach area, plus a number of other facilities discussed on the next page, and also major shopping in Panama City, including numerous fine restaurants, theaters and a fair range of entertainment. The four main beaches are Punta Chame, Gorgona, Coronado and Punta Barco. There is also the resort town of El Valle in close proximity to Altos, which is connected by paved road, and which is also accessible by horse back or four wheel drive through the back side of Altos.

Altos is a gardeners' paradise as everything grows in the rich volcanic soil. While the soil is volcanic, there are no active volcanos in Panama, nor have there been for all of recorded history. They are a thing of the far distant past. No earthquakes and no volcanos is the reason that Panama was picked as the location for the canal and not Nicaragua. There are flowers everywhere, and in areas where there are not indigenous trees, pines have been planted, making large areas of the upper sections into pine forest. Many houses had potting sheds, and the project itself has its own greenhouse for residents and for common area maintenance.

In addition to Altos being a gardener's dream come true, the resort town of El Valle just a short drive away has a major nursery that is famous throughout Panama. There is also a weekend street market in El Valle where fresh produce, nursery products and a wide range of handicrafts are sold. The soil from this region is sold all over Panama. It is a black soil so rich that when ranchers put fence posts into the ground the fence posts grow branches and leaves. (I know this sounds like the wildest hyperbole, but I'm willing to bet anyone reading this five hundred dollars that it is a fact.) It is the best soil I have ever seen and it has not been subject to pollution, over population, nor pesticides. Panama is an ecologically sound nation with one of the lowest population density to land mass ratios in the Americas if not the world.

*Courtesy of **www.escapeartist.com**. This site is the world's best for anyone thinking of living abroad.

country's highest peak. The view is amazing. On a clear day you can see both the Pacific Ocean and the Caribbean. Some adventurous souls hike from the nearby community of **Cerro Punta** to **Boquete**. Both **Cerro Punta** and **Volcán** are two beautiful towns in the area.

Lately much has been written about the town of Boquete as an ideal expatriate and retirement haven. In late 2001, *Modern Maturity* magazine rated Boquete as the 4th best place in the world to retire because of the excellent quality of life found there.

To quote the article, "If you love tropical lushness and don't need big city stimulation, this lively little community near the Costa Rica Border may be just the place for you." The Town's many American and European expats appreciate the modest cost of living (you will need about 25 percent less to

Beautiful Boquete in all its splendor

live here than in a suburb of a medium-size U.S. city), the clean air, outdoor activities, river rafting, tennis and golf.

In Boquete land costs between $8 and $15 per square meter. A decent three bedroom home may be purchased for around $50,000. Of course, larger properties are more expensive.

A three-bedroom house rents from about $450 monthly; a simple meal can be found for $4-5. There are a few restaurants, a pizzería, a bank, small hotels, a post office, and an a good supermarket. However, for special products it is necessary to travel to the city of **David**.

Basic medical care is available at the **Centro Médico San Juan Bautista**. People with major problems or need to see a specialist you will need to go to David or Panama City.

If you are a laid back type then you'll feel right at home living in the town of Boquete.

Valle Escondido or Hidden Valley is a nice development with Spanish colonial style buildings located near Boquete. This gated community offers a whole slew of amenities including a 9-hole Executive Golf Course and Proshop (opening January 2004), private country club with Tennis, swimming, beautiful parks and walking paths, jacuzzi and dayspa (opening January 2004), a 750 seat outdoor amphitheater with year round schedule of events, a serviced equestrian center, Valle Escondido Pueblo shopping center with over 20 retail shops, services and restaurants (opening January 2004) and fully furnished two and three bedroom Golf Vista Residences. Finally, by 2005 they plan to have an on-site world-class health facility with medical professionals including health insurance, prescription drugs and other services are all available at a fraction of the cost.

David is Panama's third most populous city, has around 100,000 residents and is the capital of Chiriquí Province. Due to the fact that this city is located in the lowlands it remains hot and humid all year. David has good infrastructure.

Shopping is excellent with such U.S. chains as Price smart and Costco. The city has major services like an airport, post office, hospital, movie theaters and more.

Beach lovers will happy to know to know there are numerous beaches within a short distance of Panama City.

Playa Kobbe is a popular beach just across the canal from Panama City. **Playa Veracruz** is another beach area.

A few hours west of Panama City lay some of the country's nicest beaches. A string of beaches extends from **Punta Chane** to **Punta Corona**. We have been told that reasonably priced home can be found in this area.

You also have the choice of living on a island. **Isla Contadora** (translated as "teller' or "counting house" for pearls), located 20 miles southwest in the Pearl Islands in Panama Bay, is another place to consider. Contadora is one of a hundred or so Pearl Islands, the seventh largest. It is famous for its turquoise water, coves, white-sand beaches, coral reefs, copious sea life, excellent fishing, snorkeling and diving and for being a retreat for the rich and famous. The late Shah of Iran chose to live in exile here after he was toppled from power. The island can be reached easily by ferry. There is adequate infrastructure including, bars, restaurants, hotels, a medical center, and 9-hole golf course.

Isla Taboga, or "Island of the Flowers" as it is known, is a 90-minute ferry ride from Panama City. The island is a beautiful spot with nice beaches and surrounded by clear water.

Farallón and **Costa Blanca** are popular beaches in **Coclé** Province. The **Azuero** Peninsula from **Chitre** to **Punta Mala** and around to **Tonosi** has some beautiful beaches.

La Playa de Las Lajas, about an hour's drive from David, is a beautiful white sand beach in Chiriqui Province.

Maria Chiquita and **Playa Langosta** are nice two beaches on the way to Portobelo in the Costa Arriba area . The Island of Isla Grande, with its crystal-clear waters, is another nice spot in this area.

A discussion of beach areas would hardly be complete without mentioning **Bocas del Toro**, located in the remote northeast coast.

Despite being the name of Panama's entire Caribbean province, most people associate it with the archipelago of six islands bearing the same name, and dozens of smaller islands within the Chiriquí Lagoon. Because of this unique geographical feature this area is sometimes called "the Venice of Panama". The archipelago is made up of six large islands and some smaller ones. The largest island is Colón Island, followed by Popa Island, Bastimientos Island, Cristóbal Island, Water Key and Carenero Key.

Bocas has some excellent beaches, a variety of water sports from which to choose, ample accommodations, restaurants featuring seafood and typical Panamanian cuisine, a marina and a lot of prime real estate. English is the main language of the friendly locals of Caribbean descent.

Isla Colón or Colón Island is the most visited and developed of the Bocas del Toro islands. On its southwest tip is its main town and province capital, Bocas del Toro. You can reach the island by boat or by air from David or Panama City.

The surrounding area is famous for its forest covered islands and having some of the most spectacular white-sand beaches in Central America and the Caribbean. Bocas is well-known for its excellent diving, snorkeling, surfing and fishing,

Drago Beach is a nice area on Colón Island. Bastimientos Marine Park is a spectacular underwater wildlife sanctuary.

Bastimientos offers pristine coral reefs and good sites for water sports at Larga Beach and Zapatilla Beach.

The archipelago has everything including European restaurants, a bank in the main town of Bocas, an airport, phone service, Internet connection, low crime, no hurricanes, and a half dozen hotels.

You will also find some of the most affordable and beautiful real estate along the beaches of Bocas del Toro. Houses rent from $200 to $1000 monthly. Lots go for as low as $20,000. You can even build your dream home for under $50,000.

The area's homes reflect the influence of the United Fruit Company as well as the immigrants from different areas of the Caribbean.

One word of caution about buying property in this area. There are a lot of people hustling real estate. Be careful with whom you deal. Another problem is that many properties are not titled. There are two types of titles here: "Right to Possession' and "Titled Land." Unfortunately many properties fall into the first category and do not have clear title.

We haven't touched on every area of Panama. If you are seriously interested in exploring the country for living and retirement, we suggest you read Lonely Planet's Panama guidebook, then visit the areas where you think you may want to live.

A One-of-a-kind Tour of Panama

One way to see Panama that is to take one of the introductory tours operated by **Live in Costa Rica Tours**, toll free 800 365-2342 or bluejeweltravel@cox.net. They have conducted relocation and retirement tours in Costa Rica and Nicaragua for the last ten years and have helped 1000s of people move successfully to the area and find new exciting lifestyles they never thought they could afford.

Below is a sample itinerary from their unique Panama tour.

Day 1:

Arrive in Panama City. Register at the Hotel . Dine together if your flight arrives before dinner.

Day 2:

Breakfast. Tour of Panama City including best areas to live, the canal, shopping centers, supermarkets, hospitals, banks and more.

Day 3:

Early morning bus trip to David. Lunch on the road. Tour of the basic infrastructure of David. Dinner.

Day 4:

A day in the beautiful mountain area of Boquete and surroundings.

Day 5:

Return to Panama City by bus. People wanting to fly can pay a higher rate and return by plane. Farewell dinner.

Day 6:

Departure.

* Those people who want to visit Bocas del Toro can book additional days or leave from David and return to Panama City by air.

Panama's History in Brief

Panama has always seemed to be under the influence of foreign peoples and nations. At the beginning of the 16th century more than 60 native tribes belonging to the Mayan civilization of Guatemala and the Chibchas of Columbia inhabited Panama.

The isthmus of Panama was discovered in 1501 by the Spanish explorer Rodrigo de Bastidas, one of the captains who accompanied Colombus on his second voyage to America. In September 1513 Vasco Nuñez de Balboa discovered the Pacific Ocean from a mountain in the Darien province of Panama. In 1519 Pedro Arias de Avila founded the city of Panama. On the Pacific side near where Panama City stands today.

By founding Panama City the Spanish established the first-European trading post on the Pacific coast. By the 16th century, goods from Asia were passing through Panama on their way to Europe. Increasing prosperity and wealth caught the eye of pirates who were roaming the Caribbean area. Despite building several fortifications the Spanish found it difficult to stem the incursions of the pirates. This forced the Spanish to abandon Panama and to start to ship their goods around Cape Horn to the western coast of South America.

On November 28, 1821 Panama declared its independence from Spain. Panama joined a new political unit of Gran Colombia, which consisted of present day Columbia, Peru, Venezuela, Ecuador and Bolivia. Later Gran Columbia split up but Panama remained a province of Columbia.

Panama began to take on increasing importance in the region when many nations realized that the isthmus was the narrowest point between the Pacific and Atlantic oceans. The year 1848 marked the beginning of the California gold rush. The east-west journey across the isthmus became a popular

The Big Ditch
by Panama Tom

Ever since 8000B.C. the 50-mile isthmus of Panama has been used as a transit route when man wanted to migrate up and down the American continent. A sea level canal crossing the isthmus had been a dream ever since Vasco Nuñez de Balboa discovered the Pacific Ocean in 1513. The advantages of a route through Panama were evident. So, in 1514, the King of Spain, Charles V, ordered the first studies for the construction of a canal through a section of the isthmus. Although this idea never materialized, the Spaniards built roads paved with stone that were used for transporting, by mule, tons of gold and silver coming from Peru and bound for Spain.

In 1880 French companies directed by Ferdinand de Diessepss, the builder of the Suez Canal, began to construct the Panama canal. But after seven years of fighting tropical diseases, the inhospitable jungle terrain, and sweltering heat, the French were forced to abandon the project.

In 1903, the province of Panama declared its independence from Colombia and immediately signed the Hay-Bunau Varilla Treaty which authorized the United States to begin construction of the canal in 1904. The canal project involved the removal of more than nine billion cubic feet of earth, creation of a 166-square-mile artificial lake and carving a channel through Panama's mountains. It was completed and started operations on August 15, 1914

It is considered one of the greatest engineering feats of the 20th century. The canal cuts thousands of miles off the trip around South America and thus saves a small fortune in fuel.

Almost 13,000 vessels from many nations use the canal yearly, The average crossing time takes about 10 hours, but the majority of the ships spend more time paying tolls, preparing paperwork and waiting their turn to cross the isthmus. Panama's abundant rainfall is essential for the canal's operation, since its six huge locks need to be filled with fresh water each time a big ship passes them. The average toll is around $50,000 per ship. Tolls are figured out by the ship's draft. Large ships can pay over $100,000. One of the best place to view ships as they pass through the locks is at the Miraflores Locks near Panama City.

Did you know?

The SS Ancon made the first official ocean to ocean transit through the waterway on August 15, 1914.

In fiscal year 2002, a total of 13,185 ships travelled through the Canal. These vessels carried 187.8 million long tons of cargo and paid $588,776,447 in tolls.

The lowest toll was paid by Richard Halliburton, who paid 36 cents to swim through the Canal from August 14 to August 23, 1928.

The Panama Canal Authority adopted a new toll structure based on the type and size of ships, and separating the cost for the use of locomotives. The first phase went to effect on October 1, 2002 and the second phase on July 1, 2003.

The tanker Arco Texas, which crossed the waterway on December, 15, 1981, carrying 65,299 tons of oil, holds the record of cargo carried through the Canal.

The longest ship to have ever used the Canal was the San Juan Prospector, later known as the Marcona Prospector. This ore-bulk-oil carrier is 299 meters long and has a beam of 32.6 meters.

The USS New Jersey and its sister ship, measuring 294.2 meters long and with beams of 32.91 meters, were the widest ships to cross the canal.

The average time for a ship in Canal waters is approximately 24 hours (including the time spent at anchorage awaiting transit). The average time spent in transit is approximately 8 to 10 hours.

Enough earth was removed when building the Canal to fill a train of flatcar that would stretch around the world.

route for those going to the gold fields. The Americans even built a railroad across Panama to speed up westward migration.

In 1881 the French, who has just finished the Suez Canal, attempted to build a sea-level canal across the isthmus. However, a combination of tropical disease and money problems doomed the project. It was abandoned in 1889.

On November 3, 1903, with the help of the US Panama declared its independence from Colombia. Shortly after, the US obtained a canal treaty giving them the right to control the canal zone and the right to intervene in Panamanian affairs. In 1904 the US began construction the "Big Ditch" as the canal is sometimes called.

Construction took 10 years with the first ship sailing through the canal on August 15, 1914.

In the aftermath of Panama's independence and the construction of the canal a series of governments succeeded each other.

The Miraflores Locks

In 1968 the elected democratic president was deposed and General Omar Torrijos Herrera became the leader until he died in a plane crash in 1981.

In 1977 a new canal treaty was signed by US president Jimmy Carter returning complete control and ownership of the canal to Panama on December 31, 1999. US military bases would also be phased out.

In 1983 General Manuel Antonio Noriega took control of the country. A combination of political corruption, involvement with Columbian drug cartels, the murders of opponents and rigged elections led to Noriega's removal by force. On December 20, 1989 US troops invaded Panama to restore democracy and bring Noriega to justice.

One interesting thing to come out of this is that Panama no longer has an army. So Costa Rica is no longer the only Latin American country without a real military force.

Manuel Noriega and his corrupt government have been out of power for more than a decade. Panama's current president, Mireya Moscoso is the country's first female president and wife of the late three-time president Arnulfo Arias.

Government

Despite having a history of military dictatorships Panama is a constitutional democracy. The government has three main branches. The executive branch consists of the president, elected by popular vote to a five year term. He is helped by two elected vice presidents and an appointed cabinet. The legislative power is vested in the Legislative Assembly composed of 72 members, also elected by popular vote to a five-year term. The judicial branch consists of of a nine member supreme court appointed to 10-year terms by the president. As previously mentioned, Panama is politically divided into nine provinces and two autonomous Indian territories. Each province has a governor appointed by the president and each is divided into municipal districts.

Economy

Panamanians have one of the highest per capita income in Central America. The country's economy has been based on the service sector which is responsible for 70 percent of the GDP (gross domestic product). This sector is composed of the Panama Canal, the banking and insurance industries and the Colon Free Zone. In 1946 Panama's business oriented environment gave birth to the Colon Free Zone, which today is an international import and re-export center. It is considered the second largest free trade center in the world after Hong Kong.

The banking sector open to foreign investment has converted Panama into the financial capital of Latin America. The presence of U.S. currency in Panama is a key factor in attracting foreign investment. Manufacturing, mining, utilities and construction are responsible for 20 percent of the GDP, while agriculture, forestry and fishing make up the rest of the total GDP (about 9 percent).

In 1995 Panama started its most important change in more than forty-five years. Wide reform of tax incentives and exemptions, labor market reforms, privatization and membership in the World Trade Organization, represented a major break with the interventionist policies that had long kept Panama isolated from free market changes sweeping through the Latin American region.

In the agriculture sector bananas are the most important product and its largest export. Other products include shrimp, sugar, coffee, dairy products and tropical fruits.

The government has made attempts to boost tourism with a variety of incentives and reforms. Tourism has increased especially the number of cruise ships which dock in Panama while their passengers disembark and tour the country. The new 20 million dollar Panama Convention Center is expected to attract more visitors. In 2001 the government planned public works programs, tax reforms and new regional trade agreements to stimulate growth.

The People

Panama's lovely people are perhaps the country's greatest resource. The country's population was estimated to be around 2,800,000 with an annual growth rate between one and two percent. The majority of the population (65%) are mestizo which is a mixture of Spanish and indigenous descent. People of African background make up about 14% of the population. The remaining population is composed of about 10% people of white or Spanish descent and 10% are Indian. The black population is made of of descendants principally from Jamaica and Trinidad. Many of these black Panamanians speak both Spanish and English. The country's several indigenous groups have their own language and culture.

Panama's constitution guarantees religious freedom. The country's main religion is Roman Catholic (85%). There are also Protestant (15%) and Jewish minorities.

Panama rates among the top three Central American countries for life expectancy. Panamanians are healthy people and have a longevity rate on a par with most first-world countries— 75.68 overall and 72.94 for men and 78.53 for women.

Panama has placed great emphasis on education. The literacy rate is 90.8 percent. The country has several outstanding universities. The University of Panama is the best of the group.

Panamanians are friendly and outgoing and will often go out of their way to help you even if you don't speak Spanish.

Because of their close ties to the U.S. they love anything American—music, TV, fashion and U.S. culture in general.

Generally speaking, the people of Panama love to have fun, like to live with "*gusto*" and know how to enjoy themselves. One has only to go to any local disco on any given night to see Panamanians out having a good time. Latin dances like *salsa* and *merengue* are very popular. On weekends many Panamanians go to the beach, mountains or engage in some type of recreational activity. Holidays are very popular with Panamanians and many normal activities grind to a halt so all Panamanians can participate in the festive atmosphere.

Just as the rest of Latin America, a strong family unit seems to be the most important element in Panamanians' lives. Social life still centers around the home. Much of one's leisure time is usually spent with family. Mother's Day is one of the most important holidays. Young adult, singles,and especially single women, tend to live with their families until they marry.

Panama's People

Just as in the rest of Latin America Sunday is the traditional family day. On any given Sunday families may be seen participating in a variety of activities. In fact, the whole weekend is usually reserved for some type of family activity.

Many Panamanians have distinguished themselves in a variety of endeavors. Roberto *"Mano de Piedra"* Durán is one of Latin America's most famous boxers. He is best remembered for his fights against Sugar Ray Leonard and Marvin Haggler. Rod Carew made a name for himself as a consistent hitter in the Major leagues.

Perhaps Panama's most famous celebrity is musician/ actor Rubén Blades. He even ran unsuccessfully for president of Panama in 1994, finishing in an impressive third place.

Unfortunately, as in most Latin American countries, *machismo* (manliness) is prevalent to some degree among Panamanian males.

Machismo is the belief in the natural superiority of men in all fields of endeavor. It becomes the obsession and constant preoccupation of many Latin men to demonstrate they are *macho* in a variety of ways.

There is no telling to what lengths some men will go in order to demonstrate their virility. A man's virility is measured by the number of seductions or *conquistas* he makes. It is not unusual for married men to have a *querida* or lover. Many even have children with their mistresses.

We suggest that you do not dwell on these negatives and hope you realize how difficult it is to generalize about or stereotype any group of people. After you have resided in Panama and experienced living with the people, you will be able to make your own judgements. The good qualities of the Panamanian people far outweigh any shortcomings they may have.

SAVING MONEY IN PANAMA

How Much Does it Cost to Live in Panama?

An important factor that determines the cost of living for foreigners in Panama is their lifestyle. If you are used to a wealthy lifestyle, you will spend more than someone accustomed to living frugally. Panama is not dirt cheap but it is affordable.

Despite having one of the highest standards of living in Latin America, purchasing power is greater in Panama than in the United States or Canada. The country is really a bargain compared to most places. The cost of living is reasonable and is much less than in the United States, Canada or Europe. Foreign residents will find their daily expenses to be significantly less than in "first world' countries. We will explain the things that make this statement true.

In most areas housing costs less than what it does in the U. S. and hired help is a steal. A full-time maid will run under

$200 monthly, a movie will cost under $4, a gardner will cost $10 a day and a good restaurant meal will cost under $25. Recently, we had lunch at an all-you-can eat buffet at a nice hotel in downtown Panama City. The bill for two was just under $25 for all the food you can eat plus beverages and a table of mouth-watering desserts.

Utilities—telephone service, electricity, and water— are cheaper than in North America. In the warmer areas air conditioning will be your biggest cost. Since most stoves are electric, it is not necessary to cook with gas. These services cost about 30% of what they do at home. Bills for heating in the winter and air conditioning in the summer can cost hundreds of dollars in the States. By the way, bills may be paid at the office of the provider, and at some supermarkets and banks.

Public transportation is also inexpensive. A bus ride across town or to the suburbs usually costs 25 -50¢. Bus fares to the provinces cost no more than $10 to the farthest part in the country. Taxi travel in Panama City is the best way to get around and also inexpensive.

A gallon of high octane gasoline costs about $2.00, making Panama's gasoline prices among the lowest in the Americas. Only oil-exporting countries like Mexico and Venezuela have cheaper gasoline. However, you do not really need a car because public transportation is so inexpensive. If you must have a new car, they are less expensive than in neighboring Costa Rica. Food and entertainment (movies cost about $3.75) are surprisingly affordable. Health care is inexpensive and quite good in Panama.

What really makes Panama affordable for retires is the special discounts program. Panama may just be the world's best deal for this group of people. According to Law 6, Panamanian or alien residents living in national territory who are fifty-five years of age or more, for women, and sixty-two years or more for men and all retires or pensioned persons or disabled people on pensions regardless of age, will enjoy generous benefits ranging from 15 to 50% on the following: buses, train, airfare, hotel rates, restaurants, medical care, professional services and more. For example:

* 1% discount on home mortgages
* 10% off the cost of prescription drugs
* 15% discount on loans made in your name
* 20% discount on your doctor's visits
* 25% discount on your water, electric and telephone bills
* 30% discount on bus, train and boat transportation
* 25% off for passengers on airlines and restaurants
* 50% discount on cultural and sporting events, movie theaters and hotels.

New Cars a less expensive than in the States or Costa Rica

When you have lived in Panama a while, learned the ins-and- outs and made some friends and contacts, you can cut your living costs more by sharing a house or apartment, house-sitting in exchange for free rent, working full or part-time (if you can find legal work), starting a small business or bartering within the expatriate community, doing without packaged and canned imported brand-name foods and buying local products, eating in small cafes or sodas instead of expensive restaurants, or buying fresh foods in bulk at the local farmer's market like Panamanians do. You will also save money by learning Spanish so you can bargain and get lower prices when shopping.

If you take lessons from the locals and live a modest Panamanian lifestyle, you can save a lot of money and still enjoy yourself. By not following a U.S.-"shop-till-you-drop" mentality you can live reasonably. Taking all of the factors mentioned above and personal lifestyles into consideration, the minimum needed for a decent standard of living for a single person ranges from $1200 to $1500 monthly. A person can indeed live for as little as $35 a day excluding housing. Some single people scrape by on considerably less and others spend hundreds of dollars more, again depending on how one is accustomed to living. A couple can live well on $1500 per month, and live in luxury for $2000. Couples with husband and wife both receiving good pensions can live even better. Remember, in Panama a couple can often live as cheaply as one person. Any way you look at it, you will enjoy a higher standard of living in Panama and get more for your money. Since Panama's currency is the US dollar you will not have to worry about confusing currency exchanges or making mistakes while shopping. This alone should save you money.

When you take into account all these factors and such intangibles as good year-round weather, the friendly Panamanian people, the lack of political strife, and a more

Automobile Prices

HONDA CBR 600,2000 (moto) azul/rojo $4,500 honda cbr,600 1999 (moto) negro/gris $4,200 ambas u/ dueño p/estado aceptamos trade-in 201-3095 int.carcenter 221-0907/9721.

HONDA CIVIC 1992, A/C P/ steering v/e, c/c, rines de lujo automático, 73km $4,200.00 pintura fábrica. 221-5705, 636-0456.

HONDA CIVIC 1995, ROJO, 2/ ptas, coupe, 5/velocidades, a/ c, bajo millaje, USA $5,595.00 ☎645-6265, 225-4703, 225-1267.

HONDA CIVIC A/C, P/S, V/E, c/c, rines de lujo automático 84,000kmh full extra, pintura fábrica $4,500.00 neg. 221-5705 636-0456.

HONDA CIVIC PARA CIRCUITO, 1992, motor 1.8, Vtec 210hp, listo para correr; ganador nova-to. Tel:201-2592

HONDA CRV, 1999, NEGRO, IMpecable, CD, equalizador, amplificadores, parrilla, spoiler trasero, R/16, alogenas. Tel.206-9197, 674-841].

HONDA CRV, 2001, AUTOMATI-co, garantizada, $13,000.00; Grand Vitara 2000, automática excelentes condiciones $11,350.00. Tel:215-2602 618-2820

HONDA PASSPORT 2000, TO-dos los extras, automático, mata burro, halogenas, llamar: 614-9886.

HONDA PRELUDE 1992, PARA piezas, rines y llantas/17", transmisión 5 velocidades, ☎645-6265, 225-4703, 225-1267.

HONDA PRELUDE SI, 1992, RIN/ 17", f/extras, bajo millaje, auto., exc/condiciones, USA $7,295.00/neg. ☎645-6265, 225-4703, 225-1267.

HYUNDAI ACCENT 1996, 2/ puertas, a/a, cd player. cam-

LEXUS LX470 1999 ASIENTOS cuero airbag sunroof suspensión electrónica perfectas condiciones mecánicas e interior color negra 201-3095 int.car center 221-0907/9721

MAZDA 323 1999, A/C, P/ steering, rines de lujo pintura fábrica, $5,900.00 260-7493, 671-0242.

MAZDA 323 2002 GARANTÍA de agencia a/ acondicionado r/casette v/ electricas p/steering 5 cambios 3 unidades $7,500 neg. 201-3095 int.car center 221-0907/9721

MAZDA 323F, 1997, MANUAL, a/a, b/kilometraje, rines d/lujo, un solo dueño, $5,000.00 negociable, 266-4993, 617-9188.

MAZDA 6 2003, AUTOMÁTI-co, cuero, airbag, rines lujo, alarma, garantía, f/extras, 8,000kms $19,500.00, ventas electricas, p/stering, r/ cassette 226-5021/8728.

MAZDA 626 1998 AUTOMÁTI-co a/acondicionado r/ casette v/electricas p/ steering c/central poco Km. $7,299 f/extras 201-3095 int.car Center 221-0907/9721

MAZDA MICROBUS, 15pasajeros, totalmente nuevo, año 1999, diesel, aa Precio de Remate $12,499.00 e-mail zperez@cwpanama.net $12,499.00. Teléfonos 290-1576/ 77.

MAZDA PICKUP B-2500, TOTAL-mente nuevo, año 2000, doble cabina, diesel, 4x2. Precio Remate: $10,799.00 e-mail: zperez@cwpanama Tel: 290-1576 290-15 77.

MAZDA PICKUP B2500, TOTAL-mente nuevo, año 1999, doble cabina, diesel, 4x2. Precio de Remate $10,399.00 e-mail: zperez@cwpanama.net Tel:290-1574/77

MITSUBISHI MIRAGE 99 A/ acondicionado p/steering v/ electricas c/central automático full extra $5,800.00 Neg. 261-5128, 671-0242.

MITSUBISHI MIRAGE LAN-cer/00 automático, full extras, p/steering, v/electricas, pintura de fábrica, p/kms, $5,900.00 221-5705.

MITSUBISHI MONTERO 1998, intercooler, turbo diesel, 4x4, asiento de cuero, sun roof, doble a/c, impecable. Auto Line 229-5732, 229-6373.

MITSUBISHI MONTERO 1999 diesel 4x4 diesel, full extras, v/ eléctricas, cd-player, a/c, cambio, óptimas condiciones, $9,900.00 neg. Auto Line 229-5732, 612-6131.

MITSUBISHI MONTERO COR-ta, 1996, 4x4, cambio, a/c, r/ cassette, rines de lujo, spoiler, impecable, $6,900, ganga. Auto Line 229-5732, 229-6373.

MITSUBISHI MONTERO DID (3.2 diesel) 2003, como nueva, con todo, 15,000kms $34,500.00 263-5633

MITSUBISHI MONTERO, 2002, Limited, p/uso, 4,000 millas, 6/cil, f/extras, sunroof, cuero, v/ eléctricas, e/estado $26,500.00. 269-9721

MITSUBISHI NATIVA 1999 blanco automatico, v/ electricas, s/roof, p/steering, a/cuero, cierre central, Precio 12,500.00 Visitenos en www.patelautos.com o 226-5021/8728.

MITSUBISHI NATIVA 99, AUTO-mática, cd, alarma, ventana eléctricas, rines, excelentes condiciones, f/extras. $11,000.00 Tel.269-9721 201-0075.

peaceful way of life, no price is too high to pay for living in a unique, tropical paradise like Panama.

Approximate Cost of Living and Prices as of January 2004 in Dollars*

Rentals - Monthly
House (small, unfurnished)..$400
House (large, luxurious) $1000–1500
Apartment (small, 1–2 bedrooms, unfurnished.....................$300+
Apartment (large, luxurious)....................................$700+
Property Taxes ....Low
Home Prices
House (small) ....$40,000+
House (large) ....$80,000+
Miscellaneous ....Monthly
Electric Bill (operating air conditioners 24 hrs.).......................$100
Water-Sewage (apt.)..Inexpensive
Telephone (calls within the country) $25
Cable TV (includes HBO, CNN, etc.)...............................$40
Direct TV $30
Internet Service (digital)...$30
Taxi (Inexpensive -no meters used)....................$1.50 to $2.50
Bus Fares (around city)..................................$.15 to $.20
Private Postal Service $25
Gasoline (super) ....$ 2.00per gallon
Maid (full time) $180.00
Restaurant Meal (inexpensive)..................................$5.00+
Restaurant (mid-range) $10.00
Movie Ticket...$3.50
Theater $10.00
Small stove $130.00
Small refrigerator $340.00
A microwave..$99.00
A small hot water heater $125.00
Banana ....$.05
Soft drink..$.50

Pineapple	$1.00
Papaya	$.70
Avocado (large)	$.50
Lettuce	$.30
Cereal (large box of corn flakes)	$3.00
Bread (loaf)	$1.00
Tuna (small can)	$.75
Rice (5 lbs.)	$2.00
Chicken 1 lb)	$1.00
Quart of Milk	$.80.
Beer	$.55
Airmail Letter	around $.35
Newspaper	$.40
Doctor's Visit (specialist)	$45
Emergency Room Visit	$100-$200
New Automobile	U.S. prices

* These prices are subject to fluctuations at any given time.

Tipping

Tips are not included in restaurant bills. You should generally leave 10% to 12% for a tip in a restaurant. Of course, employees such as bellhops and taxi drivers are appreciative of any additional gratuity for excellent service. It is also customary to give a small tip to the parking attendants who watch your car on the street, called *cuidacarros*.

Money

Panama's greatest asset, which may be more important than the canal, is the American dollar. Panama's currency has been the US dollar since 1904. Thus, Panama was the first Latin American country to dollarize almost one hundred years ago. The real official currency of Panama is the *Balboa*, but bill are never printed.

All Panama's bills come in standard American denominations. Panamanian mints its own version of American coins. They are the same size and value as US coins, so both can be used interchangeably. Coins are, one, five, ten, twenty-five, fifty and one hundred cents which is the equivalent of a one-dollar bill. The term *Balboa* is used interchangeability with the word dollar, so do not get confused if someone should charge you in the local money.

Since Panama's currency is the US dollar, you will not have to worry about devaluation and converting US currency to local money as you have to do in the majority of Latin American countries

Banking in Panama

When any sophisticated investor thinks of Panama, the first thing that comes to mind is the country's well-developed international banking center. With an increase in banking activity Panama is now considered the financial capital of Latin America. Around 130 banks take advantage of the country's favorable bank regulations and confidentiality, free currency convertibility and movement, use of the U.S. dollar as legal tender, favorable fiscal legislation, good international communications, a well-trained workforce, stable economic, political and social environments, and the high degree of utilization of modern technology. In 1959 Law 18 provided numbered bank accounts.

A banking decree in 1970 increased the number of banks operating in the country. Banks may be licensed under three conditions: Those doing business only in Panama; Those that are offshore; those that have banking activity within or outside of Panama.

Of the 130 banks operating in the country, 62 operate under a general license, which enables them to do domestic and international business; 30 under international license, limited to off-shore business and 17 are representative offices.

Banco Nacional is the largest bank operating in Panama and works like the Federal Reserve Bank of the US,

Close to 75% of deposits are from abroad, which underlines the important service international banking center provides to the region, as a converging point for credit facilities and safe haven for deposits.

Bank secrecy and confidentiality laws and numbered accounts are features Panamanian banks offer. Do not get the wrong idea, since Panama's excellent banking system is not set up for criminal use. Confidentiality is still in place but when criminal activity is suspected there will be intervention by the proper authorities.

One of Panama's banks

If you are really worried about privacy be sure to stay away from US and Canadian banks operating in Panama.

It is very hard to just walk off the street and open an account in Panama. You usually to need to be a resident or at least live in the country to open a bank account. However, non-residents with the right contacts may be able to open accounts in some instances. An American friend of ours who resides in Costa Rica managed to open a dollar savings account or *cuenta de ahorros* in David. He had to provide three letters of recommendation from Costa Rican banks and wait a few weeks. The procedure is similar to open a checking account or *cuenta corriente*. The amount of money needed to open an account varies from bank to bank.

To open an account you will probably be asked to provide some of the following: A copy of your passport, bank references from your home country and from a local Panamanian resident, a description of your business, origin of funds, and reasons for opening an account.

All of this information will be reviewed by the appropriate bank personnel to see if you meet the requirements.

There are a variety of standard banking services available in Panama. Banks offer savings accounts, checking accounts and certificates of deposit. Interest rates are slightly higher than the U.S. You will be happy to know foreigners as well as residents pay no tax on interest generated from bank accounts.

In general, banks are open Monday through Friday from 8:00 a.m. until 3:00 p.m. There are few banks offering services on Saturday.

ATM machines can be found in banks and grocery stores all over Panama. They work just like the machines in your home country. You can withdraw cash and make deposits. Both international and local debit and credit cards may be used to withdraw cash from ATMs. Visa and Master card are the most common cards that work with ATMs in Panama. Limits are around $500 per day. Local debit cards will also work in Panama's ATMs. When you open a local bank account you can link your debit card to your account. Most business establishments will accept debit cards inline of cash. Panamanian banks offer credit cards but interest rates are astronomically high. Therefore a debit card is more adventagous.

If you desire to open a corporate bank account using a Panamanian Corporation you will have to provide the following:

(1) A clear copy of the beneficial owner's passports (photograph page only) which will also be required for all signers on the account. The signature that appears on the passport page must be notarized and then authenticated by the nearest Panamanian consul.

(2) Two commercial or personal references and two bank references are required for each account owner and signer to be addressed to the bank. The bank references should confirm the satisfactory conduct of accounts and that the relationship have been at least two years in duration. Each bank letter must:

(a) Be within a month from the date it was issued.

(b) Mention the approximate account balance

(c) Mention the period of the relationship.

(d) State if the relationship has been satisfactory.

(3) You must also supply brief details of the applicant's business. This will be reviewed by every local bank's Compliance Officer who is required to review all new account applications in accordance with the monitoring procedures stipulated. The information required is:

(a) The nature of the company's business, or intended business, and the approximate annual volume of business that the company does or will do.

(b) The locations of the business.

(c) The origin of funds to be deposited in the new account.

(d) The reason for opening the new account in Panama.

(e) The approximate annual volume of monies which will pass through the account.

4) A resume of each beneficiary of the account as well as all signers on the account. The resume should be brief and provide academic and work experience.

In certain instances, additional information or documentation may be required. Debit or visa cards may be obtained for the account. Debit cards can be used for many ATM machines anywhere in the world.

THE BANKING ASSOCIATION OF PANAMA The Hong Kong Bank Building 15th Floor Ave. Samuel Lewis Panama City, Panama Phone: (507)263-7044 Fax: (507)263-7783, (507)263-763

Banks with a General License:

ABN AMRO BANK, N. V. Apartado 10147, Panama 4, República de Panama Tel. 2636200 Fax (507) 2690526 JOSE LUIS PELAEZ PEREZ, Gerente General JULIO E. PASTOR D., Subgerente

BANCAFE (PANAMA), S. A. Apartado 384, Panama SA, República de Panama Tel. 2646066 / 2646377 / 2646777 / 2646577 Fax (507) 2636115 ALVARO NARANJO SALAZAR, Gerente General KATHYNA DE FABREGA, Gerente Sucursal Panama

BANCO ALIADO, S. A. Apartado 552109, Paitilla, Panama, República de Panama Tel. 2639777 / 2639757 Fax (507) 2639677 ALEXIS A. ARJONA, Gerente General GABRIEL DIAZ H., Gerente de Administración.

BANCO BILBAO VIZCAYA (PANAMA), S. A. Apartado 3392, Panama 3, República de Panama Tel. 2636922 Fax (507) 2636483 JAVIER LEJARRAGA, Gerente General AURELIO PEREZ PALOMINO, Subgerente General

BANCO CENTRAL HISPANOAMERICANO, S. A. Apartado 8381, Panama 8, República de Panama Tel. 2639044 / 2639127 Fax (507) 2695824 JOSE

MANUEL FRADE, Gerente General GRISELDA DE DE LA GUARDIA, Gerente Area Comercial

BANCO COMERCIAL ANTIOQUENO, S. A. Apartado 1630, Panama 1, República de Panama Tel. 2636577 / 2636125 / 2636648 Fax (507) 2637534 / 2636865 LUIS FELIPE HOYOS, Gerente General ANNETTE FIERRO DE DE OBALDIA, Subgerente Operativo

BANCO COMERCIAL DE PANAMA, S. A. BANCOMER Apartado 7659, Panama 5, República de Panama Tel. 2636800 / 2634433 Fax (507) 2638033 EMANUEL GONZALEZ REVILLA, Presidente y Gerente General CARLOS R. HENRIQUEZ L., Vicepresidente GABRIELA DE OBARRIO DE NAVARRO, Presidente Honoraria

BANCO CONFEDERADO DE AMERICA LATINA, S. A. COLABANCO Apartado 7547, Panama 5, República de Panama Tel. 2699888 Fax (507) 2633518 JUAN ANTONIO NI8O, Vicepresidente Ejecutivo y Gerente General DAVID L. PLATA, Vicepresidente de Operaciones y Sistemas

BANCO CONTINENTAL DE PANAMA, S. A. Apartado 135, Panama 9A, República de Panama Tel. 2635955 / 2635153 / 2635580 Fax (507) 2643359 PAUL SMITH A., Gerente General RAFAEL REYES E., Gerente de Crédito ROBERTO MOTTA C., Presidente

BANCO DE BOGOTA, S. A. Apartado 8653, Panama 5, República de Panama Tel. 2646000 Fax (507) 2638037 ANDREW L. CLARKSON R., Gerente General FABIO GUILLERMO RIA8O A., Subgerente General

BANCO DE COLOMBIA, S. A. (PANAMA) Apartado Postal 4213, Panama 5, República de Panama Tel. 2640359 / 2645382 / 2645428 Gerencia General: 2643581 Fax (507) 2641285 JORGE HUMBERTO VIDELA RICO, Gerente General RIGOBERTO NOLAN FORBES, Tesorero Contralor

BANCO DE IBEROAMERICA, S. A. Apartado 6553, Panama 5, República de Panama Tel. 2635366 / 2635983 / 2635379 Fax (507) 2691616 JUAN MANUEL LIMA B., Gerente General GINA G. DE SAENZ, Gerente de Planificación y Control JOSE MARIA CHIMENO, Presidente

BANCO DE LA EXPORTACION, S.A. BANEXPO Apartado 3844, Panama 7, República de Panama Tel. 2235333 Fax (507) 2235338 IGNACIO FABREGA O., Gerente General YESSICA ROJAS URIBE, Subgerente General

BANCO DE LATINOAMERICA, S. A. BANCOLAT Apartado 4401, Panama 5, República de Panama Tel. 2640466 / 2640676 Fax (507) 2637368 RAFAEL ARIAS CHIARI, Gerente General SANTIAGO DUQUE Z., Subgerente General

BANCO DEL ISTMO, S. A. Apartado 63823, El Dorado, Panama, República de Panama Tel. 2695555 Fax (507) 2695168 ALBERTO VALLARINO, Vicepresidente Ejecutivo L.J. MONTAGUE BELANGER, Gerente General SAMUEL LEWIS GALINDO, Presidente

BANCO DISA, S. A. Apartado 7201, Panama 5, República de Panama Tel. 2635933 / 2639950 / 2639954 Fax (507) 2641084 RAFAEL C. ENDARA, JR., Vicepresidente Ejecutivo y Gerente General ROBERTO E. THOMAS S., Gerente de Crédito

BANCO DE BRASIL, S. A. Apartado 871123, Panama 7, República de Panama Tel. Central telefónica: 2636566 / 2636170 / 2636470 Gerencia General: 2636302 Gerencia Adjunta: 2693742 Money Desk: 2640495 Fax (507) 2635542 TELEFAX DE RELACIONES BANCARIAS: 2699867 CELSO DE MEDEIROS DRUMMOND, Gerente General MELANIA MEDEIROS FERNANDES, Gerente

BANCO EXTERIOR, S. A. Apartado 8673, Panama 5, República de Panama Tel. 2271122 Fax (507) 2273663 RAFAEL SANCHEZ GARROS, Gerente General RAMON TWEED MOTLEY, Gerente de Operaciones

BANCO FEDPA, S.A. Apartado 6218, Panama, República de Panama Tel. 2633233 Fax (507) 2633240 MIGUEL A. GALDAMES B., Gerente General FRANCISCO MORENO, Gerente de Operaciones

BANCO GANADERO, S. A. Apartado 63567, El Dorado, Panama, República de Panama Tel. 2690659 / 2690134 / 2637933 Fax (507) 2638985 ABEL MERCADO JARAVA, Gerente General EDUARDO BREWER C., Subgerente Bancario y de Mercadeo

BANCO GENERAL, S. A. Apartado 4592, Panama 5, República de Panama Tel. 2273200 / 2270150 / 2270260 2274757 / 2272289 / 2273690 Fax (507) 2273427 TELEFAX DEL DEPTO. INTERNACIONAL: (507) 2274618 RAUL ALEMAN Z., Vicepresidente Ejecutivo y Gerente General JOSE DIAZ SEIXAS, Vicepresidente

BANCO HIPOTECARIO NACIONAL Apartado 222 Panama 1, República de Panama Tel. 2270055 Fax (507) 2256956 WINSTON RODOLFO WELCH B., Gerente General AZAEL PURCAIT, Gerente de Finanzas

BANCO INDUSTRIAL COLOMBIANO DE PANAMA, S. A. Apartado 8593, Panama 5, República de Panama Tel. 2636955 (buscador automático) Fax (507) 2691138 JORGE DURAN OSPINA, Gerente General SANTIAGO EDUARDO VILLA CARDONA, Subgerente

BANCO INTERNACIONAL DE COSTA RICA, S. A. Apartado 600, Panama 1, República de Panama Tel. 2636822 / 2635240 Fax (507) 2636393 JOSE FRANCISCO ULATE, Gerente General FEDERICO ECHANDI GURDIAN, Subgerente General

BANCO INTERNACIONAL DE PANAMA, S. A. BIPAN Apartado 11181, Panama 6, República de Panama Tel. 2639000 Fax (507) 2639514 RENE A. DIAZ A., Gerente General ANNABEL DE TERAN, Subgerente General

BANCO LATINOAMERICANO DE EXPORTACIONES, S. A. BLADEX Apartado 61497, El Dorado, Panama, República de Panama Tel. 2636766 Fax (507) 2696333 JOSE CASTA8EDA VELEZ, Vicepresidente Ejecutivo HAYDEE A. DE CANO, Primer Vicepresidente Administración

BANCO MERCANTIL DEL ISTMO, S. A. Apartado 484, Panama 9A, República de Panama Tel. 2636262 Fax (507) 2637553 / 2636431 MANUEL JOSE BARREDO MARTINEZ, Gerente General RODOLFO MIRANDA VERGARA, Gerente de Promoción

BANCO NACIONAL DE PANAMA Apartado 5220, Panama 5, República de Panama Tel. 2635151 Fax (507) 2690091 / 2647155 JOSE ANTONIO DE LA OSSA, Gerente General

BANCO PANAMENO DE LA VIVIENDA, S. A. BANVIVIENDA Apartado 8639, Panama 5, República de Panama Tel. 2274020 / 2250128 / 2250155 Fax (507) 2275433 MARIO L. FABREGA AROSEMENA, Gerente General

BANCO PANAMERICANO, S. A. PANABANK Apartado 1828, Panama 1, República de Panama Tel. 2639266 Fax (507) 2691537 / 2645357 GUIDO J. MARTINELLI, JR., Vicepresidente Ejecutivo y Gerente General CARLOS R. BARRIOS I., Gerente de Operaciones

BANCO REAL, S. A. Apartado 7048, Panama 5, República de Panama Tel. 2691444 / 2691104 / 2691596 Fax (507) 2691716 LUSIVANDER F. LEITE, Gerente General MILTON AYON WONG, Gerente

BANCO TRASATLANTICO, S. A. Apartado 7655, Panama 5, República de Panama Tel. 2692318 Fax (507) 2694948 RAUL DE MENA C., Gerente General ANTONIO FOTIS TAQUIS, Subgerente

BANCO UNION, S. A. C. A. Apartado "A", Panama 5, República de Panama Tel. 2649133 / 2649091 Fax (507) 2639985 MARIA M. DE MENDEZ, Gerente Encargada ANA BERTA DE VILLANUEVA, Subgerente General

BANK LEUMI ISRAEL B. M. Apartado 64518, El Dorado, Panama, República de Panama Tel. 2639377 / 2693113 / 2693812 Fax (507) 2692674 ALBERT BITTON, Gerente General DAVID MAMANN, Subgerente

BANK OF CHINA (Sucursal Panama) Apartado 871056, Panama 7, Panama Tel. 2635522 / 2636383 Fax (507) 2239960 / 2691079 QI RE HE, Gerente General XIU RONG YIN, Subgerente General

BANQUE NATIONALE DE PARIS (PANAMA), S. A. Apartado 1774, Panama 1, República de Panama Tel. 2636600 Fax (507) 2636970 / 2639472 PIERRE THOME, Vicepresidente y Gerente General JORGE DIXON DE LEON, Director Comercial

BANQUE SUDAMERIS Apartado 1847, Panama 9A, República de Panama Tel. 2272777 Fax (507) 2275828 GIANCARLO PANICUCCI, Gerente General JULIO A. CORTES, Gerente Adjunto

CAJA DE AHORROS Apartado 1740, Panama 1, República de Panama Tel. 2636233 / 2691544 Fax (507) 2693674 JAVIER ARTURO VINCENSINI, Gerente General ANIBAL ILLUECA HERRANDO, Asistente a la Gerencia General

CITIBANK, N. A. Apartado 555, Panama 9A, República de Panama Tel. 2638377 Corporativo / 2364044 del Consumidor Fax (507) 2694171 Corporativo / 2362574 del Consumidor EDUARDO C. URRIOLA, Gerente General ROXANA DE RICHA, Vicepresidenta

CREDICORP BANK Apartado 871338, Panama 7, Rep. de Panama Tel. 2635600 Fax (507) 2639314 CARLOS GUEVARA, Gerente General MAX JOE HARARI, Gerente de Finanzas

DEUTSCH SUDAMERIKANISCHE BANK AG Apartado 5400, Panama 5, República de Panama Tel. 2635055 Fax (507) 2691877 PETER NHR, Gerente General KLAUS MFLLER, Gerente

GLOBAL BANK CORPORATION Apartado 551843, Paitilla, Panama, República de Panama Tel. 2699292 Fax (507) 2644089 JORGE E. VALLARINO S., Presidente y Gerente General OTTO O. WOLFSCHOON, JR., Vicepresidente Ejecutivo

KOREA EXCHANGE BANK Apartado 8358, Panama 7, República de Panama Tel. 2699966 Fax (507) 2644224 MENG BOK LEE, Gerente General SUN GAP WHANG, Gerente

LLOYDS BANK P.L.C. Apartado 8522, Panama 5, República de Panama Tel. 2636277 Fax (507) 2647931 JORGE FRANKE, Gerente Principal GILDA C. DE TEDMAN, Gerente (Comercial)

METROBANK, S. A. Apartado "B", Panama 5, República de Panama Tel. 2231666 / 2231325 Fax (507) 2232020 ALBERTO JOSE PAREDES, Vicepresidente Ejecutivo y Gerente General ALFREDO E. BAIZ B., Subgerente General

MIDLAND BANK PLC Apartado 5322, Panama 5, República de Panama Tel. 2636200 / 2695477 Fax (507) 2695577 / 2695133 JOSEPH L. SALTERIO, JR., Gerente General LORENZO J. RIVERA, Gerente de Tesorería e Instituciones Financieras

MULTI CREDIT BANK, INC. Apartado 8210, Panama 7, República de Panama Tel. 2696763 / 2690188 / 2692779 / 2692812 Fax (507) 2644014 / 2693921 PEDRO OLIVA, JR., Gerente General BENITO AVERSA, Gerente de Crédito ALBERTO SALOMON, BTESH, Presidente

PRIMER BANCO DE AHORROS, S. A. PRIBANCO Apartado 7322, Panama 5, República de Panama Tel. 2272225 / 2272666 Fax (507) 2274037 JOAQUIN DE LA GUARDIA G., Gerente General OSWALDO A. DIAZ A., Subgerente General

REPUBLIC NATIONAL BANK, INC. Apartado 8962, Panama 5, República de Panama Tel. 2647777 / 2647904 Fax (507) 2643722 INES T. DE LEW, Gerente General JULIO C. QUINZADA, Asistente

STATE BANK OF INDIA Apartado 64526, El Dorado, Panama, República de Panama Tel. 2636866 Fax (507) 2696780 KISHORE KUMAR SAXENA, Gerente General GABRIEL O. AROSEMENA, Subgerente de Operaciones

THE BANK OF NOVA SCOTIA Apartado 7327, Panama 5, República de Panama Tel. 2636255 Fax (507) 2638636 ALBERTO R. TARABOTTO, Gerente General AMELIA Z. DE CASTILLERO, Gerente de Operaciones

THE BANK OF TOKYO, LTD. Apartado 1313, Panama 1, República de Panama Tel. 2636777 Fax (507) 2635269 KAZUTOSHI HOSHINO, Gerente General HORACIO O. MARQUINEZ, Gerente SR.

THE CHASE MANHATTAN BANK, N. A. Apartado 9A76, Panama 9A, República de Panama Tel. 2635855 / 2635877 / 2635180 Fax (507) 2636009 OLEGARIO BARRELIER, Vicepresidente y Gerente General ANIBAL HENRIQUEZ, Vicepresidente Contralor

THE DAIICHI KANGYO BANK, LTD. Apartado 2637, Panama 9A, República de Panama Tel. 2696111 / 2696360 Fax (507) 2696815 YUTAKA KOYAMA, Gerente General MARTHA DE DE WOLF, Gerente de Operaciones

THE FIRST NATIONAL BANK OF BOSTON Apartado 5368, Panama 5, República de Panama Tel. 2642244 / 2642225 Fax (507) 2647402 LUIS A. NAVARRO L., Vicepresidente y Gerente General SONIA R. DE NEWELL, Vicepresidente Asistente

THE INTERNATIONAL COMMERCIAL BANK OF CHINA Apartado 4453, Panama 5, República de Panama Tel. 2638108 / 2638217 / 2638565 Gerencia: 2649911 / Subgerencia: 2649022 Fax (507) 2638392 TAIHSIUNG LEE, Vicepresidente y Gerente General FELIX CHEN, Gerente

TOWERBANK INTERNATIONAL, INC. Apartado 66039, El Dorado, Panama, República de Panama Tel. 2696900 Fax (507) 2696800 / 2641536 / 2692964 G. ANTONIUS DE WOLF, Gerente General ROSEMARIE DE AYALA, Gerente de Operaciones

BANKS with INTERNACIONAL Licenses:

ATLANTIC SECURITY BANK Sucursal Panama Apartado 68934, El Dorado, Panama, República de Panama Tel. Central: 2695944 / 2695862 / 2695367 / 2695865 Fax (507) 2695391 / 2642392 JORGE PONCE, S. Vicepresidente Senior y Gerente General MARISOL E. SIERRA V., Vicepresidente y Gerente de Operaciones

AUSTROBANK OVERSEAS (PANAMA), S.A. Apartado 63197, El Dorado, Panama, República de Panama Tel. 2695275 / 2695372 Fax (507) 2646135

NICOLAS LATORRACA E., Apoderado ENRIQUE JAEN CHONG, Gerente de Operaciones

BANCO AGRICOLA COMERCIAL DE EL SALVADOR, S.A. SUCURSAL PANAMA Apartado 62637, El Dorado, Panama, República de Panama Tel. 2635863 / 2635762 Fax (507) 2635626 JOSE ALFONSO ESPINOZA, Gerente RUTH BARNES DE ARAUZ, Gerente de Operaciones

BANCO ALEMAN PLATINA, S. A. Apartado 6180, Panama 5, República de Panama Tel. 2238005 / 2692666 Fax (507) 2690910 ALDO O. ZAVAGNO, Gerente General LETICIA S. DE URRUTIA, Subgerente

BANCO ANDINO (PANAMA), S. A. Apartado 61061, El Dorado, Panama, República de Panama Tel. 2691084 / 2695587 / 2637682 Fax (507) 2637749 HUMBERTO ARCIA W., Subgerente ZAYDEE DE MIRANDA, Secretaria

BANCO DE LA NACION ARGENTINA Apartado 63298, El Dorado, Panama, República de Panama Tel. 2694666 Fax (507) 2696719 HUGO O. CRESPI, Gerente General OLGA SOLIS, Gerente de Operaciones y Crédito

BANCO DE LA PROVINCIA DE BUENOS AIRES Apartado 64592, El Dorado, Panama, República de Panama Tel. 2272167 Fax (507) 2278378 / 2250431 JUAN CARLOS STURLESI, Gerente General EDUARDO E. CARO, Adscripto a Gerencia

BANCO DEL PACIFICO (PANAMA), S. A. Apartado 63100, El Dorado, Panama, República de Panama Tel. 2635833 Fax (507) 2692640 LUIS A. SANTAMARIA, Presidente JOSE CHUNG H., Vicepresidente y Contralor

BANCO DE OCCIDENTE (PANAMA), S. A. Apartado 67430, El Dorado, Panama, República de Panama Tel. 2638144 / 2638240 Fax (507) 2693261 / 2643198 OSCAR LUNA G., Gerente General MARITZA F. DE BARSALLO, Subgerente de Operaciones y Administración

BANCO DE PRESTAMOS (PANAMA), S.A. Apartado 66670, El Dorado, Panama, República de Panama Tel. 2643000 / 2643891 / 2643797 Fax (507) 2234530 MIGUEL YEPEZ, Gerente de Operaciones

BANCO DE SANTA CRUZ DE LA SIERRA (PANAMA), S. A. Apartado 64416, El Dorado, Panama, República de Panama Tel. 2638477 Fax (507) 2638404 / 2637704 JULIO ANTELO S., Gerente General PERCY ZEBALLOS IBA8EZ, Gerente Adjunto

BANCO MERCANTIL, C. A., S.A.C.A. Apartado 62898, El Dorado, Panama, República de Panama Tel. 2636191 Fax (507) 2692055 RAMIRO MOLINA, Gerente General TERESA DE BOYD

BANCO POPULAR DOMINICANO (PANAMA), S. A. Apartado 5404, Panama 5, Panama, República de Panama Tel. 2694166 / 2694374 Fax (507) 2691309 LUCIA DE AIZPURUA, Vicepresidenta Ejecutiva y Gerente General JOSE A. SEGOVIA, Vicepresidente y Gerente Asistente

BANCREDITO (PANAMA), S. A. Apartado 66010, El Dorado, Panama, República de Panama Tel. 2232977 / 2232918 Fax (507) 2646781 RAISA GIL DE FONDEUR, Vicepresidente GIOVANNA DE ZISOPULOS, Gerente

BANK OF COMMERCE & FINANCE, INC. Apartado 4310, Panama 5, Panama, República de Panama Tel. 2236323 Fax (507) 2648795 ROBERTO R. ALEMAN Z., Presidente MARIA DE LOURDES CHANIS TEJADA, Gerente

BANQUE NATIONALE DE PARIS SUCURSAL PANAMA Apartado 201, Panama 1, Panama, República de Panama Tel. 2648555 Fax (507) 2636970 / 2636559 PIERRE THOME, Vicepresidente y Gerente General JULIO SAMIT, Vicepresidente Senior

CREDIT LYONNAIS Apartado 1778, Panama 9A, República de Panama Tel. Central: 2636522 / Tesorería: 2635814 / 2635956 Fax (507) 2635904 MICHEL CHATELAIN, Gerente General YVES BARES, Apoderado

FILANBANCO TRUST & BANKING, CORP. Apartado 873940, Panama 7, República de Panama Tel. 2694080 / 2239251 Fax (507) 2699141 ERIC A. CASTRO G., Gerente CARLOS CA8IZARES, Asesor Ejecutivo

SOCIETE GENERALE Apartado 63689, El Dorado, Rep. de Panama Tel. 2699611 / 2649191 Fax (507) 2640295 JEAN FRANCOIS GUEX, Gerente General ALAIN HOURCADE, Gerente Comercial

SWISS BANK CORPORATION, S. A. Apartado 61, Panama 9A, Panama, República de Panama Tel. 2637181 Fax (507) 2695995 LEONARDO CASTRO, Director, Banca Comercial y Tesorera

Housing and Real Estate Investments

Rentals

Housing is affordable and plentiful in Panama. Rentals are inexpensive compared to what you would pay in the U.S., Canada or Europe.

Prices of rentals can vary greatly depending on where you choose to live and the amenities. In the lower range— from $300 to $700—you can expect to find a two to three bedroom house or apartment in a middle class neighborhood. Since the majority of Panamanians pay less than $150 monthly for rent, a few hundred dollars should rent a nice place to live. Most affordable houses and apartments are unfurnished. However, you can usually buy a complete household of furniture from someone who is leaving the country. This way you can save money.

Many of the upper end apartments have such amenities as parking, elevators, 24-hour security, a swimming pool, a doorman, recreational area, a gym and a social area for parties or entertaining friends.

When looking for a place, remember to check the phone, the shower, the closet size, kitchen cabinets, electrical outlets, light fixtures, the toilet, faucet and water pressure, locks, general security of building, windows and the condition of the stove, refrigerator and furniture, if furnished. Look at ceilings for telltale leaks and stains.

Also, check for traffic noise, signs of insects and rodents and what the neighbors are like. Ask about the proximity of buses and availability of taxis. If you have a pet make sure there are no restrictions about having animals. Have anything you sign translated into English before you sign it. **Do not sign**

anything you do not understand based on the landlord's word of honor.

With the implementation of Law No. 93 (1973), the owner of an apartment and/or office unit, with a monthly rent between $250.00 and $500.00, is not permitted to raise the rent unless first approved by the Housing Ministry. All other leasing contracts, with rents superior to the monthly amounts mentioned above, are free to be governed by agreements between the parties. This law remains in force today. Resulting from private sector criticism surrounding Law No. 93, and due to the lack of new investment by developers on rental buildings, Law No. 38 (1984) was enacted, and with it came deregulation in the leasing market. However, this modification only applies to new rental buildings which commenced construction after November 16th, 1984.

Whether you rent or lease, you will most likely have to pay a security deposit equivalent to one month's rent. If the apartment is in good condition when you vacate it, your deposit will be returned.

When reading the ads in the Spanish newspapers, you should be familiar with the following words: *Se Alquila*-for rent, *agua caliente*-hot water, *alfombrado*-carpeted, *amueblado*-furnished, *sin muebles*-unfurnished, *baño*-bathroom, *cocina*-kitchen, *cochera* or *garaje*-garage, *contrato*-contract, *depósito*-deposit, *dormitorio*-bedroom, *guarda*-guard, *jardín*-garden, *seguro*-safe, *patio*-patio, *parqueo*-parking, *verjas*-bars, *zona verde*-grassy area.

How We Found our Piece of Paradise
By Angela Hollister

Contadora is a great place to get away from the world and recharge your batteries. We can socialize and enjoy the dining spots and companionship of other islanders, or just pick up a book and a margarita and enjoy the beautiful views from our deck or the beach.

My husband and I are from the New England area. To escape harsh winters, we have vacationed in Grand Cayman for a number of years, renting a condo on Seven Mile Beach. The condo gave us the luxury of not spending our beach time elbow to elbow with all the other hotel guests. We enjoyed our time in Cayman, but the cost of real estate and the worry of hurricanes were discouraging.

We prefer to get away when the weather is cold at home. Bermuda's climate is best in June, July or August--when the weather is nice at home. The Bahamas can also be quite cool during the winter/early spring months. And St. Bart's is extremely expensive and language was also an issue there--neither of us speak French. On Contadora, the year round warm climate without the worry of hurricanes is a big plus.

With Contadora, the investment cost is low compared to areas in the Caribbean that we have considered. Here we have all the advantages of a private home with everything we need, but can lock it up and leave without the worry of maintenance.

We had been looking to purchase an island getaway for quite some time when information regarding Contadora arrived from International Living. It looked very intriguing, but we had never been to Panama. I mentioned it to my oldest stepson, who had actually visited Contadora. He encouraged us to check it out.

Contadora is attractive for many reasons. For one, it is not commercialized and is a great place to get away for quiet relaxation; the island is primarily residential. It is remote, but easily accessible from Panama City by plane and barge (for freight). The infrastructure, particularly for such a location, is fantastic.

For the next few years, we will try to get down there 3 or 4 times per year. Our older sons and their families will probably take advantage of it as well. In a few years, we will probably escape the cold winters here by spending more time on the island.

It's also very nice to have what amounts to a brand new house that should not need any major work for quite some time.

Having never purchased real estate outside this country, buying property that needed a lot of work on a remote island in a foreign country has been a much smoother process than some of the less complicated transactions we have had here in the States.

And it is very nice to have International Living's local office there as a resource for us.

We have already met a lot of very nice, helpful people on the island. I've been told that once people know you are an owner there, you become a part of the community. We had a very warm welcome from one of the restaurant owners this past trip. This is a refreshing change from the cold attitudes of New England.

This has been a good experience for us and we look forward to enjoying our little piece of Paradise.

*Courtesy of International Living. See **www.international living.com** for more information.

Buying Real Estate

As we alluded to in Chapter 1, there is a variety real estate for everyone's taste. You will have the choice of many different housing options in Panama City; mountain areas like El Valle and Boquete; numerous beaches and island areas like Bocas del Toro and Contadora. Once you decide on the area you want you will be pleased to know that as a foreigner you are afforded the same protection as a Panamanian land owner.

Now is a good time to invest in Panamanian real estate for a variety of reasons. Panama has had a stable democratic government for over ten years. The country has excellent infrastructure and communications systems and boasts one of the wonders of the world, the Panama Canal which is an economic mainstay and constant source of revenue. The Canal and its importance to world trade make Panama one of the most solid economies in the world. The country also boasts a thriving Free Trade Zone, a bustling modern city of over 1.5 million people, the dollar as the official currency and a first world banking system. In addition, non-citizens may purchase property and have the same rights as Panamanians. The country has a variety of real estate for the retiree, investor and entrepreneur. Easy residency requirements and attractive tax advantages for investors and businessmen add to the country's appeal.

It's easier to get a mortgage in Panama than anywhere else in Latin America. Other than Puerto Rico, Panama is the only Latin American country where private lenders are willing to make 30-year, fixed-rate mortgages. Why? Because the economy is stable, there is little chance of default, and the banks know they will get their money back even if someone cannot pay back a loan. This is not the case anywhere else in this part of the world.

Panama has some of the most inexpensive real estate bargains found in Latin America. As we mention in Chapter 1 many investors are interested in the old section of Panama City or *Casco Viejo*. The gentrification process is already under way. Furthermore, the government provides incentives for

Prices of Homes

OBARRIO GANGA 198M2, 2/R c/b, s/comedor, c/b/e, 2/ estacionamiento, a/a, todo remodelado, cocina nueva, $105.000.00, 614-5631.

OBARRIO, EDIF LA FONTANA, PISO ALTO, 3/REC, ESTUDIO, C/B/E, $190,000.00 INTERESADOS LLAMAR 213-8822 223-0843

OBARRIO: P.H. MILLENIUM, PISO 20 con vista al mar. Remodelado, $170,000.00. 613-4493.

P.PAITILLA 350MT2, EXONERAdo, v/panorámica, a/social, piscina, sauna, seguridad, p/ eléctrica, 3r, estudio, salas. 269-9721/ 633-9721. $246,000.00.

P.PAITILLA: LUJOSO APARTAmento, recien remodelado, 2/ cuartos, 2/b, c/b/e, 140mts2, piscina, vista mar, seguridad 24hrs. 614-5838.

P/PAITILLA APTO 83MTS² 1REC, 1b, ½baño adicional, remodelado, seguridad, conserje, avalúo $55,000.00 acepto oferta, tel.672-4325.

PAITILLA PLATINIUM TOWER, apartamento, lujosos acabados, linea blanca, a/a, incluido, para información llamar, 612-6042, 269-5994.

OBARRIO: P.H. MILLENIUM, PISO 20 con vista al mar. Remodelado, $170,000.00. 613-4493.

PARQUE LEFEVRE APARTAMENto 54mt2, balcón, dos recámaras, Motivo viaje, ganga $28,500.00, 2 piso. 200-1712, 200-7817.

PARQUE LEFEVRE VENDO APARtamento 2/r, 1/b, balcón, 67.66M2, casi nuevo $36,000 Teléfonos 649-4511 607-1466.

PARQUE LEFEVRE: PARK PLACE Torre B, preventa increíbles, 3r, 2b, c/b/e, $59,350.00; 2r, 2b, desde $47,650, piscina, gimnasio, seguridad, 224-7617

PLAZA DORADA/II, 138MT², NUEvo. Enero/2004, 3/rec, c/b/ emp, por urgencia, s/ intermediarios. Por favor no b/ raices. 672-7874

CONSTRUCCION, REMODELADA, A/C, C/B/E, JACUZZI, PISCINA, ALARMA 612-1884.

ALTOS DEL GOLF: CASA 660MTS cercana a ex-General Noriega, avaluo $215,500.00, remato $165,000.00. P/viaje, negociable. 221-6097, 617-7885.

ARRAIJAN ARBOLEDA DE CACEres 3r, 2b, s/c, lavandería, terraza y estacionamiento techado, cercada 600mts2 avaluó $68,000.00 "Ganga $49,000.00" Q.Inversiones, 214-3136/8833.

AVANCE. GANGA 387.29MTS, 3r, estudio, terraza, jardín, casa huesped, garaje grande, $115,000.00neg 260-7771, 236-9751, 615-5167.

BALBOA $52,089.00, DIABLO $62,344.00, L/Boca $150,294.00. Farfán $60,451.00, L/Rios $90,816.00, Gamboa $22,343.00, Corozal $95,499.00. 236-3217.

BARRIADA SANTA LUCIA BOquete, vendo casa nueva 2 recámaras, teléfonos 771-4586, 776-0082 precio muy razonable.

AVANCE. GANGA 387.29MTS, 3r, estudio, terraza, jardín, casa huesped, garaje grande, $115,000.00neg 260-7771, 236-9751, 615-5167.

BALBOA $52,089.00, DIABLO $62,344.00, L/Boca $150,294.00. Farfán $60,451.00, L/Rios $90,816.00, Gamboa $22,343.00, Corozal $95,499.00. 236-3217.

BRISAS D/GOLF, DUPLEX 467.73mts2, esquina, 3r, principal w/closets, terraza, estacionamientos techado. $115,000.00 Remate 99,900.00 F/disponible. 224-9827/ 214-3136/ 236-2016/ 671-4188 – 671-9554.

CASA LAS LOMAS CHORRERA 2/r, 1/baño s/comedor, cercada, otras mejoras 260-2557 239-3937.

CHANIS COMODA RESIDENCIA 2 pisos, amplia s/c, 3r, c/b/e, la-

V/FUENTES 2, $137,000.00 4/R, 3/b, estudio s/familiar, amplia terraza 325m2 terreno 285m2 construcción, 4/ estacionamiento. 236-0323.

VENDO CASA DOS RECAMAras, sala comedor, cocina, Alto Verde, David, vía Aeropuerto $14,000.00 721-1732 noche profesora Gloria.

VENDO CASA EN PRADERA DE S/Antonio remodelada, accesible llamar al 270-2411 Luis Alberto.

VILLA L/FUENTES GANGA REMAto 285mts construcción, remodelada, 3r, estudio, cbe, terraza $95,000.00 260-7771, 236-9751, 615-5167.

VILLA ZAITA: LUJOSOS DUPLEX, imponente arquitectura en área exclusiva, 3r, 21/2 baños, cbe, finos acabados, importados, estacionamiento techado. $92,500.00 224-7617.

APROVECHE LA MEJOR AREA V.Zaita, majestuosas casas 2 pisos, 3r, 2-1/2b, cbe, estacionamiento techado, acabados de primera calidad 224-7617. $92,500.00

640-duplexs venta

ALBROOK: DUPLEX EN ESQUINA, 3/REC, 3½/BAÑOS, C/B/E, AMPLIA TERRAZA, LAVANDERIA TECHADA, PISCINA, JARDIN TEL.265-0891, 616-0025 LIC. TEJEDOR

COLINAS DEL GOLF: VENDO/ alquilo dúplex 4r, estudio, 3b, terraza grande. Buen Precio 674-2527, 224-5401, 223-6694.

MIRAFLORES, BETANIA, 3/R, 2/B, c/b/e, terraza, depósito, sala familiar, 229-6834, 614-7675. $95,000.00.

RESIDENCIAL SANFERNANDO, 3/rec, 3/b, c/b/e, estudio, amplia cocina, seguridad, alarma, $109,500.00 negociable 229-8612 608-2993

investors in this unique area of the city. Whether you are a real estate investor or someone just looking for an interesting place to live or retire, Casco Viejo might just be the place you are seeking.

Because military and canal personnel have left the country, there are hundreds if not thousands of apartments and houses available. Some of the best deals can be found in and around the Fort Clayton area.

In Chapter 1 we mentioned other suitable areas for living such as **San Francisco, Marbella** and **El Dorado,** among others.

Cerro Azul and **Altos de María** are desirable places near Panama City where affordable real estate may be found.

We have already alluded to the real estate bargains that may be found in the **Boquete** and **Bocas del Toro** areas of northern Panama.

If you cannot afford to buy a house in the U.S. or Canada, prices of decent homes in Panama will seem like a bargain. However, like anyplace in the world, you will end up paying more for a house in an upscale neighborhood. If you wish to live outside the city in a rural setting, then check out Chirique. Panama is not a densely populated country, so there is a great deal of raw land in the countryside.

Sky scraper

As you already know foreigners are entitled to the same ownership rights as citizens of Panama. This means your purchase here can be fully secured and safe.

To find property look in local newspapers, contact a broker, try by word of mouth, from friends or pound the pavement in the area of your choice looking for 'For Sale" signs.

If you decide to buy real estate, an attorney is absolutely necessary to do the legal work for purchasing property. We strongly recommend that your lawyer do a thorough search of all records before you make your purchase, and make sure there are no encumbrances (*gravámenes*) on it. You can obtain information about property at the *Registro de Propiedades* (like our land title office). You can obtain information from the *Registro* at **www.registro-publico.gob.pa, rpinternet@registro-publico.gob.pa**. You can visit them in person at: Vía España Calle 67A, frente a la Clínica Hospital San Fernando, Tel: 278-6000, Fax: 278-1014.

You can also find the status and ownership of a piece of property and get any title documents and surveys you may need at this office. If the property is registered in the name of

Homes on former U.S. army bases are an option

a corporation, the legal representatives must be verified, since they have power of attorney to make the sale.

Title verification should be done for any property especially outside of Panama City. If your property is free and clear it will have a *título de propiedad*. If not, stay clear of the property.

It is best to own property through a Panamanian Corporation to limit your liability in case of legal disputes. Buying and registering a property in a corporation has many advantages, mainly, asset protection in the event of a divorce or a lawsuit, which could result in you losing the property.

The final advice is do **not hire the same lawyer used by the seller of the property**. Also, do not forget to check that you are buying the land from its rightful owner. There are some people who will try to sell you property to which they do not have title. Some owners have sold their land to several buyers. You can protect your real estate investment further if you talk with neighbors about water shortages, safety and burglaries in the area.

Remember, never buy a property sight unseen. Do not forget to see if you need special permits to build. Be sure to check the comparative land values in your area to see if you are getting a good deal. If you are thinking of living in a remote area, check to be sure that roads, electricity and telephone service are available.

When buying rural or farm land, be careful of squatters. They can gain title to the land if they have lived on the property for a number of years. If you cannot live on your property year-round, then you will have to hire a guard, caretaker or a reliable house sitter to watch it for you. Make sure boundary fences and limit signs are well maintained and visible.

We suggest that in some cases, you rent for at least six months. However, whether you rent or buy first really depends on your comfort level. Make sure to buy where it's easy to rent or sell your home or condominium in case you change your plans or in the event of a personal emergency.

To find a house or land, first find a realtor with a good reputation. Your real estate agent should be able to identify true market value of any property.

In order to get a good buy you should study the market. Do not depend so much on the newspaper. Talk to as many people as you can. Nothing works better than word of mouth for finding good deals. Since Latinos love to haggle, practice your negotiating skills. You may be better off having a trustworthy, bilingual Panamanian search for you and do your negotiating. Your realtor or lawyer should also be able to assist you.

Building A Home

If you do decide to build a home on your land, there are several steps required. First, conduct a preliminary study, which should be completed before you buy the land. Also, be sure to see if your lot has access to water, drainage, electricity and telephone services. You will have to hire an architect or civil engineer to oversee the construction of your home. Be sure to get several bids and ask for references. Expect to visit the construction site almost everyday to ensure things are getting done.

If you cannot be there have a reliable person inspect the construction site for you on a daily basis.

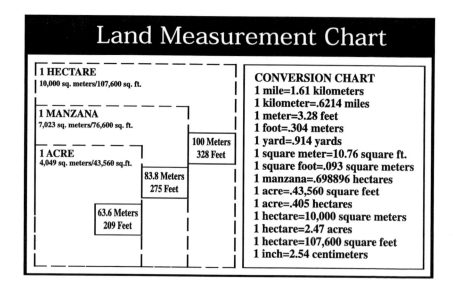

Land Measurement Chart

1 HECTARE
10,000 sq. meters/107,600 sq. ft.

1 MANZANA
7,023 sq. meters/76,600 sq. ft.

1 ACRE
4,049 sq. meters/43,560 sq.ft.

100 Meters
328 Feet

83.8 Meters
275 Feet

63.6 Meters
209 Feet

CONVERSION CHART
1 mile=1.61 kilometers
1 kilometer=.6214 miles
1 meter=3.28 feet
1 foot=.304 meters
1 yard=.914 yards
1 square meter=10.76 square ft.
1 square foot=.093 square meters
1 manzana=.698896 hectares
1 acre=.43,560 square feet
1 acre=.405 hectares
1 hectare=10,000 square meters
1 hectare=2.47 acres
1 hectare=107,600 square feet
1 inch=2.54 centimeters

Before you build, you should seriously weigh the costs of building a home yourself or buying a ready-made home.

As in the rest of Central America most construction in Panama is done with cinder block. However, more and more sheet rock is being used in the interior of homes for ceilings and walls. Most floors are covered with ceramic tile. Wall to wall carpeting and rugs are rarely found in homes.

Property Ownership

Foreigners can own property in Panama with few restrictions. Currently ownership can be conveyed in two ways: title and rights of possession.

Titled property is treated very similar to U.S. real estate law. Deeds are recorded in the public registry or "Registro Público". Rights of possession are handled by the agriculture department and also recorded. This system was originally set up in the land reform of 1971 to encourage homesteading of unclaimed, untitled land. Most of the land traded in the islands is by right of possession with the exception of town, property.

The most important difference in the two forms of ownership is that rights cannot be mortgaged.

Constitutionally the government cannot take possession of private property without following a condemnation process similar to the U.S.; the owner must be compensated for land and improvements at fair market value.

Regarding waterfront property, by law all beaches are public, hence all beachfront properties most provide a right of way starting from the highest tide to the property line. (The distance may vary).

The technical aspects of property ownership and your best options are best discussed with a qualified Panamanian lawyer.

Building Restrictions

Environmental impact studies may be required in some instances, but there are currently no zoning laws or building restrictions in some areas. Building permits are required and obtained locally. Permits to build on stilts over the water require a concession from the maritime authority.

Construction Costs

There is a vast range here depending on accessibility of the building site and degree of finish-out. The average cost, on Colon, is estimated between $30- 40/sq. ft.

Property Taxes

You will be pleased to know that property taxes for newly constructed homes are not applicable for the first twenty years you own the property.. A 2% (of acquisition cost) transfer tax is charged upon the sale of titled property.

Affordable Hired Help

As you know, full or part-time domestic help is hard to find and prohibitively expensive for the average person, not to mention a retiree, in the United States. This is not the case in Panama. A live-in maid or other full-time help usually costs about $150 to $200 per month. Often you can hire a couple for a bargain price with the woman working as a maid and the man working as a full-time gardener and watchman.

In Panama a maid usually does everything from washing clothes to taking care of small children. You can also use your maid to stand in line for you or run errands and bargain for you in stores since foreigners often pay more for some items because of their naively and poor language skills.

General handymen and carpenters are also inexpensive. If you are infirm, one of the above people can assist you with many daily tasks.

Labor laws in Panama are very strict. All domestic help have the right to Panama's Social Security, bonuses and severance pay. As an employer you are obligated by law to pay benefits for all types of help including domestic workers. It is imperative to file a work contract with the "**Ministerio de Trabajo**" when you hire an employee. It is highly advisable to do everything legally and in accordance with Panama's labor law when hiring employees. This way you will avoid misunderstandings and headaches at a later date. Social Security benefits for employees are between 5 and 6% of their monthly salaries.

There are two new books to help you communicate better with your hired help: Crown Publishers *Home Maid Spanish* and Barron's *Household Spanish*. Both books enable you to converse with your Spanish-speaking help without being fluent in the language. They are filled with all of the essential words and phrases you need to know.

Below is a brief summary of the main points of Panama's Labor Law. It is highly advisable to contact the Labor Ministry (*Ministerio de Trabajo*) or a competent lawyer if you have any specific concerns regarding your responsibilities as an employer.

Salaries - Employees have to be paid at least two times per month. In Spanish this is called *la quincena*. The government sets the minimum wage in Panama. Wages for skilled employees is higher than those set for unskilled. Wages are usually higher in Panama City.

Worker's Compensation - Every employer has to enroll their employees in the social security system which includes worker's compensation.

Maternity - Female employees have to receive benefits in accordance with Panama's Labor Code. Maternity leave is granted for at least 14 weeks, at least six weeks before delivery, and eight weeks after childbirth.

Sick Leave - Disability or paid sick leave has to be provided for each employee up to one and a half days per month. This equates to 18 days yearly. Sick leave may be accumulated for up to two years and be used entirely or partially during the third year of service. Employees covered by social security may receive additional sick leave.

El Aguinaldo - All employers are required to pay their employees a special thirteenth month bonus called an *aguinaldo*. This thirteenth month Christmas bonus is equivalent to one month's pay.

Amounts paid by the employer for the thirteenth month bonus are tax deductible.

Vacations - Usually an employee receives one month or 30 days of annual leave yearly. Annual leave may be accumulated for up to two years. Employees can take the annual leave in two 15 day blocks.

Overtime - An employee cannot be required to work overtime except under special circumstances. Three hours per day and nine hours weekly are the maximum amount of overtime hours. If the employee works more than this amount of overtime, additional salary must be paid. Overtime can range from 25% to 150% depending if the employee is working day or night shifts or holidays.

Maids

Work Day - The standard day shift is eight hours with a maximum of 48 hours weekly. Night shifts are seven hours with a maximum of 42 hours per week.

Purchase a **Panamanian Work Code** or *Código de Trabajo*, which lists all of the above regulations. After reading it, if still you have any questions or problems with employees rights we suggest you consult an attorney. This you will reduce the possibility of having misunderstandings with your hired help.

Health Care
Staying Healthy

Panama is considered to have one of the best health care systems in Latin America. Life expectancy is around 75 years. Along with Costa Rica Panama has some of the best private medical facilities in Central America. Many of their private medical facilities are affiliated with hospitals in the U.S.

Unlike other countries in Latin America, especially Mexico, Panama's water supply is good and perfectly safe to drink in most areas of the country. In most places you can drink the water without the fear of Montezuma's Revenge (diarrhea) or other intestinal problems. However, be careful when you drink water in the countryside. We have not heard many people complain about the quality of the country's water. If you prefer, bottled water is available. Just as in the U.S. there are about twenty brands of bottled water in all size containers sold at the supermarkets. Some of the more popular brands are Evian and Perrier which are available in supermarkets, restaurants and at hotels. Due to the country's hot climate it is important to drink a lot of liquids to avoid dehydration. Furthermore, health standards are good in most areas of the country due to the sanitation programs put into practice during the construction of the Panama Canal.

Malaria is no longer a problem in Panama. It has been completely eradicated. However, *mosquitos* can be a problem around sunrise and sunset. So, it is still a good idea to use repellent in jungle areas or at the beach.

Although the Panamanian government takes precautions to monitor the quality of the water and the country has high standards of sanitation, there are some precautions you should take. Wash and peel all fresh fruits and vegetables. Avoid drinking fruit drinks made with water that are sold in stands on the street. You should also watch out for raw seafood dishes served in some bars and restaurants.

Even if you are in good health, the probability of needing medical care increases with age. The security of knowing that good health services are available represents an enormous relief.

Most Panamanian doctors are excellent and have been trained in Europe, Canada or the United States. If you do not speak Spanish, you do not have to worry since many local doctors speak English, but most receptionists and nurses do not.

Doctor's fees for office visits vary. A typical visit to the doctor will set you back $10 to $20 dollars. A good private specialist usually charges between $30 and $45 for each visit, although some specialists charge a little more and others a little less.

Medical care is inexpensive because the average Panamanian earns only a few hundred dollars monthly. Also doctors do not have to pay high malpractice insurance premiums as in the United States.

To find a good English-speaking physician or specialist talk to other retires, look in the Yellow Pages under *Médicos*. Consultorios Médicos Paitilla (Tel: 269-522), in Panama City, has over 100 specialists.

A number of local insurance companies offer medical coverage in Panama for around $50 monthly. There are a number companies based in other countries which will cover you worldwide. Panama even has a Social Security System or **Caja de Seguro Social** similar to its U.S. counterpart. Members may obtain free medical at a Social Security hospital. The public or Social Security hospitals; located all over the country, can only accept those people who are members of Panama's Social Security system.

These public medical facilities are so good that you do not usually need private care. Most private specialists are required by law to work part-time in public hospitals. However, private clinics and hospitals do provide quicker services with more privacy enabling you to avoid long lines and the bureaucracy of the public system.

Private hospitals with the best facilities and equipment are **Centro Médico Paitilla**, **Clínica San Fernando** and **Hospital Nacional**. Panama's private hospitals accept insurance from most foreign insurance companies. Do not take this for granted and be sure to check with both the hospital in Panama and your private insurance company .

Centro Médico Patilla (Tel: 265-8800,269-5222 Calle 53 Este and Avenida Balboa) is the country's best and most expensive Hospital. This private hospital accepts foreigners. Depending on their amenities, rooms cost between $100 to $200 per day. All rooms have air conditioning, a private bathroom, telephone, color TV and usually have a sofa where a relative can spend the night. Most of the doctors who practice there have their own offices located across the street in front of the hospital.

Clínica San Fernando (Tel: 229-3800/229-2004, E-mail:elisalew@panama.phoenix.net). They have all the same facilities as the Paitilla hospital. In fact, many specialists practice in both hospitals.

Hospital Nacional (Tel: 207-8100 E-mail: mercadeo@hospitalnacional.com). This full-service hospital and medical center is located in Panama City.

Clínica Bella Vista (Tel: 227-1266 Avenida Perú at Calle 38) is another good hospital.

Centro Especializado y **Hospital Pediátrico San Fernando** (Children's Hospital) Tel: 229-3800 ext. 5300.

Clínica Hospital América Tel: 229-2221/229/1627

Hospital del Niño (Children's Hospital) Tel:225-1546.

Hospital Santo Tomás Tel: 227-4122 Avenida Balboa at Calle 34. This hospital is a public hospital under the Social Security system.

Hospital Centro Médico Mae Lewis Tel: 775-4616 or775-5566, E-mail: maelewis@pty.com. Located in David.

One of Panama's City's private hospitals

Care for the Elderly

Panama there also has full service custodial health care available for the elderly at a very low cost. Care for less independent senior citizens is around $1000 per month. Some of the better facilities offer comprehensive medical care and assistance which includes all medicines, lab work, dental care, ambulance service, a nutritionist, indoor and outdoor recreation, physical therapy, rehabilitation, permanent short and long-term stays, bilingual personnel, and special diets.

These programs are some of Central America's best and are considerably less expensive than in the United States. However, if these facilities are beyond an elderly person's means, a full-time live-in domestic worker can be hired as a nurse for a couple of hundred dollars monthly. In addition to caring for an infirm person this worker can manage other household chores.

To find care for the elderly look under asilos in the Panama City telephone directory, contact your consulate in Panama, or ask a local doctor.

Medicines and Pharmacies

Pharmacies are numerous in Panama and they stock most standard medicines available in Europe, Canada and the U.S. In general, the cost of most medicines is lower than those in the U.S.

A large number of drugs requiring a prescription in North America are freely available "over the counter" in any Panamanian pharmacy. Exceptions are strong pain reliever and narcotics that require a special prescription. Pharmacists are highly trained and are permitted to prescribe medicines as well as administer on-the-spot injections. Many pharmacies are open 24-hours.

They are also available to answer your questions and give free medical advice about less complex conditions.

Pharmacies:

Farmacia Arrocha Tel: 236-4023 is open 24 hours.
There are 12 stores in the Panama City area.
Farmacia Metro Tel: 221-6573
Super Farmacia Patilla Tel: 264-7584
Farmacia San Fernando Tel: 261-6945

Laboratories:

Laboratorio San Fernando Tel: 229-1610/229-3800
Laboratorio Clínica De Sedas Tel: 263-7121/263-8786
Laboratorio Clínica Pasteur Tel: 269-5653/269-6367

A Panamanian Pharmacy

Insurance

Life insurances, Medical insurances, car insurance, fire, theft , etc. are available in Panama. Contact the agents below if you have questions about different coverage.

Kevin Bradely
Tel: (507) 263-6450
E-mail: kevin@centraldeseguros.com

Seguros Fedpa, S.A.
Tel: (507) 264-0326
E-mail: segfedpa@sinfo.net

IS Internacional de Seguros
Tel: (507) 206-4000

Rodríguez R., Nilka Z.
Phone (507) 261-2131
(507) 635-5152
Fax (507) 261-2131
E-mail: nilkaz@mail.com

Taxes

Foreign income is exempt from taxation in Panama. Foreign retires are not required to pay Panamanian taxes on their income generated abroad. Bank account interest is 100% tax free as is capital gains on the sale of securities. So you can see why Panama is considered to be a tax haven by many expatriates.

Real estate taxes are reasonable. Sellers of real estate pay a low tax for the transfer of property.

Income tax for individuals who work is also reasonable. According to the tax law, any income generated from a source within the Republic of Panama is subject to income tax. Article

694 of Panama's Tax Code states what activities are not considered as income-producing within Panama and not subject to taxes. Article 708 and Decree 60 of the Tax Code list types of income not subject to income taxes in Panama: Interest on savings accounts, time deposits, Panamanian securities and some types of loans.

The first $3,000 of net taxable income is exempt from taxes. People making over $3,000 are taxed progressively on their total net income. Tax payers can take advantage of many deductions. All deductible expenses must be generated in Panama. Corporate income tax rates are around 20% to 40% as stipulated by the tax code. If you have any questions about taxes, you should contact a Panamanian attorney or accountant.

Property Tax is regulated by Article 766. The maximum annual percentage of assessment is 2.10% over the value of the land (land value under US$20,000.00 is exempt of this particular tax, as per Law No. 36 of 1995). The property tax is also levied on the declare value of the improvement build on the land. The owners must pay according to the official assessment value (which is usually the declare (commercial) value on the last purchase Deed).

Transfer Tax on Real Property is regulated under Article 701, and was amended in 1991 with the implementation of Law No. 31 and in 1995 by Law No. 28. The Law confirms that all sellers are obligated to pay, at the moment of a transfer of a real property, the transfer tax, but allows the seller to apply one of two options. Option 1) the seller could select the 2% tax of the declared commercial sale price, which is understood as an advance payment on the capital gain or the 5% tax of the assessment value, which is established by adding a 10% increase per annum on the purchase value.

You will be pleased to know that interest payed on a mortgage is deductible from your U.S. taxes.

Capital Gain Tax is applicable if the alternative of 2% for Transfer Tax is used for the transfer of real property and if there is a capital gain. This tax is regulated by Article 699 and for corporations acting a sellers, a 30% flat tax payment on the profit will be applicable, notwithstanding, if shareholders are foreigners. Another percentage will be applicable if the seller is a natural person. If there is no capital gain on the transfer of a property, the 2% transfer tax paid in advance for the sale, is to be considered as a credit for the seller and will be lost.

Inheritance Tax was regulated under Article 819 until 1985, at which time it was abolished with the enactment of Law No. 22.

U.S. citizens are subject to income tax wherever they are living. You must file your U.S. income tax returns yearly through the American Embassy. You have to declare all income earned abroad but you may claim a tax exemption up to $ 80,000 on overseas-earned gross income. The $80,000 applies to individual, unmarried taxpayers. If you are married, you and your spouse may exclude up to $144,000 of foreign income, but you cannot combine the two exemptions. This exclusion does not apply to passive income such as interest, dividends, capital gains or overseas pensions. It only applies to a foreign earned income. You must reside outside of the U.S. for at least 330 days a year or be a legal resident of a foreign country to qualify for this exemption. Your primary business must also be located abroad to qualify for the foreign-earned income exemption.

Fortunately, if you live outside the U.S., you qualify for a 2-month extension and may wait to file your taxes until June 15th. However, if you mail your return from outside the U.S., it is best to mail your return at least 2 weeks before the due date. You can speed this up by using DHL, FedEx or UPS. You need to use a U.S. tax form 2555 to apply for this extension. Even if you earn no income in Panama, it is imperative to file a standard 1040 tax form to avoid problems. The biggest mistake made by individuals is assuming that since their income is under the exclusionary amount, they do not have to file a return. Payment of taxes, interest and penalties can now be done by credit card by dialing **1-888-2PAY-TAX**.

If you have any tax questions, contact the U.S. Embassy or IRS. Call either the Consular Section of the U.S. Embassy 227-1777, or the nearest IRS office in Mexico City at 525 211-0042, ext. 3557. You may consult the IRS Web site at: www.irs.gov. There is also book titled *The Expats Guide to U.S. Taxes*. It may be purchased through www.amazon.com. Another good resource is found at: www.filetax.com/expat.html.

If you need help with your tax forms and returns while living in Panama, contact **H & R Block** Tel: 011-(507) 260-1052 or see www.hrblock.com for income tax assistance or for help with IRS problems.

If Canadians want to be exempt from income taxes in Canada they need to have severed major residency ties for at least two years. These "residency ties" can include an un-leased house, Canadian health coverage, automobile registration, spouse or child support in Canada, banking or investment ties.

A foreign tax credit is often available for taxpayers who pay tax in another country, i.e. Panama. To find out your tax status, consult form IT221R3 on the Canadian Customs and Revenue Agency Web site: www.ccraedrc.gc.ca. Canadian tax returns should be in by April 30th. Self-employed people have until June 15th.

Canadians will have to contact the local Canadian Embassy concerning their tax obligations while living abroad.

Panamanian Corporations

Offshore corporations enable you to act as an international citizen with complete confidentiality, privacy and safety. Offshore corporations can legally open offshore bank accounts, brokerage accounts, hold credit cards, trade securities, hold titles to cars or other hard assets, own property, stocks, etc., and in many cases, completely exempt you from any tax reporting requirements with complete confidentiality.

Why Panama?

For many years, Panama has been recognized worldwide as a major international offshore banking center offering very attractive legal and tax incentives to Panamanian corporations. For example, Panamanian law allows Panamanian corporations to issue "bearer" stock certificates. This means the owners who control the corporation do not have to be named in any public record, since ownership is through physical possession of the "bearer" shares. Panamanian Corporations are not subject to Panamanian tax on income earned outside of Panama. Stated another way, as long as you are not earning money within Panama, your money will be 100% tax free. If your business derives its monies from within Panama, some taxes will have to be paid. Panama allows you to name your corporation with an English name, which has many advantages when using your Panamanian Corporation in English speaking countries. These are just a few of the more important reasons why Panamanian corporations are so popular.

Forming a Panamanian Corporation:

First we recommend you select a name in English followed by Corp., Corporation Inc. or Incorporated. You cannot use the words Bank, Trust, Foundation or Insurance in the name of your corporation. You may use any name as long as it is not being currently used in Panama. If you own a U.S. Corporation, you may find some advantages in using the same name for your Panamanian corporation, if available in Panama. This would allow you to have identically named offshore and onshore bank accounts as well as other similar advantages.

Panamanian corporations are typically formed with nominee directors, president, secretary and treasurer. All corporations must have these officers. The law allows one person to hold one or more offices within the corporation. A nominee is someone who is lending his or her name for the corporation. The nominee is basically a "front man." Nominees are usually Panamanian citizens who are modestly paid officer workers. If you wish, you may select your own directors and officers. However, the original directors and officers selected are registered with the Panamanian public registry and becomes public information available to anyone who inquires. Therefore, if you wish confidentiality, we recommend you select the nominee director option. Officers and directors can always be changed later.

A corporation does not have to have a registered office in Panama. However, every corporation must have a resident agent in Panama who must either be a lawyer or a law firm.

Panamanian law allows corporate shares to be issued in "bearer" form. This means that whoever physically possesses the shares owns the company. This allows for total confidentiality of ownership, since the person who physically possesses the shares is not identified in any public or even private record. Having a Panamanian corporation with "bearer" shares also makes transfer of ownership completely private and not a matter of public record, since transfer of ownership is a simple process of physically transferring the "bearer" shares to a new owner. This is very similar to passing a $20 bill to someone else versus writing them a check. This feature makes it very easy to sell or transfer properties confidentially by simply transferring the "bearer" shares and ownership of the Panamanian corporation, and thus avoiding many forms of taxes and closing costs because title of the property remains in the name of the Panamanian corporation. Essentially, you are simply selling the corporation that owns the property.

Your Panamanian Corporation comes with a notarized General Power of Attorney (in English) signed by two officers named in the articles of incorporation. This power of attorney provides a blank space for you to fill in the name of any person you want to act as the legal agent for the corporation with the authority to open and sign on corporate bank accounts, enter into contracts for the corporation, sign and transfer assets for the corporation, etc. Although you fill in your name or another person name as having Power of Attorney, this is not evidence of ownership. The person named is simply an agent, similar to an employee empowered to act for the corporation. You may order as many additional Power of Attorney forms as you wish.

Older Panamanian corporations with established bank accounts sell for thousands of dollars or more. Selling your Panamanian corporation is a matter of physically transferring the "bearer" stock certificate together with the other corporate records to the new owner.

The one-time cost for setting up a simple Panamanian Corporation is around $ 700. You will have to pay an annual Registered Agent and Director's fee of $150 , due one month before the anniversary date of the corporation. An annual fee of around $150 must also be paid plus a few administrative costs.

We recommend **Roberto I. Guardia R** if you want to form a Panamanian corporation or foundation. A number of Americans we interviewed speak very well of him. Please see his ad in this book. Tel: (507) 263-3917, Fax: (507) 263-3924 Cel: 612-5429 E-mail:rig@orcag.com, www.orcag.com.

*A copy of the entire Panamanian Corporation Law may be found in Chapter 10.

Private Interest Foundations

A foundation is another legal entity for doing business. Panamanian Law 25, which was passed on June 12, 1995, created Panamanian Foundations. This law was made for tax planning and created foundations which work similarly to a Liechtenstein Foundation. A foundation of this type is sort of a combination of a trust and an International Business Company (IBC). The advantage of a foundation is that when its assets are from outside Panama, no taxes have to be paid. A foundation is not suppose to take part directly in a commercial venture for profit. However, it can own shares of a business or IBC under the condition that the profits from the business will be used to benefit the foundation. This way an IBC can be put in a foundation.

There are some annual fees associated with owning a foundation. A private foundation must be formed with an amount to no less than $10,000. The name of the beneficiaries, the objectives, and board members of the foundation must be listed. The founder of the foundation may select the name in any language, but it has to contain the word "foundation." It must also be specified if the foundation is fixed for life or perpetual.

For additional details and all of the nuances of a Panamanian Foundation, we suggest you contact a Panamanian attorney.

MAKING MONEY IN PANAMA

Investing in Panama

Let's review a few of the reasons Panama has such magnetism for qualified foreign investors. The country boasts a democratic elected government and enduring political stability.

The presence of US currency in Panama is a key factor in attracting foreign investment. Since Panama is on the dollar system, investors do not have to worry about having their money devaluated as in many Latin American countries.

The trend towards an open economy and possible trade pacts with such nations as the U.S. and Mexico are conducive to investment in Panama. There are also no government expropriation or interference as in many Latin American countries. Foreign investment is encouraged by a business oriented government. All investment is backed by a government that realizes the value of private business to a developing country. In 1946 Panama's business oriented mentality led to the creation of the Colón Duty Free Zone, considered to be the second largest free trade center in the world, after Hong Kong. In addition, the Panamanian government offers foreigners who invest in Panama many attractive incentives such as legal residency and tax privileges.

To promote tourism the government passed Law Number 8 in 1994, whereby for a minimum investment of $30,000 in Panama City or $50,000 you receive accelerated depreciation on real estate assets of 10% per year, a 20-year exemption of import duties for materials, equipment and vehicles, and a 20-year exemption on real estate taxes for your business.

With over 130 banks, Panama is a considered an international banking capital and one of the most important offshore business centers in Latin America.

Panama is easily accessible from all parts of the world by land, sea, or air. A world class international airport is located only 35 minutes from the capital. Fast internet access is available in metropolitan areas. Outstanding phone, telex, and telegraph systems link Panama internationally to other parts of the world. Easy access to shipping, air transportation and proximity to North American and Latin consumers markets and a modern labor code also make the country attractive to investors.

Also, let's remember that investors in Panama have equal rights and laws to protect them. When you start a business a Panamanian partner is not required nor is residency necessary. Ownership of real estate and/or private investment is guaranteed and protected by Panama's constitution under Article 44 applicable to both Panamanians and foreigners alike.

The regulations for conducting business in Panama are the same for both local and foreign corporations, which can fully own and control local corporations as well as real estate without any access limitations or restrictions.

Real estate has always been a good investment for United States citizens and other foreigners. In Panama all real estate property titles must be registered in the *Registro Público* (Public Registry).

Many opportunities await foreigners who start new businesses previously nonexistent in Panama. As you know the cost of labor is low.

Additional reasons for investing in Panama are: asset protection (creditors, judgments, liens, bankruptcy and divorce), privacy from individuals and governments and fewer taxes (income tax, inheritance tax, estate taxes and probate fees).

When the U.S. bases were operating in Panama a lot of revenue and jobs were generated by the soldiers and their dependents. After the U.S. closed its bases all of this came to an abrupt end and the economy began to suffer the effects of the withdraws. Consequently, the government is now promoting tourism to compensate for the loss of revenue and jobs. With the government's help tourism has finally finally started to grow. This governmental support has created many opportunities for savvy entrepreneurs in the field of tourism.

On June 1994 Congress enacted Law No. 8 to further promote tourism investment in Panama. This law was later modified in April 1995 and is now similar to that which regulates tourism investment in Costa Rica, more specifically, allowing investors, both foreign and local, to obtain tax breaks for up to 20 years under certain circumstances.

This decree regulates public lodgings, receptive tourism agencies, tourist transport services of passengers, tourist restaurants, discos, nightclubs, specialized tourism centers, recreational parks, theme parks, zoos, convention centers, marine complexes, tourist development zones of national interest, etc.

Once an interested party or corporation has completed the necessary forms, they must submit the forms to IPAT (Panama

Tourism Department), where they will be reviewed by IPAT's Board of Directors. This board meets once a month, at which the Minister of Commerce serves as the Chair person. Upon approval, the benefits are granted to the developer.

Some of the tax incentive are:

a) 20 years of full exoneration from import duties for the introduction of any material, vessels, automobile and/or equipment to be used to build and furnish public lodging establishments.

b) 20 year exoneration from real property tax.

c) Exoneration from any tax or assessment on its capital.

d) Exoneration from warfare or any fee for landing on piers, airport, etc.

e) Exemption from payment of income tax on any interest earned by creditors, etc.

f) Annual rate of 10% will be allowed for real property depreciation, not including the cost of the land.

Foreigners can invest with Panama's banking system, private banks, or finance companies. Interest rates are higher than in the United States and there are many attractive savings accounts and time deposit programs from which to choose. There are some degrees of bank secrecy, liberal money transfer regulations, and favorable tax laws for foreigners (see the section in this chapter titled "Taxes").

You may also invest profitably in blue chip offshore mutual funds. Most people do this to protect their assets from creditors, judgments, liens, bankruptcy, malpractice claims, divorce and separation claims, liability claims not covered by insurance, and seizure by the U.S. government.

RELOCATION, INVESTMENT and RETIREMENT CONSULTANTS is a firm we highly recommend to any newcomer or potential investor. They have many years of experience, will steer you in the right direction and save you a lot of headaches and money. Their expertise, network of reliable contacts, and insider information have already helped hundreds of people find success, prosperity and happiness in Central America. Most importantly, they can show you how to really make money in Central America by hooking you up with time-tested investments with low tax liability. Most savvy investors here have their money in one of these programs. You may contact them at Tel/Fax: 011-(506)-261-8968, E-mail: **centralamericaconsultants@yahoo.com**.

Before investing or starting a business, you should take the time to do your homework. Under no circumstances should you invest right off the plane, that is to say, on your first trip to Panama. Unscrupulous individuals will always prey on impulsive buyers anywhere in the world. Be wary of any sales persons who try to pressure you into investing. Remember it is hard to start a business in your own home country; do not imagine it will be any easier in Panama, where both language and customs are different.

We also suggest you ask a lot of questions and get information and assistance from any of the organizations listed below in order to thoroughly understand the business climate of the country. However, do not solely depend on the help of these organizations. You will have to garner a lot of information and learn on your own by some trial and error. This way you can find out what works best for your particular situation.

American Chamber of Commerce of Panama
P.O. Box 128
Balboa Ancon, Panama RP
Panama City, Panama
Tel: (507) 269-3881 Fax: (507) 223-3508

Panama Chamber of Commerce
Avenida Cuba No. 33a Panama City
P.O. Box 74, Panama
Tel: (507) 25-0833 Fax: (507) 64-8513

Panama Banking Association
P.O. Box 4554 Zona 5
Panama 15/F
Banco Union Building,
Samuel Lewis Avenue, Panama
Tel: (507) 263-7044 Fax: (507)263-7783

U.S. Panama Business Council (in USA)
Ronald Reagan Bldg. and International Trader Center
1300 Pennsylvania Avenue.,
Washington DC 20004-3021
Tel: (202) 312-1645 Fax: (202) 312-1646
E-mail: information@us-panama.org
www.us-panama.org

U.S.-Panama Business Council (in Panama)
Global Bank Tower
Calle 50, Piso 22, Oficina 22F
Panama City, Panama
Tel: (507) 269-2178 Fax: (507) 269-0534

PANAMA'S STOCK MARKET

Foreigners can also invest in the local Stock Exchange (Bolsa Nacional de Valores) to get better returns than from traditional financial systems. The stock market presents a safe investment alternative with great opportunities for the investment to grow through stock appreciation, dividends, stock splits, mergers and acquisitions.

For almost a century, Panama's dollar-based monetary system has fostered a stable, open economy based on a modern banking center, a nationwide trade zone and broad infrastructure of corporate and financial products successfully serving Latin America.

The Panama Stock Exchange emerges as the natural development of this unique economy. It stands as the only dollar-based securities market in the region. Its mission is to increase and complement the stability that Panama provides to Latin America and to provide a unique regional niche for investors, issuers and broker/dealers seeking global challenges.

Since its creation in 1990, the Panama Stock Exchange has been an important part of the development of Panama's role as a regional financial center. This self-regulated institution is supervised the **National Stock Market Commission**.

In August of 1999, an electronic trading system was introduced, through which the stock market exchanges are interconnected by means of a fiber optic system. This permits negotiations and trades to be made from an individual's office. This system has increased trading volume and added more liquidity to the market.

The **Bolsa Nacional de Valores** offers the investor the opportunity to acquire stocks, short-term corporate debt, government documents, closed end mutual funds and corporate bonds and mortgages.

Investors can diversify their investments so as to reduce risk by placing their capital in such sectors as banks, telecommunications, insurance companies, financial services, mutual funds, commerce, construction, tourism, and entertainment.

The main targets are the many companies of Central America and the northern countries of South America that have strong balance sheets but are too small to issue shares in New York. In Panama, these companies find ready sources of capital in the foreign investors who have billions of dollars deposited in Panamanian banks.

This regional business is showing promise. El Salvador's Taca Airlines pioneered last year with a $30 million-share issue on the exchange. Banco Ganadero of Colombia issued $20 million in shares in December 1995, and Banco de Colombia followed with a $10 million offering.

As part of the effort to develop a regional equities market, the Panama Stock Exchange has taken a leadership role in financially integrating Central America through a regional exchange known as the Bolcen. As a first step, clearing and settlement systems are being harmonized to bring delivery and payment in line with world standards.

Currently, most transactions center on government bonds. Banco Disa recently issued bankers' acceptances through the stock market.

Requirements:

Companies must obtain the authorization of Panama's National Securities Commission to sell or underwrite an initial public offering of securities. Companies must also apply to have securities listed on the Panama Stock Exchange.

To obtain the Securities Commission's authorization, companies must file through an attorney with the Commission and the Stock Exchange.

The main filing requirements are: The articles of incorporation and by-laws of the company, which must be registered with the National Public Registry.

Certification from the National Public Registry of the names of the company's directors and legal representative, the authorized share capital and the term of the maturity of the company.

A prospectus or selling memorandum in compliance with the rules and regulations of the National Securities Commission.

To list in Panama securities initially issued by a company abroad, the main requirements are:

An information memorandum describing details of the issue, which must comply with the rules and regulations of Panama's securities commission and the exchange.

Copies of the most recent financial statement, which may be no more than 120 days prior to the application date, and statements for the past three fiscal years. Statements must be audited by an independent certified public accountant and comply with generally accepted accounting principles.

The issuer or agent who requests the listing on the Panama Stock Exchange must appoint a legal agent with full power of attorney to permanently represent the issuer in Panama.

All documentation issued in a foreign country must be authenticated by the competent authorities or diplomatic representative of Panama in the country of origin of the document.

Registration with the National Securities Commission in Panama is free. The Panama Stock Exchange registration fee is $250, plus an annual maintenance fee of $100.

Direct enquires or further questions for the Panama Stock Exchange can be addressed to:

General Manager
Panama Bolsa de Valores
Calle Elvira Méndez y Calle 52,
Edificio Vallarino, Planta Baja
Apartado Postal 87-0878,
República de Panamá
www.panabolsa.com
E-mail: bvp@pmabolsa.com
Tel: (507)269-1966 Fax: (507)269-2457

There are more than 150 companies listed on the stock market. Among those listed, there are some foreign companies which negotiate stocks as well as bonds.

Panama Stock Exchange Members:
Cambios, S.A. Manuel D. Cabarcos G. Juan Manuel Cabarcos C. Tel: (507) 264-6655 Fax: (507) 264-5204 Apdo, 4341, Panama 5, Rep. de Panama

Negocios En Valores Mariana de Detresno-Pedro Detresno Thomas Abrahams Tel: (507) 269-5135/264-4301 Fax: (507) 264-2878/264-7395 Apdo. 6-497 El Dorado, Rep. de Panama

Capital Traders of Panama Dulcidio De La Guardia Tel: (507) 264-2044 Fax: (507) 223-5147 Apdo. 7201 Panama 5, Rep. de Panama

Inversiones Bursatiles De Panama, S.A. Ramon E. Fabrega G. - Americo Quintero M. Julieta G. de De Diego-Samuel Espinosa Tel: (507) 263-7150 Fax: (507) 263-7995 Apdo. 6646, Panama, Rep. de Panama

Tower Securities Inc. Ricardo Sosa Tel: (507) 269-6900 Fax: (507) 269-2964 Apdo. 6-6039 El Dorado, Rep. de Panama

Banistmo Brokers Inc. Alvaro Tomas A. - Alberto Alvarez A. Aura Beitia Tel: (507) 269-9555 Fax: (507) 264-5881 Apdo. 6-3823 El Dorado, Rep. de Panama

Bantal Brokers, S.A. Javier Carrizo-Paul A. Smith Monica de Chapman-Vicente Pascual Francisco Escoffery-Carolina Guardia Tel: (507) 263-7072 Fax: (507) 264-7106 Apdo. 135, Panama 9A, Rep. de Panama

BG Investment Co., Inc. Juan Rafil Humbert A.-Francisco Sierra Eugenia de Jimenez-Rosa Duboy Tel: (507) 227-3200/3169 Fax: (507) 225-2868 Apdo. 4592, Panama 5, Rep. de Panama

LAFISE Jorge Rosania Tel: (507) 264-7100/5416 Fax: (507) 264-7528 Apdo. 55-2654 Paitilla, Rep. de Panama

Citi Valores Eduardo Jimenez-Ema M. de Zarak Giselle de Tejeira-Omar Alvarado Tel: (507) 263-5544 Fax: (507) 264-0659 Apdo. 555, Panama 9A, Rep. de Panama

Banco Nacional de Panama Maria Isabel Fraser Calamari Militza Hernandez Santiago Carmen Herrera Tristan Tel: (507) 263-5151/7527 Fax: (507) 269-0091 Apdo. 5220, Panama 5, Rep. de Panama

Bicsa Valores (Panama), S.A. Arturo Cuevillas Leon Jose Francisco Ulate Federico Echandi Gurdian Guillermo Clark Cano Tel: (507) 263-6822 Fax: (507) 263-6393 Apdo. 600, Panama 1, Rep. de Panama

Courtesy of www.explore Panama.com

Finding Work

Foreigners can only work when they are legal residents. Once they have residency they will not need a work permit. The only exception to this rule is when a non-resident can do a job a Panamanian is unqualified to do. In this case a work permit is usually granted (see Chapter 4). These kinds of jobs are few and far between.

We have some discouraging news for those living on small pensions and hoping to supplement their income with a part or full-time job or for others who need to work just to keep busy. Finding work can be difficult but not impossible. In the first place, it is not easy for a Panamanian, not to mention foreigners who do not speak fluent Spanish, to find permanent work. Unless you have excellent Spanish language skills and offer a skill not found in the local job market, you will find it difficult to procure a traditional job.

If you are one of the few foreigners who has mastered Spanish, you will probably have a fair chance of finding work in tourism or some other related field. However, your best bet may be to find employment with a North American or European firm doing business in Panama. The best-paying jobs are with multinational corporations. Many foreign companies in Latin America have a need for native English speakers. Many Panamanians have studied English well. But few speak it with native fluency. Your English skills can be a real advantage when looking for work. It is best to contact one of these companies before moving to Panama. Depending on your qualifications, you may be able to find a job as a salesman, an executive, or a representative.

When local companies hire foreigners, they are generally looking for a solid educational background and an entrepreneurial spirit that some companies find lacking in Panamanians. It helps to have a degree from a well-known U.S.

university—preferably an MBA. If you have worked in a modern company in North America or Europe, the knowledge and skills you have learned can give you an advantage over the locals and open some important doors.

Even if you know little or no Spanish, you have a chance of finding work as an English teacher at a language institute or private school. Do not expect to earn more than a survival salary from one of these jobs because the minimum wage in Panama is low. Working as a full-time language instructor will not bring you more than a few hundred dollars monthly.

As supplemental income or busywork, this is fine, but you will not make a living, given the kind of lifestyle to which you are probably accustomed to. If you can find work at a private bilingual school, you can earn over $1000 a month. The competition for these jobs is very stiff, preference is given to bilingual Costa Ricans and most foreigners hang on to these coveted positions.

Try putting one of your skills to use by providing some service to the large expatriate community in Panama. Everyone has a talent or specialty they can offer. Unfortunately, if you are a retired professional such as a doctor or lawyer, you cannot practice in Panama because of certain restrictions but can offer your services as a consultant to other foreigners and retires.

As if finding work were not hard enough in Panama, a work permit or residency is required before foreigners can work legally. Labor laws are very strict and the government does not want foreigners taking jobs away from Panamanians. You are only allowed to work if you can perform specialized work that a Panamanian cannot. However, many foreigners work for under-the-table pay without a work permit.

If you do not seek remuneration, you can always find volunteer work to keep yourself busy. This kind of work is legal, so you do not need a work permit or run the risk of being deported for working illegally.

Starting a Business in Panama

An important thing to remember is that Panama is a land of abundance. This plenitude can translate into opportunities for the savvy investor or creative entrepreneur.

Panama literally means "the place of abundant fish," but the locals like to say everything abounds in Panama. And it is true, as visitors and residents will discover for themselves. There is an abundance of wildlife throughout the country, vast expanses of land, a copious amount of white sand beaches, hundreds of islands, more banks and shopping centers than you have ever dreamed possible and a huge amount of seafood. In addition, Panama City has an abundance of restaurants, hotels, convention centers and night clubs.

No other country in Central America has a highly developed urban area with dense tropical rain forest at a short distance. Last but not least, you will find an abundance of smiles, from Panama's friendly helpful people.

If you plan to go into business here it is very important to be aware of the local consumer market in order to succeed. Most of the country's purchasing power is located in the Panama City area. Intelligent business people will try to meet the needs of this group.

You may also think about targeting tourists and upper-class Panamanians. Panama has world class fishing, diving and opportunities in ecotourism. There are a wealth of opportunities as well as incentives available in tourist-related businesses. Upper-class Panamanians have a large disposable income and the greatest purchasing power. They do not mind spending a little more on good quality products. Just look at their expensive designer clothing like Tommy Hilfiger, their expensive imported automobiles and many palatial homes. Even used American

Success Stories in Panama and Central America

A Place for Expats

Roger Gallo is an international investment consultant. Years ago he realized that there was a world of adventure and business opportunities awaiting people who relocated countries outside the U.S. Mr. Gallo's interest in alternative expatriate life-styles led him to write the classic expat handbook, Escape from America. It gives the whole scoop for anyone who wants to relocate and seek a better quality of life for less money or for those who want to make more money outside of America. Mr. Gallo also runs the best internet resource for anyone seeking information about moving abroad. His site may be found at: www.escapeartist.com.

An Enterprising Gringo

Jim moved to Panama several years ago from Costa Rica. He really liked Costa Rica but had trouble finding his niche there. He started a magazine about tourism which had moderate success. It was a good publication but the market and timing were not right. So, he decided to test his luck in Panama and found success in a couple of ventures.

A Real Estate Genius

Sandy Perkoff came to Nicaragua about two years ago after residing in Costa Rica for over 20 years. He ran a successful car rental company and dabbled in real estate during his stint in Costa Rica. Presently he lives in the colonial city of Granada with his Costa Rican wife, Lucía. He is a personable man who knows everyone in town. Sandy is a highly -skilled creative entrepreneur working in real estate. He has brokered several properties and was involved in the sale of a multimillion dollar project at the beach. His pet project is the restoration of a colonial style house in downtown Granada.

A Service for Expats

About 10 years ago Jim Fendell realized the need for a fast reliable mail service as an alternative to the regular Costa Rican mail system. Thus Aerocasillas was born. His company has now expanded to Panama and other countries in the region.

A Costa Rican Transplant

Clayton Schmitt moved to Panama from Costa Rica about eight years ago. The retiree from Denver rents a 1,500-square-foot, four-bedroom home for $250 a month. "I priced a Nissan Sentra in Panama," recalls Schmitt,70 "It cost $10, 545 including sales tax. The same car woul have cost more in other Central American countries."

Schmiit says, The grocery stores have everything you want. We buy meat by the pound, gas by the gallon and we pay for it in dollars."

Costs are dramatically lower than in the US. Schmidt's wife had a kidney stone removed last year in a Panama hospital for $1,600. The same operation would cost nearly $28,000 in the US, she says." (Courtesy of USA TODAY)

A Travel Business

Rob, another friend of ours from Florida has had a successful travel business based in Costa Rica and Florida for many years. He is a visionary and is well aware of Panama's impending travel boom. It is only a question of time before he dominates the travel scene in Panama like he has done in Costa Rica. His website can be found at www.centralamerica.com.

A Hidden Valley

Sam Taliaferro, from the U.S., is said to have discovered Boquete's Valle Escondido(Hidden Valley) while horseback riding. He was the first developer and made his dream come true. Now the area is considered one of the country's prime retirement havens.

A Place to Learn Languages

American David Kaufman is the founder of Conversa, Costa Rica's oldest and most successful language schools. David had a Masters Degree in linguistics and served in the Peace Corps in the Dominican Republic. At his school's two campuses, Spanish is taught to foreigners and English to Costa Ricans.

A Dedicated Educator

Mary Ellen Norman is the director of the American-Nicaraguan School in Granada. Mary originally came to the school over ten years ago on a short-term basis. However, she fell in love with Nicaragua and her job and has never left. Under her auspices the school has flourished, offering a complete accredited academic program with all subjects in English. Her school is located on a hill overlooking the city of Managua. The academic program is excellent and the school is on the American calendar.The campus is very impressive. All of the rooms have air conditioning, there is a huge gymnasium, running track and much more.

clothing is an excellent business for Panamanians who cannot afford designer brands.

The majority of the country's middle-class consumer's values are now more akin to their U.S. counterparts. Middle and lower upper class Panamanians seem to want all of the goodies.

One group to target is the lucrative foreign residents market. There are many full-time foreigners living in Panama. All you have to do is look for a product to fill their needs. Most yearn for some hard-to-find-products from home and would rather buy them in Panama than go to the U.S. to shop.

Panama is ripe for innovative foreigners willing to take a risk and start businesses that have not previously existed. Start-up costs for small businesses are less than in the U.S. or Canada. Many of the same types of businesses which have been successful in the U.S. and Canada will work if researched correctly. There is definitely a need for these types of businesses. You just have to do your homework and explore the market. Be aware that not everything that works in the U.S. will work in Panama. Also you may have to adapt your idea because of the vagaries of the local market and different purchasing power. Do not get any grandiose ideas since the country has only around 2 million people. You cannot expect to market products on a large scale as in the States.

Panama's local artisans make scores of beautiful handcrafted products. With so many choices, a smart person can find something to sell back home.

These are some of the potential business opportunities worth exploring: building and selling of small homes for middle-class Panamanians or foreigners; an import-export business; desktop publishing; computer services and support; U.S. franchises; importing new foods; specialty bookstores; restaurants and bars; an auto body and paint shop; consulting;

or specialty shops catering to North Americans and upper-class Panamanians.

Panamanians love anything novel from America. There are many stores selling both new and used trendy U.S.-style clothing. Local teenagers dress like their counterparts in the States and even watch MTV. U.S. Fast food restaurants like Taco Bell, Burger King , Pizza Hut and McDonald's are extremely popular. Real estate speculation can be lucrative if you have the know-how and capital.

You may also think about targeting tourists and upper-class Panamanians. There is a wealth of opportunities available in tourist-related businesses. Upper-class Panamanians have a large disposable income and the greatest purchasing power. They do not mind spending a little more on good quality products. Just look at their expensive designer clothing like Tommy Hilfiger, their expensive imported automobiles and many palatial homes.

The majority of the country's middle-class consumer's values are now more akin to their U.S. counterparts. Middle and upper lower class Panamanians seem to want all of the goodies.

One group to target is the lucrative foreign residents market. There are around thousands full-time foreigners living in Panamanian. This number is bound to increase as Panama's reputation grows as a retirement haven. All you have to do is look for a product to fill their needs. Most yearn for some hard -to-find-products from home and would rather buy them in Panama than go to the U.S. to shop.

These are some of the potential business opportunities worth exploring: building and selling of small homes for middle class Panamanians or foreigners; an import-export business; desktop publishing; computer services and support; U.S. franchises; importing new foods; specialty bookstores; restaurants and bars; an auto body and paint shop; consulting;

Live in and Make Money in an Architectural Treasure
By Roger Gallo

Casco Viejo languished and decayed. For over half a century no one with any sense would invest money in it. Certain functions still took place in Casco Viejo. The exotically beautiful presidential palace Las Garzas, (The Herons) was there, and still is, but all the modern functions of government were done somewhere else. Las Garzas, one of the most beautiful buildings imaginable, features a "Moorish Patio" that has a fountain with live herons. The Presidential Palace remained in Casco Viejo even as Casco Viejo declined, for if Casco Viejo was anything it was Panamanian. There were other buildings also lovely and as pain-stakingly maintained. The French Embassy for one. As Casco Viejo declined around it, the French Embassy remained in flawless condition as befits an emblem of pride, for if Casco Viejo was anything it was French. Other buildings stood up and maintained. Some families never retreated. (See photo above.)

But the overall trend for Casco Viejo was downhill. Most buildings were not maintained, nor was the neighborhood itself. Only a few building were maintained amidst a sea of decay. Those that stood the test of time however, have been proved right. Casco Viejo might have been knocked down, but it was not out. Within the past few years money has begun to flow back into Casco Viejo. As Panama closes in on the 21st century, it looks forward to ownership of the canal, and there has been a growing pride in things that are Panamanian. Casco Viejo is the birthplace of Panama City and there is little question that it's incredible charm make it an international treasure. The government of Panama has decided that Casco Viejo will be renovated and they are providing incentives to encourage investment.

The incentives offered by the government make the purchase and renovation of these properties a fairly exciting investment. I've heard three versions of the incentives so the reader should verify legal details before proceeding with a purchase. My understanding is that payment of 10% of the purchase price will qualify as a down payment. Banks in Panama will loan on the properties at 3% below the current interest rate. The current rates in Panama are on par with U.S. rates, as Panama uses the U.S. dollar as a means of exchange. This also means that there are no exchange controls. This all means that current rates on loans for Casco Viejo are 7% on 15 year loans.

I have also been told that there is a tax holiday on any property purchased in Casco Viejo. Again, please verify these factors before purchasing. I am including a rough translation of these statues at the end of this article. Please note that the translation is not a legal translation. The statue is included as an navigational aid to help the reader, not as a legal statement of fact.

Casco Viejo's development for most of 1998 was restricted to what is called the "prime area." The prime area is at the point of the peninsula. Already this year (1999) I've seen several projects begun some distance from the prime area. (The area closest to the French Plaza. See Photo.) Areas away from the prime area are less expensive than those on the tip of the point. In my opinion, it does not make any long term difference. In the short term it means that the less than prime areas will not experience gentrification as quickly. It also means that properties are less expensive in those areas away from the point. (As you travel away from the point prices fall.) The areas closest to Chorrillo are bargains. Chorrillo is the first neighborhood that fronts on Casco Viejo. Chorrillo also has interesting buildings and it may some day be encompassed in the renovation. See photo.

The prices of property in Casco Viejo varies widely, as does the availability of the properties themselves. As research for this article, I attempted to purchase houses in Casco Viejo. On my first attempt to buy property in Casco Viejo I managed to line up two very nice properties. One was a building near Chorrillo of about 12,000 square feet for $120,000. It was bigger than anything that I would want for myself. The second was a smaller house which was priced at $40,000. It would have been a fun project.

*Courtesy of Escape Artist and Roger Gallo. For more information see: www.escapeartist.com

or specialty shops catering to North Americans and upper-class Panamanians and tourists.

(ommon Business Sense In Panama

It is important to keep in mind that running a business in Panama is not like managing a business in the United States because of unusual labor laws and the Panamanian way of doing business.

In order for a foreigner to own a business, a Panamanian corporation or *Sociedad Anónima* must be formed (see the section titled "Taxes" in the last chapter).

If you do choose to establish your own business, keep in mind that what works in the U.S. will not always be successful in Panama.

Check out restrictions and the tax situation. And most important to choose a business in which you have vast prior experience. It is much more difficult to familiarize yourself with a new type of business in a foreign country.

Remember a trustworthy partner or manager can mean the difference between success and failure. Make sure you choose a partner with local experience. Do not trust anyone until you know him or her and have seen them perform in the workplace.

You will be doomed to failure if you intend to be an absentee owner. We know of someone who founded an English book distribution business in Central America which initially did very well. However, they moved back to the States and put a couple of employees in charge and everything eventually fell apart: sales began to lag, money went uncollected, checks began to bounce, expenses were unaccounted for and incompetent salesmen were hired. Their potentially successful business just could not be run from abroad.

You have to stay on top of your business affairs. At times it is hard to find reliable labor and the bureaucracy can be stifling. If you have a business with employees, be aware of your duties and responsibilities as an employer. To avoid problems, know what benefits you need to pay in addition to salary to avoid problems. Remember the more employees you have, the more headaches.

In case things get rough, be sure you have enough money in reserve in case of an emergency. You should have an ample reserve of capital to fall back on during the initial stage of your business.

Talk to people, especially the "old timers," who have been successful in business and learn from them. Profit from their mistakes, experiences, and wisdom. Do not rush into anything that seems too good to be true. Trust your intuition and gut feeling at times. However, the best strategy and rule of thumb is to "Test before you invest."

Newcomers find themselves seduced by the country's beauty and friendly people and are often lured into business and investment opportunities that seem too good to be true, and often are.

During the time we have lived in Central America, we have seen many foreigners succeed and fail in business in Central America. There are few success stories and a lot of failures in areas as diverse as bars, restaurants, car-painting shops, language schools, real estate, tourism and, bed & breakfasts to name a few. People have impossible dreams about what business will be like in Panama. It is a gigantic mistake to assume that success comes easy in Panama. Initially starting any business usually takes more time and more money. Also many unexpected problems are surely to arise.

If you decide to purchase an existing business make sure that it is not over priced. Try to find out the owner's real motives for selling it. Make sure you are not buying a "pink

Common business Lingo

A pagos...Payments, buy on time
Abogado, Licenciado..Lawyer
Acciones...Stocks
Accionista..Stockholder, Shareholder
Activo..Asset
Agrimensor..Surveyor
Al contado...For cash
Anualidad...Annuity
Año Fiscal ....Fiscal year
Anticipo, prima, depósito ....Down payment
Arrendamiento..Lease
Autenticar ....Notarize
Avalúo..Appraisal
Certificado de depósito ....C.D.s.
Cheque...Check
Cláusula ....Clause
Comprador..Buyer
Contrato ....Contract
Corredor............................Stockbroker, real estate broker
Costo...Cost
Cuenta ....Bank account
Cuenta Corriente ....Checking account
Déficit ....In the red, deficit
Depreciación..Depreciation
Deuda...Debt
Divisas..........................Foreign exchange (hard currency)
El Justo Valor del Mercado.........................Fair market value
Embargar, Enganchar.......................................Attach assets
En efectivo..Pay in cash
Escritura ....Deed
Estado de Cuenta.......................Bank statment, statement
Facilidades de Pago ....Payment plan
Fideicomiso ....Trust
Fidecomisario ....Trustee

Financiamiento	Financing
Gastos	Costs, expenses
Giro	Money order
Hipoteca	Mortgage
Impuestos	Taxes
Intereses	Interest
Impuestos Prediales	Property taxes
Inversiones	Investments
Lote	Lot
Montar, Poner Un Negocio	Start a business
Negocios	Business
Notario	Notary
Pagaré	Promisory note
Parcela	Parcel of land
Plazo	Term, period of time
Precio	Price
Préstamo	Loan
Principal	Principal
Propiedad	Property
Registro	Record of ownership
Renta	Income
Rentabilidad	Profitability
Saldo	Balance of an account
Seguros	Insurance
Socio	Partner
Sociedad	Corporation
Subcontratar	To subcontract, farm out
Superávit	In the black, surplus of capital
Tasa de interés	Interest
Testaferro	Person who lends a name to a business
Terreno	Land
Traspaso	Transfer
Timbres Fiscales	Tax stamps
Valor.	Value
Vendedor	Seller

elephant." Ask to see the books and talk to clients if you can. To ferret out a good deal, look for someone who is desperate to sell their business. Check the newspapers and ask everyone you know if they know of someone selling a business. Finally, make sure there are not law suits, debts, unpaid creditors, or liens against the business.

After reading the above, if you still have questions or are confused, we advise you to consult a knowledgeable Panamanian attorney for further information. If you plan to invest or do business in a Spanish-speaking country, you should definitely purchase *Wiley's English-Spanish Dictionary*, Barron's *Talking Business in Spanish*, or Passport Books *Just Enough Business Spanish*. All of these guides contain hundreds of useful business terms and phrases.

PANAMA LAW 54 PROTECTING FOREIGN INVESTMENT IN PANAMA (July 22,1998)

Whereby provisions for the Legal Stability of Investments are adopted.

Chapter I Investment Protection

Article 1. The State promotes and protects investments within the country, in all areas of economic activity established in the Law, and in any enterprise or contractual form in accordance with national legislation.

For the purpose of this Law, an investment is the disposition of capital, in cash or credit facilities, capital goods or transfers of assets designated to the effective production of goods and services, in accordance with activities establishes in article 5 of this Law.

Article 2. Foreign investors and the enterprises in which they participate, have the same rights and duties as national investors and enterprises, with no other limitation than those established in the Political Constitution and the law, including those that refer to the freedom of trade and industry, and export and import.

Furthermore, the freedom to dispose of the profits obtained in their investments, the freedom to repatriate their capital, dividends, interest, and profits produced by their investments and the freedom to commercialize their production is guaranteed hereby to said investors.

Article 3. Property rights for investors have no limitations other than those established by the Political Constitution and the law.

Article 4. Copyrights and trademark rights of foreign investors are subject to the same regulations as established for national investors.

Chapter II Application Scope

Article 5. The present legal stability regulation is granted to individuals or private entities, foreign of domestic, who carry out investments within the national territory to develop the following activities: Tourism, industrial, agricultural, exports, forestry, mining, export processing zones, commercial and petroleum free zones, telecommunications, constructions, port and railroad development, and all activities approved by the President's Cabinet, previously recommended by the Ministry of Commerce and Industries.

Article 6. The Ministry of Commerce and Industries is the authority in charge of enforcing this Law and the regulations that develop it.

Article 7. Except for information protected by law, government entities and public offices have to provide the information and assistance required by the Ministry of Commerce and Industries to enforce this Law.

Article 8. To receive the benefits of this Law, the investor must develop the investment in accordance with the investment plan presented for such purposes, must be duly registered in the entity in charge of promoting and supervising such investments, if it is the case, and must comply the other duties established in article 16 of this Law. Said entity, on sight of the petition of party in interest, shall certify the existence of the investment and shall send copy of it to the Ministry of Commerce and Industries, entity that shall decide to file or deny the file of the investment in the Registry, through a motivated opinion, within a term of six months.

Foreign and domestic investors who, previous to the promulgation of this Law, have been engaged in investments in accordance with the requirements as prescribed by article 16 and who are interested to receive the benefits of this Law, shall have a term of six months to do so, after the promulgation of this Law.

The legal and tax stability provisions in effect at the moment of their inscription in the registry provided for in this article shall be guaranteed to these investors, in the event that they were duly registered in the entity responsible for promoting and supervising the respective type of investment.

For the purposes of the previous paragraph, the entity responsible for promoting or supervising the activity, duly required by the interested party, must send to the National Board of Enterprise Development of the Ministry of Commerce and Industry, identified with the acronym "DINADE", copy of the inscription, in order that the Board may file or deny the file of said investment in the Registry.

In the case of activities which investment does not require to be registered in an entity in charge of promoting and supervising it, the investor request from DINADE the authorization for the corresponding inscription, which may be denied or accepted by the Board, in order to obtain the benefits of this Law.

All inscription requests must follow the guidelines established in this article.

Article 9. The following are not allowed to obtain the benefits of this Law.

Individuals or juridical entities who have been or might be convicted by domestic or foreign authority or court for tax or customs crime, those with outstanding, clear and due fiscal debts, or when a final judicial or administrative decision has been passed declaring the firm's failure to comply with customs, tax or social security statues.

Individuals who have been convicted or might be convicted by a foreign or domestic court for any of the crimes established in articles 255,257,258,260,262,263a,263b,263c,263ch,263e and 263g of the Criminal Code, which refer to crimes related to drugs, money laundering, or legitimization, entities in which said individuals act as directors, officers, or representatives. Those who have been convicted for crimes described in articles 190,197,265, and 267 of the Criminal Code, respectively, which are related to fraud, misappropriation, and forgery of public and private document.

To validate this numeral, a final judicial or administrative conviction declaring said person criminally responsible must exist.

In the event that, after being registered in the DINADE Registry, an investor protected by this legislation incurs in any of the crimes outlined in numeral 1 and 2 of this article, the registration will be cancelled after the corresponding verification process has been accomplished and a motivated resolution has been issued. The same treatment will be dispensed to investors which have incurred in the situations established in numeral 1 and 2 of this article, when these circumstances are made known to the corresponding authorities after the registration, even if the crimes were incurred before the inscription. The cancellation of the registration will produce the extinction of all benefits the present Law offers the investor and the latter will be punishable law.

Chapter III Guarantees

Article 10. The individual or entity who develops investments in the activities prescribed in article 5 and who comply with the obligations set forth in article 16 of this Law, since its promulgation, shall receive the following benefits for the term of ten years.

Legal stability in such a manner, that even though new regulations that might vary its acquired rights herein be enacted, said new regulation shall not affect its constituted regimen, unless public utility or social interest causes shall exist.

Tax stability within the national territory, subject only to existing tax laws at the time of its registration at the Ministry of Commerce and Industries, Indirect taxes are excluded from the tax stability contemplated herein.

Municipal tax stability, to the extent that possible changes to the regulation on how to determine and pay municipal taxes could only affect investments protected under this Law every five years.

Stability in customs statutes derived from special laws, when these are enacted for special tax refund situations, exonerations, temporary admissions, and similar. The President's Cabinet faculty, to modify all customs legislation, shall not constitute a violation of this guarantee.

Stability in labor statutes in relation to the laws in force at the time of the contract, pursuant to the Panamanian law and to the international pacts and agreements on the matter, ratified by the Republic of Panama.

Article 11. To assure the effects of the previous article, the DINADE shall send to the pertinent municipal and government authorities a copy of the filed registry, which act as a proof in favor of the investor.

Article 12. If, during the enforcement of the law for the legal stability of investments, any exoneration or modification of the national taxes, which constitute part of the guaranteed tax statute, should expire, the investor shall pay taxes in accordance with the tax statute in effect at the time of its registration in the DINADE, unless the modification answers to public or social interests.

If the abolishment of any of the taxes that form part of the guaranteed tax statute result from its substitution with a new tax, that investor shall pay the new tax up to an amount which does nor exceed the amount that he would have has to pay annually under the abolished law.

Exoneration and their enforcement period will be regulated by the legal norms that enacted them.

Article 13. At any moment, investor registered in the DINADE shall elect, only once, to benefit from the tax statute applied to the investors or protected by this Law. In that case, said statute will constitute, for the investor, the new parameter the same shall remain in force without modification, unless public or social interest mediate, for the rest of the ten year period provided by article 10 of the present Law.

The investor who elect to change the tax statute, in accordance with the aforementioned, shall notify such change to the DINADE, who shall issue the respective resolution, which shall be notifies to the Ministry of Finance and Treasury.

Likewise, investors who have elected to receive the benefits guaranteed by this Law, shall, at any time, after duly having notified DINADE, waive such guarantees and thus become bound to normal conditions that, in legal and tax matters, are in force for other investors not protected by this Law.

Chapter IV Counsel Board

Article 14. The Counsel Board for Investment Legal Stability herein named as the Counsel is created under the jurisdiction of the Ministry of Commerce and Industries, and shall be integrated as follows:

The President of the Panamanian Association of Corporation Executives (APEDE), or a designated representative of that association.

The President of the Panamanian Chamber of Commerce, Industries and Agriculture, or a designated representative of that association.

The President of the National council of Private Enterprises (CONEP), or a designated representative of that association.

The President of the Panamanian Syndicate of Industrialists (SIP), or a designated representative of that association.

The President of the National Union of Agricultural Producers (UNPAP) or a designated representative of that association.

The President of the Panamanian Food Merchants Association (ACOVIPA), or a designated representative of that association.

The President of the Panamanian Association of Exporters (APEX), or a designated representative of that association.

A representative of any other association or body determined by the counsel. The members of the Counsel shall or receive remuneration for the service renders.

Article 15. The duties of the Counsel Board shall be as follows:

To advise the Ministry of Commerce and Industries on investment matters related to the interest of the investors protected.

To support, through recommendations, opinions and analysis of the respective groups, all efforts conducted by DIANADE.

To recommend to the Ministry of Commerce and Industries the inclusion of new activities in the present stability regulation, pursuant to article 5 of this Law.

Chapter V Investor's Obligations

Article 16. All investors interested in receiving the benefits of this Law shall comply the following procedure:

To present to the competent authority in charge of regulation and supervising the investment, whichever the case may be, an investment plan which includes the obligation to invest two million dollars ($2,000.000.00), which shall be developed in the period established by the law that regulates the respective activity or in other cases.

The amount of the planned investment. Number of employment planned to be created.

Execute, maintain, and develop the pertinent investment, during the agreed term and according to the investment plan.

To faithfully fulfill the group of norms, strategies, and actions established by or to be established by the Government, to orient, condition, and determine the conservation, use, administration, and utilization of the environment and natural resources, taking the necessary provisions as ordered by the pertinent authorities in order to avoid any negative effect on the environment.

To strictly comply with the laws and regulations, regarding the activity linked to the type of activity in reference to pay on time the taxes, fees, and contributions and other social and labor charges which the business may be funded.

To waive any diplomatic claim, whenever the enterprises are totally or partially held by foreign capital or wherever foreigners are the owners or control the stock or participation in them, with the exception of cases of denial of justice.

Article 17. The investor's default of whichever of the obligations outlined in the previous article shall produce the loss of the protection system a term that shall not exceed a two years term, computed from the time of the registration, except that the nature of the investment demands a term extension, that DINADE shall determine.

Once the term for the investments have elapsed, the investor must accredit the amount invested and the activity developed, which shall be done through an affidavit, the certification of a certified public accountant and the corresponding evidence annexes. The affidavit certification shall be presented to the authority in charge of supervising the investment or to the DINADE in the case of activities that does not require to be registered with an authority in charge of promoting and supervising their investment:

For the purpose of this Law, with the exception of those activities where the authority in charge of supervising the investment has disposed the content of the respective investment plan, the plan should contain at least the following information.

If the investor is an individual, the name and personal description of the investor, including the number of the personal identity card or passport number.

If the investor is a juridical entity, foreign or domestic, or must include a copy of the Articles of Incorporation and a certification signed by the Public Registry certifying the names of the directors, officers, legal representative,resident agent, authorized capital stock and any other information of the corporation. This certification is valid for two months.

A detailed and precise description of the activity, including the feasibility studies, blueprints, and any technical studies the project might require or need guaranteed by this Law, unless force major can be proven.

This decision shall only be adopted after the investor's default has been proven, through summary proceeding, and it shall be decreed through a motivated resolution issued DINADE, who will notify the investor, who might appeal in the manner provided in article 20.

Article 18. The Government shall indemnify the investor in the event that, for social or public interest, an investment protected by this Law be expropriated, as long as that decision causes damages which can be proven. The indemnity shall be determining in the manner provided in article 22 of this Law. The investor will not receive said indemnity if the investment has been insured against country risk by a foreign government by the World Bank Multilateral Guarantee Agency (MIGA) or any other local insurance company. The government will encourage local insurance companies to offer investment insurance for the activities described in this Law.

Article 19. When, in accordance with this Law, a foreign government, an international organization, or a foreign or domestic insurance company has issued the investor any insurance or financial guarantee against country risk, the Government shall recognize the investor's subrogation rights when that insurance or financial guarantee has been paid out.

Chapter VI General Rules

Article 20. Any controversies, claims, and differences that arise between the government and investors with regard to the application, execution, or interpretation of this Law will be settled in a direct and friendly manner through conciliation in accordance with the conciliation Rules of the Panamanian Center of the Conciliation and Arbitration. Supervisory actions from national and municipal tax administrations and administrative acts of interpretation and tax collection and other public order rules are excluded from the conciliatory and arbitration process referred to herein.

Through a decision of the competent governmental or judicial authority.

Through judgement, in accordance with the Arbitration Rules of the Panamanian Center of Conciliation and Arbitration. Arbitration judgement shall be definite and obligatory for the litigating parties and shall be definite and obligatory for the litigating parties and shall be executed in accordance with national legislation.

These cases in which exist the causes of causation based on form or annulment based on prevarication exists, as provided in articles form or annulment based on prevarication exists, as provided in articles 1151 and 1441 of the Judicial Code, respectively, are excluded from the above paragraph.

Article 21. The Government shall or take direct or indirect measures of modification or derogation of laws which carry the same effect against investments developed under the protection of this law, unless such measures the adopted under the following criteria.

That paid measures be adopted based on public utility or social interest and in accordance with the Political Constitution.

That said measure is not discriminatory. That paid measure implies the payment of adequate indemnity.

Article 22. The indemnity referred to in the previous article shall be based on the market value, according to fiscal laws, of the investments effective on the date immediately previous to that in which the adopted measure is communicated to the affected party.

When there is a difficulty to determine said value, the indemnity may be fixed according to the principles of evaluation generally applied, taking into account the amount of capital invested, its depreciation, the amount of repatriated capital up to date, replacement value, and other relevant factors.

In any of the cases deserved in the previous article, the procedure for payment of the indemnity shall adjust to that established in Part II, Title XVI, Book II of the Judicial Code.

Article 23. This Law shall or affect the rights, conditions or benefits granted to investments by virtue of treaties for the promotion and protection of investments undersigns by the Republic of Panama.

Article 24. The Executive Branch will regulate the precision contained in this Law.

Article 25. This Law shall be effective as of its promulgation and it revokes law regulation, that contravenes it.

Note: The above is a translations from the original spanish version.

RED TAPE

Dealing with Bureaucracy in Latin America

Just as in the rest of Latin America, Panama is plagued by a more inefficient bureaucratic system than is the U. S. This situation is exaggerated by the Latin American temperament, seemingly lackadaisical attitude of most bureaucrats, and the slower pace of life south of the border. The concept of time is much different from that in the U. S. or Canada. When someone says they will do something *"ahorita"* (which literally means right now), it will take from a few minutes to a week, or maybe forever. It is not unusual to wait in lines for hours in banks and government offices and experience unnecessary delays that would seldom occur in the U. S.

This situation is very frustrating for foreigners who are used to fast, efficient service. It can be especially irritating if you do not speak Spanish well. Since very few people working in offices speak English and most North Americans speak little else, it is advisable to study basic Spanish. However, if language is an insurmountable obstacle at first, use a competent bilingual lawyer with Panama's bureaucracy . Above all, learn to be patient and remember that you can get the best results if you do not push or pressure people. Try having a good sense of humor and using a smile. You will be surprised at the results.

Since bribery and pay offs are common in most Latin American countries and government employees are underpaid, some people advise paying them extra money to speed up paper work or circumvent normal channels. This bribery is illegal and not recommended for foreigners; they can be deported for breaking the law. However, in some instances it may be necessary to pay extra money to get things done. Use your own discretion in such matters. A tip here and there for a small favor can accelerate bureaucratic delays.

Everyone planning to live, retire, or do business in Panama should know that the **American Embassy** Tel: (507) 227-1777, can help with Social Security and Veterans benefits, notarizing documents, obtaining new U. S. passports, registering births of your children and getting a U.S. visa for your spouse (if you choose to marry a Panamanian). They also assist in obtaining absentee ballots for U.S. elections and getting U.S. income tax forms and information. However, if you get into any legal trouble in Panama, do not expect help from the U.S. Embassy.

How to Become a Legal Resident of Panama

Tired of the hectic pace or the cold weather? Discover the newest retirement destination: the Republic of Panama!

Law 9 of June 1987 and Executive decree 62 of August 1987 provide a whole slew of benefits, rights, tax, and customs exemptions for retired foreigners provided they take up residence in Panama and prove they have enough income. In order to obtain said benefits the applicant has to apply for a

Retired Tourist Visa at either the **National Department of Migration** or at a **Panamanian Consulate**.

Panama's Retired Tourist Visa is one of the best deals going. What makes this program so attractive is the generous discounts of up to 50% off almost everything. Panamanian or alien residents living in the country, who are fifty-seven or older, if they are women, and sixty-two or more, if they are men, will enjoy a myriad of benefits.

People find Panama attractive and want to live in the country for a many of reasons: good year-round weather, tired of the rat race and hustle-bustle, a new start in life, inexpensive living and retirement, tax benefits, the country's low-cost health care system, start a business or invest, learn Spanish, separation or divorce, enjoy the country's large expatriate community and even find companionship. Whatever your motives may be for wanting to move to Panama, there are a number of ways to remain in the country on a long-term basis.

Tourists from North America and many countries in Europe may remain legally in the country for three months without having to apply for legal residency. You may own property, start a business, or make investments with no more than a tourist visa.

We know many Americans, Canadians, and other foreigners who started businesses as tourists. If you plan to reside in Panama full-time, however, one of Panama's residency programs will appeal to you.

Becoming a legal resident will by no means affect your U.S. or Canadian citizenship.

<u>Retired Tourist Visa</u> - Retiring in Panama is relatively easy. A retired tourist visa is granted to foreigners retired or pensioned by foreign governments, international organizations, or private corporations, wishing to establish their residence, permanently with their families and dependents in the Republic of Panama.

With the application of the visa, the applicant must prove that he/she earns an income sufficient enough to cover the expenses which he/she or his/her dependents may incur in the Republic of Panama. Sufficient income is deemed to be earnings of not less than five to eight hundred dollars (US$ 500.00 to US$ 800.00) monthly or its equivalent in foreign currency, plus one hundred dollars (US$ 100.00) monthly, for each dependent.

Once the visa is granted, the beneficiary must, on an annual basis, inform the Immigration Department that his/her income has been maintained or has increased the amount originally declared. If a reduction of the income is evident, it is possible that a cancellation of the respective visa may result.

In addition of permitting the beneficiaries to reside indefinitely in the Republic of Panama, this visa offers significant benefits, such as:

1.   Total exemption of import duties of personal or domestic articles only once, for the amount of ten thousand dollars (US$ 10,000.00).

2.   Total exemption of import duties of one (1) car every two (2) years, if destined for personal or family use.

3.   Total exemption of any tax, deposit or immigration duties in connection with obtain of this visa.

The retired tourists wishing to work in the Republic of Panama may only do so in the following cases:

1.   When rendering specialized services not offered by Panamanians to the national government or its autonomous institutions.

2.   When considerable investments have been made in Panamanian corporations, previous authorization by the Ministry of Labor, in accordance with the Labor Code regulations.

3. When becoming members of the Board of Directors of the corporations in which their investments have been made.

The necessary requisites to obtain this visa are the following:

1. Power of Attorney in favor of the attorney presenting the petition.

2. Proper documentation evidencing your condition as a retired person stating the monthly income derived, which must not be less than five hundred dollars (US $500.00) or its equivalent in foreign currency, plus the amount of one hundred dollars (US$ 100.00) for each dependent.

3. In case of foreigners retired from private corporations, a document certifying that the corporation operates outside the Republic of Panama, duly countersigned by the proper authorities. Payment receipts of the pension must also be provided.

4. Good health certificate of the applicant and each dependent, including a laboratory test for H.I.V., which must indicate the method used for the test, issued by a Panamanian physician and laboratory.

5. Police record of the applicant and each dependent over eighteen (18) years old, issued by the authorities of the place of residence for the last two (2) years.

6. Police record of the applicant and each dependent over eighteen (18) years old, issued by the Police Department of the Republic of Panama (PTJ) (NOTE: FOR THIS PARTICULAR MATTER THE APPLICANT MUST GRANT A POWER OF ATTORNEY).

7. Marriage certificate of the applicant and birth certificate of each dependent, or an acceptable equivalent document, IF APPLICABLE, as the case may be.

8. A letter whereby the applicant assumes responsibility of his dependents, IF APPLICABLE.

9. Original and two (2) copies of the applicant's passport, duly authenticated by a notary public.

10. Affidavit of personal data.

11. Four (4) photographs, passport size (Gentlemen are required to wear tie).

12. An additional copy of all documentation, including the passport.

IMPORTANT: Please note that all foreign documents must be authenticated by the nearest Panamanian Consulate to your home town.

Fees and expenses in connection with obtaining this type of visa can vary between US$ 1,200 to $2,000. The reason this visa is a little more expensive than some of the others is because it is granted indefinitely.

Holders of this visa may invest money in the country but cannot work unless: they offer special services which cannot be performed by Panamanians; they have large corporations and are on the board of directors.

After this visa is granted, it is recommend that the applicant obtains a multiple exit and entry permit that will allow you to travel in and out of the country freely without requesting any authorization to the Panamanian Government. This special permit is granted for a period of one (1) year, renewable for equal periods of time, indefinitely. Expenses and fees in connection with this permit are US$ 200.00. This permit has to be renewed every year.

Additional Methods of Obtaining Panamanian Residency

Once in Panama there are several types of visas you can apply for depending on the purpose of your stay.

(1) **Retiree Visa** - This program is for the foreigner who has retires from his own private activities and is able to make a deposit in the National Bank. People in this category do not meet the monthly pension requirement for a Retired Tourist Visa, so a certificate of deposit is required that generates a minimum income of $750 per month. Said amount may vary depending on the interest rate being offered by the National Bank of Panama. At present, you will need to buy a certificate of around $100,000 to generate $750 monthly. Although this amount is higher than the $500 required for the standard *pensionado* visa, no additional monies need to be paid for your spouse and children under eighteen years of age. If you decide to leave the country permanently, this deposit will be returned in full.

(2) **Investment Visa** - You may obtain this type of visa by investing in a corporation or creating one. This is less expensive than the prior method of obtaining residency. What you have to do is set up a business with a minimum of $10,000. Then you will have to establish a Panamanian Corporation for your business. A cash deposit of $10,000 will then have to be made to your company's bank account. The whole process should not take long under this visa category.

This program was made to create jobs for Panamanians. Therefore you will required to have at least three Panamanian employees. It is easy to find then since you can even include your domestic help to fulfill this requirement.

(3) **Temporary Visa for Technicians** - This visa is granted to foreigners who work in Panama as business executives or technicians for private businesses. This visa may also be granted to the spouse and children of the business executive or technician. A labor permit through the Ministry of Labor must also be obtained.

(4) **Student Visa** - temporary visas are given to students workers not staying in Panama permanently.

(5) **Immigrant Visas** - Individuals wanting to reside permanently in Panama may obtain several types of immigrant visas provided they meet the requirements.

(a) **Immigration Visa for the Spouse of a Panamanian Citizen** - For the foreigner married to a Panamanian, the immigration laws of Panama offer the possibility of applying for an immigration visa, which is granted for a term of one year, after which permanent residence is given with thee right to obtain a personal identity card or *cédula*.

(b) **Immigrant Visa for Investors** - This visa is for those foreigners who invest their own capital, not less than $100,000 in the Republic of Panama for the purpose of engaging in commercial, financial or industrial activities. The applicants wife and minor children may obtain the same benefits.

(c) **Immigrant Visa for Forestry Investors** - This visa is given to foreigners who wish to invest their own capital, not less than $40,000, in forestry and reforestation enterprises within the Republic of Panama. The applicant's spouse and minor children may obtain the same benefits as dependents.

(d) **Immigrant Visa for Self-sufficient Individuals** - This visa is given to foreigners who have enough income to cover the expenses for all their families needs. In order to apply for this visa, the applicant must deposit and maintain the sum of $100,000 in a local bank.

We suggest that you contact a Panamanian attorney to help you with these and any other programs that may interest you. Your attorney can explain all of the nuances of each category.

For the above visas you will need:

(1) A blood test for HIV Aids (S.I.D.A.)

(2) Medical Certificate of good help from a local doctor issued within three months of application.

(3) Four original copies of your birth certificate

(4) A police report from your local police department. This must be certified by the Panamanian Consulate in your home country.

(5) Four passport photos

(6) Birth and marriage certificates in case you have a family.

All applications must be made through a lawyer. The cost usually cost between $500 to $800.

Immigration and Other Matters

Visas

Requirements for entering Panama are different for people of each country and are subject to change. It is highly advisable to contact the Panamanian Consulate in your home country to obtain the most up-to-date information on entry requirements. Some countries have special agreements with Panama that eliminate the need to get a visa or tourist card.

Everyone needs a valid passport, onward ticket, and proof of solvency to enter Panama. Visitors from the U.S. and Canada only need tourist cards, which are issued at border crossings, from embassies and consulates, and at the airport.

People with passports from certain countries will have to obtain a visa. If entering by land from Costa Rica, it is also a good idea to have a visa and onward ticket.

All non-Panamanian citizens must have a tourist visa and can stay up to 90 days in the country. Initially, everyone can stay in Panama for 30-days. After 30-days, visas and tourist cards can be extended for an additional 60 days up to a 90-day total.

Information about immigration matters may be obtained from the **Ministerio de Gobierno y Justicia** Tel: (507) 212-2000 or see **www.gobiernoyjusticia.com.pa**.

Extending Your Stay

To extend your stay (up to 90 days) you will need to visit the immigration office or **Oficina de Migración y Naturalización** on Avenida Cuba at calle 29 este Tel: 225-1373. There are also offices in David, Changuinola, Santiago, and Chitré. You will need two passport-size photos, an onward air or bus ticket, you passport showing your most recent entry into Panama and $10. Next, you will need to fill out an extension form called a *prórroga de turismo*. It's written in Spanish, so you may need help filling it out.

Leaving The Country

If you have stayed longer than 30 days, you will need to obtain a *permiso de salida* (exit permit) to be able to leave the country. But first, you will have to obtain called a *paz y salvo* (peace and safety. It's an official form stating that you do not owe the Panamanian government money. You can get this document from the **Ministerio de Hacienda y Tesoro** (tax department) calle 35 at Avenida Perú Tel: 227-3060.

The next step is to take your *paz y salvo* form to the immigration office to obtain the *permiso de salida* stamp in your passport. If you do not have the time to spend the day running around, you can hire an attorney to the job for you. We also understand there are attorneys who hang out around the immigration office who can do this for you.

All foreigners with residency in Panama will need a re-entry permit to travel abroad and to return to the country. Permits of this type are good for multiple entry.

Work Permits/Visas

Foreigners planning to work for a local company must obtain a work permit from the Ministry of Labor. The government will only let you work if there are no qualified Panamanians to do a specific job. To obtain a work visa you must have a letter from a local company offering you employment stating your work specialty.

To obtain a work permit you will need a series of documents. Since the requirements are subject to change, you will have to check with an attorney to see which documents and certificates are required. Once you have obtained all of the required papers your attorney will apply for the work permit through the Ministry of Labor. He/she then has to go to the ministry Labor to apply for a Visa. When the Ministry of Labor eventually grants the work permit, the Immigration department will issue a temporary Visa for a year.

Perpetual Tourist

Staying in the country illegally after your tourist card or visa has expired is not advisable. Bear in mind that it is always better to have your papers up-to-date because you may be deported almost instantly at the whim of a Immigration official or if you get into any kind of trouble and are in the country illegally.

Due to a lack of money for some other reason a few people try to live as a perpetual tourist in Panama or other Central American countries. They just leave the country for at least 72 hours every three months to renew their tourist visa.

You can repeat this process over-and-over again to stay in the country indefinitely. The only disadvantage is that as a tourist you may not work in Panama and it is almost impossible to become a legal resident unless you marry a Panamanian or have immediate relatives in Panama.

Panamanian Citizenship

The following individuals may request Panamanian citizenship by naturalization:

(1) Foreigners having resided for five consecutive years in Panama and who have Panamanian residency.

(2) Foreigners with three consecutive years of residence, after obtaining a permanent residency permit, that have children born in Panama of a Panamanian father or mother.

(3) Citizens by birth of Spain or any Latin American country if they meet the same requirements that a Panamanian has to meet in order to become a citizen of their country.

Getting Married

Getting married in Panama is easy provided you have all the necessary paperwork and follow the correct procedures. This is what a foreign citizen has to do:

(1) You must provide both birth and bachelorhood certificates which have to be authenticated by the Panamanian Consulate in your home country. Next, both documents have to be delivered to the **Ministerio de Relaciones Exteriores** in Panama. Once you are there give said papers to the **Department of Legalizaciones y Autenticaciones** to be authenticated.

(2) You will also need a medical certificate called a *Dictamen Médico* issued by a Panamanian doctor within 15 days prior to the wedding. The physical exam must include the following lab tests: urinalysis,HIV, blood test and V.D.R.L.

(3) A Valid passport or *Carnet de Migración* if you have been in the country for more than 30 days.

(4) Two witnesses of adult age with a passport, who are not family members of the people being married.

All of the above must be presented to the **Juzgado de Turno en Matrimonios** (Marriage Court), ideally two or three days before the wedding .

It is essential that both birth and bachelorhood certificates be authorized prior to arriving in Panama. Otherwise, the documents will have to be mailed back to your home country for the process to be complete.

If you plan to marry a Panamanian citizen, he/she has to do the following:

(1) Provide a birth certificate from the Civil Registry or *Registro Civil*.

(2) A divorce decree if pertinent from the Civil Registry.

(3) You will also need a medical certificate called a Dictamen Médico issued by a Panamanian doctor within 15 days prior to the wedding. The physical exam must include the following lab tests: urinanalysis, HIV and blood test.

(4) A birth certificate for your children , if they are from the marrying couple.

(5) Two witnesses of adult age who are not family members of the people being married.

Purchasing an Automobile

You will be better off if you buy a vehicle locally. New car prices are real bargain in Panama. Prices are not as high as neighboring Costa Rica or many other countries in Latin America. All of the major U.S. and Japanese manufacturers have dealerships in Panama. Furthermore, shipping a car can be a real "pain in the neck."

Another reason to buy locally is to ensure your vehicle will be under warranty in case anything goes wrong. Most local dealers offer good warranties on new cars.

The majority of automobiles in Panama are made in Japan. Most replacement parts are for Japanese automobiles. Spare parts for U.S. cars have to be imported, are expensive and sometimes hard to come by. If you do decide to bring a car from the U.S. or Canada, it is best to bring a Toyota, Nissan, Honda, or some other Japanese import for the reasons just mentioned.

If you decide to bring a car to Panama, there are two ways to do it—by sea or by land. If you ship your car to Panama by boat, contact a shipping company near to where you have your car in the U.S. This method of transportation is relatively safe since your car can be insured against all possible types of damage. You may ship your car in a container with your household goods or ship it separately. Before you ship you vehicle you will also have to contact a custom's agent in Panama. All of the required taxes and other fees will have to be paid. You will need to provide the correct documents including the bill of sale and the registration. The amount of tax you pay on your vehicle depends on the value of your car and your particular visa status.

To determine the value of your vehicle agents use a guide similar to the Kelly Blue Book. Customs agents refer to the market value based on their "Black Book," a manual published in the U.S. with a listing of new and used car wholesale auction prices. The book is a bible for U.S. car dealers, loan officers and Panamanian customs agents. For additional information about the Black Book, contact National Auto Research at 2620 Barrett Road, PO Box 758, Gainesville, GA 30503. Tel: (800) 554-1026, Fax: (770) 532-4792, www.blackbookguides.com. Shipping companies at both ends can help you with all of the steps.

Driving an Automobile to Panama

If you have sufficient time and enjoy adventure, drive your automobile to Panama. The journey from the U.S. to Panama (depending on where you cross the Mexican border), takes about three weeks if driving at a moderate speed. By road it is about 4000 miles from Panama to Brownsville, Texas, the nearest US city.

Take your time so you can stop and see some of the sights. We recommend driving only during the day since most roads are poorly lighted, if at all. At night, large animals—cows, donkeys and horses— can stray onto the road and cause serious accidents.

Your car must be in good mechanical condition before your trip. Carry spare tires and necessary parts. Take a can of gas and try to keep your gas tank as full as possible because service stations are few and far between.

Do not leave anything of value in your car unless you are with it. Keep your US license plates inside the car since they are valuable items to thieves for transporting stolen cars.

Have your required visas, passports, and other necessary papers in order to avoid problems at border crossings. Remember, passports are required for all U.S. citizens driving through Central America. You also need complete car insurance, a valid driver's license and a vehicle registration.

You can buy insurance from AAA in the U.S., or contacting **Sanborn's Insurance** in the U.S. Tel: (210) 686-0711, Fax:

A stretch of the Pan-American Highway

(210)686-0732 or www.sanborns.com. They offer both Mexican and Central American policies.

Instant Auto Insurance offers a 24-hour 800 number and fax service, so you can have your policy ready. In the U.S. and Canada, call 1-800-345-47-01 or fax 619-690-65-33.

You can also buy insurance at the border before entering Mexico. Having an accident in Mexico is a felony not a misdemeanor, do not forget to be fully insured.

If you are missing a driver's license, a vehicle registration, or insurance, border guards can make your life miserable. Also, remember some border crossings close at night, so plan to arrive at all borders between 8 a.m. and 5 p.m. just to be safe.

When you finally arrive at the Costa Rican/Panamanian border, expect to be delayed clearing customs. The crossing at Paso Canoas is the most frequently used exit and entry point on the border with Costa Rica. The border is open from 6 am to 11pm.

To bring a vehicle into Panama, you have to pay $5 for a *tarjeta de circulación* (vehicle control certificate) and an additional $1 to have your car fumigated. You will also need to show proof of ownership and have a valid driver's license. You passport will also be stamped indicating you brought a vehicle into the country.

In order to drive a vehicle in Panama, any foreign citizen will need a driver's license. Tourists can use a license from their own country for up to 90 days.

For additional information about driving from the U.S. to Panama, you can purchase a useful guidebook, We recommend *Driving the Pan-American Highway to Mexico and Central America*, by Raymond and Audrey Pritchard. You can now order this one-of-a-kind book by writing to **Costa Rica Books**, Suite 1 SJO 981, P. O. Box 025216, Miami Fl

33102-5216. Also see **www.drivetocentralamerica.com** and **www.costaricabooks.com**.

Bringing Your Boat to Panama

As you may know, Panama is a boaters paradise. The country has oceans on both sides, a canal, lakes, and offshore islands. If you have a yacht or sail boat you can dock at any of the of country's yacht clubs. In Chapter 5 there is a list of some of the county's yacht clubs.

If you enter Panama in a foreign vessel, you will be able to keep it in the country for 90 days. Beyond 90 days, you may apply for an extension, which essentially is a rubber stamp process. You are given a photo ID enabling you to keep the vessel in the country for an additional 90 days. However, you must obtain the proper form the **Panamanian Maritime Agency** (Tel: 507-232-5396) if you plan to visit Panama for a limited time only. The charges are listed on the form for obtaining a permit in order to legally navigate in Panamanian waters.

In addition, the owners of yachts that navigate in Panamanian waters have to pay an annual tax, based on Law 56. Fees are based on the size of the boat.

Those people who wish to permanently reside in Panama or leave their vessel in the country for an extended period of time must use the same form mentioned above. However, prior to completing the form you must pay the import taxes for registering your boat in the country. Customs officials will determine the cost.

Shipping Your Household Goods to Panama

One of the largest expenses you incur when moving is shipping your furniture and other household goods. However, after taking high shipping costs into consideration, you may be reluctant to ship any household items from the U.S. This is a matter of personal choice. Most foreign residents and even Panamanians prefer U.S. products because of their higher quality. However, many retires live comfortably and happily without luxuries and expensive appliances.

You can rent a furnished apartment excluding stove and refrigerator, for a few hundred dollars monthly. You can also purchase good used furniture and appliances from expatriates and others who are moving out of the country. Check the local newspapers. What you need to import depends on your personal preference and budget.

Make an effort to get rid of "clutter" and bulky items and do not ship what can be easily or cheaply replaced. Try to leave large appliances and furniture at home. You will be able to buy most everything you need in Panama and it is usually less expensive. You pay more for a few selected items in Panama, but in the long run they turn out to be less expensive when you take shipping costs and taxes into consideration. Also remember Panama has the second largest free trade zone in the world located in Colón. Talk to other foreign residents and retires to see what they think is absolutely necessary to bring to Panama.

We have a friend who saved 1000s of dollars by eliminating about 90 percent of what he originally intended to bring from the U.S. With the money he saved, he was easily able purchase the same items in Panama.

Ways to Bring Your Belongings to Panama

If you still want to bring items from your home country after reading the last section and taking Panama's low prices into consideration, then we suggest you follow the advice in this below.

(1) First, when entering the country as a tourist by plane, you can bring in a lot of personal effects and small appliances. A tourist is sometimes waved through customs without ever having to open any luggage.

The government understands that tourists come here to enjoy the country and have many different hobbies and reasons for visiting. They know that tourists need such items as surfboards, bicycles, kayaks, musical instruments photographic equipment, small stereos, and more. The government permits items for personal use only and not intended for resale. The number of these personal items has to be reasonable in relation to the length of the stay or needed for the exercise of one's profession during his or her trip. Finally, all items have to be portable and considered as luggage.

The amount of luggage allowed on the plane by airlines is limited in most cases to 2 pieces which must not exceed 66 pounds. Sometimes they allow excess luggage for an additional fee. If they do allow you to take more, do so because it is the cheapest way of bringing items into Panama.

Have friends bring a few things when they come to visit you in Panama. Always try to take as much as possible with you on the plane rather than shipping items by boat because most used personal things are not taxed at the airport. Even used appliances have a good chance of clearing airport customs if you can fit them on the plane.

(2) If you have a small amount (less than 500 pounds) of items that you cannot take with you as luggage you should consider sending it as air cargo.

If you choose to ship your belongings by air, try American Airlines. Call their 800 toll-free number. They will ask you your intended destination. You will then have to give them the number of boxes you are planning to ship, and the respective weight and dimensions of each box.

The operator will then figure the approximate cost. (All of the items will be weighed at the airport cargo facility.) The cost is based on either the total weight or the combined dimensions of all your boxes—whichever is greater.

You will then be given the choice of sending your things by express or standard freight. The latter is your best bet if you are not in a hurry since it only takes two to five days to reach Panama from the U.S. The only drawback to shipping standard rate is that it will be on a space-available basis, so, your merchandise may be slightly delayed. The cost works out to be about a dollar per pound.

We recommend packing your belongings in unmarked plain boxes. Especially if you are shipping computers, stereos, or other electronic equipment. Number each box and put the name and address of the person who will be receiving them in Panama. Make a list of the contents of each box for yourself, the airlines, and customs. This will help ensure your boxes get there intact. All of your boxes should be made of thick cardboard and have plenty of packing materials to protect any fragile items. Airline employees often heap heavy boxes on top of other cargo. Be sure to write on any paperwork and air bills "Not for resale." This will save you a lot of money when the customs people figure out how much you will pay in taxes.

(3) If you have over 500 pounds and large items like refrigerators, it is too expensive to ship by air. Your best option will be to send your things by boat in a cargo container. It is more cost effective to use a large container and the transit time will be shorter. It usually takes about three weeks to arrive from the States. Your customs agent can get all of your

household items and belongings out of customs. Expect to pay $3,000 to $4,000 for a 40-foot container. Everything you bring must be itemized. If you have retiree status, you will be able to get your belongings into the country without paying taxes. Do not ship anything until your status has been approved.

4) Driving through Mexico and Central America is another way to bring your household goods and personal belongings to Panama. However, due the length of the journey, delays at border crossings, and other hassles this method is not recommended.

How to Find a Lawyer

If you plan to start a business, work, buy or sell property, or seek long-term residency status in Panama, you will definitely need the services of a good attorney.

Your attorney can help you understand the complexities of the Panamanian legal system. You are guilty until proven innocent, just the opposite of our system in the U.S.A. A lawyer is one of the best investments you can make because he can assist you with bureaucratic procedures and handle other legal matters that arise.

If you are not fully bilingual, be sure to choose a lawyer who is. The secretary should be bilingual too (Spanish/English). This helps avoid communication problems, misunderstandings, and enables you to stay on top of your legal affairs.

It is very important to watch your lawyer closely since most lawyers in Latin America tend to drag their feet as bureaucrats do.

Never take anything for granted. Refuse to believe that things are getting done, even if you are assured they are. Check with your lawyer on a regular basis and ask to see your file to make sure he has taken care of business. As you might imagine, paper work moves slowly in Panama so you do not want a procrastinating lawyer to prolong the process.

When you first contact a lawyer, make sure he is accessible at all hours. Make sure you have your lawyer's office and home telephone number in case you need him in an emergency. If you are told your lawyer is always "in meetings" or "out of the office", this is a clear sign your work is being neglected and you have chosen the wrong lawyer.

Roberto I. Guardia's Panama City La Firm

Know your lawyer's specialty. Although most attorneys are required to have a general knowledge of Panamanian law, you may need a specialist to deal with your specific case. Some people find it's a good idea to have several lawyers for precisely this reason.

Take your time and look around when you are trying to find a lawyer. You should ask friends, other people, retires and other knowledgeable people for the names of their lawyers. Above all, make sure your attorney is recommended from a reliable source. Then try to inquire about your potential lawyer's reputation, his work methods, and integrity. Throughout the world, there are always a few incompetent, unscrupulous attorneys, so be careful with whom you are dealing before you make your final choice.

Remember, one of the most important people in your life in Panama is your lawyer, so it is imperative that you develop a good working relationship.

Most attorneys charge from $25 to $50 an hour depending on your problem and their expertise. It is inadvisable to select your lawyer solely on the basis of legal fees. Lawyer's fees, or *honorarios*, vary. Just because a lawyer is expensive does not mean he is good. Likewise, you should not select an attorney because his fees are low.

In Panama it is not uncommon to hire a lawyer on a full-time basis by paying what amounts to a small retainer.

However, if you speak fluent Spanish and have a lot of patience, you can do your residency paperwork yourself. Just pick up a list of the requirements from the immigration office.

Do not pay them all the money up front. If you choose this route you can save yourself hundreds of dollars in attorneys' fees. All a lawyer does is just sign a couple of papers, turn them in at the immigration office and take your money.

There is a small amount of paperwork involved in giving your lawyer power of attorney (*poder*) so he can take care of your personal business and legal affairs.

This is not a bad idea when you may have to leave the country for a period of time, or in the event of an emergency. However, first make sure your lawyer is completely trustworthy and competent. You may either choose to give your attorney poder general (General Power of Attorney) or poder especial (Special Power of Attorney). You may revoke both of these types of power of attorney at any time.

We recommend purchasing a copy of *Diccionario de Términos Jurídicos* by Enrique Alcaraz. It is a complete English/Spanish dictionary of legal terms.

Here is a partial list of bilingual attorneys who have many North American clients:

Roberto I. Guardia R. (Bilingual and our lawyer. We highly recommend this firm. Please see his ad in this book))
Orillac, Carles & Guardia
Ave. Samuel Lewis y Calle58
P.H. ADR Torre ADR Technologies, Piso 7, Oficina 7-A
Apartado 0818-04373
Panama 3, República de Panamá
Tel: (507) 263-3917, Fax: (507) 263-3924
Cel: 612-5429
E-mail:rig@orcag.com
www.orcag.com
Practice areas: Commercial Law, Corporations, Mari time, Civil Law, Tax Consultancy, Patent and Trade Mark Registration

BUFETE BERROCAL Bocas del Toro
Ubaldo Vallejos
Changuinola
Tel: (507)-758-7582 beeper: 758-5155
E-mail: u_vallejos@yahoo.com
Courtesy Explore Panama

Panamanian Consulates and Embassies Abroad

Panamanian Consulates provide information about visas, work permits, marriage, and residency. They can issue tourist visas, authenticate documents, and assist Panamanian Citizens living abroad.

Anyone seeking permanent residency in Panama needs to have certain documents notarized by a Panamanian consulate or embassy in their country of origin. Documents that must be notarized are a birth certificate, police certificate (stating you have no criminal record), and a proof of income statement. All this paperwork should be taken care of before coming to Panama.

If you apply for permanent residency in Panama, it may take months to get notarized documents from your home country if it is possible at all. If worse comes to worst, you may even have to make a trip home to take care of these matters. While you are waiting for papers from abroad, other documents may expire and you will have to start all over again. Bureaucracy is slow enough as it is in Panama and it is foolish to delay this process any more than necessary.

Each Panamanian has its own business hours and its area of coverage. Please locate your nearest consulate for personal attention. If there is no consulate in your state, please locate the state or city nearest to your residence in the list below.

Argentina - Avenida Santa fe 1461, 5to. Piso C.P. 1060 Buenos Aires, Argentina. Tel: 00-54-1-8111254 Fax: 00-54-1-8140450 E-mail: epar@ba.net

Austria - ELISABETHSTRASSE Tel: 00-43-1-5872347 Fax: 00-43-1-5863080 E-mail: mail@empanvienna.co.at

Belgium - Ave. LOUISE, 390 - 392 1050 Bruselas, Belgica Tel: 00-322-6490729 / 00322-6492879 Fax: 00-322-6489216 E-mail: panama@antrasite.be

Bolivia - Calle Julio Patiño No.1526 Entre Calles 21 22, Calacoto, Zona Sur Apdo. Postal 678, La Paz. Tel: 00-591-2-797290 Fax: 00-591-2-799974 E-mail empanbol@ceibo.entelnet.bo

Brazil - SHIS, QI 11, Conj. 06, Casa 06 CEP71625, Brasilia D. F. Tel: 00-55-61-2487309 Fax: 00-5-61-2482834 E-mail: empanama@nettur.com.br

Canada - 130 Albert St. Suite No.300 Ottawa, ON. Kip 5G4 Tel: 00-1-613-2367177 Fax: 00-1-613-2365775 E-mail: pancanem@travel-net.com

Panama Investment Bureau S.A. in Canada - 20 Bay Street, Suite 1205 Toronto, On. M5J 2N8 Canada, Tel: 416-367 0458 Fax: 416-367 0511

China - 6-1-11, Tayuan Diplomatic Compound No.1, Dong Zhi Men Wai Xin Dong Lu Chao Yang District, 100600 Beijing Rep. Popular China - Tel: 8610-65325981 Fax: 8610-65326822 E-mail: panachin@public3.bta.net.cn

Colombia - Calle 92 No.7-70 Apartado 90094 Santa Fe de Bogotá. Telephone: 00-57-1-275068 0057-1-2574452 Fax: 00-57-1-2575067 E-mail: embpacol@openway.com.co

Costa Rica - Del Centro Colón, 275 mts., al norte, San José. Tel: 011-506-257-3241 Fax: 506-257-4864

Cuba - Calle 26 entre 1ra y 3era, No.109 Miramar La Habana Tel: 00-537-241673 , 00-537-240858 Fax: 00-537-241674, 00-537-249011 E-mail: panaembacuba@ip.etecsa.cu

Chile - Calle Lota No.2257, Departamento 203, Comuna de Providencia Casilla 16404, Correo 9. Tel: 00-56-2-2344086 00-56-2-2311641 Fax: 00-56-2-2344086

Dominican Republic - Calle benito Monción255 casi esquina Bolívar en Gazcue, Santo Domingo. Tel: 00-1-809-4767396, Fax: 00-1-809-6853665 E-mail; emb.panama@codetel.net.do

Ecuador - Ave. Diego de Almagro 1550 y Pradera, Edificio Posadas de las Artes, 3er piso, Quito. Tel:00-593-2-565234, Fax:00-593-2-566449, E-mail: pmaemecu@interactive.net.ec

Egypt - 4-A, IBN Zanki St. Apart. No.3 P.O. BOX 62 - Zamalek 11211 El Cairo Tel: 00-20-2-3400784 Fax: 00-20-2-3411092

El Salvador - Alameda Roosvelt No. 2838 y 55 Ave. Norte Altos de la Compañía Panameña de Aviación, Apartado 01-104, Tel: 503-298-0884, Fax: 503-260-5453

France - 145 Avenue de Sufren 75015 Paris Tel: 00-33-1-45664244 Fax: 00-33-1-45679943 E-mail: panaemba@worldnet.fr

Germany - Lutzowstrasse 1   53173 BONN, Alemania Tel: 00-49-228-361036 Fax: 00-49-228-363558 E-mail: panama@lg.elge.de

Greece - Calle Panepistimiou 42, 7 Piso 10679 Atenas Tel: 00-30-1-3636121 Fax: 00-30-1-3631089 E-mail: panpirl@hol.gr

Guatemala - 5a.Avenida 15-45 Zona 10 centro Empresarial Torre II, Oficinas No. 708 y 709 Apartado Postal 369. Tel: 502-2-3337182 Fax: 502-2-3372446

Honduras - Colonia paalmira, Edificio palmira segundo piso, frente al Hotel Honduras maya, Apartado Postal 397 Tegucigalpa. Tel: 504-232-8174 Fax: 504-232-8174

Hungary - TGLOT U. 6/b. 2. 1118 Budapest Tel: 00-36-1-4669817 Fax: 00-36-1-4669817

India - EMBAJADA DE PANAMA C-550, Defence Colony New Delhi-110024, India Tel: 00-91-11-4642518 00-91-11-4627890 Fax: 00-91-11-4642350 E-mail: mirta@del2.vsnl.net.in

Israel - Calle Hei Be´iyar No.210 Tercer Piso Aptdo 3, Kikar Hamedina Apartado Postal 21260 Tel Aviv - Tele: 00-972-3-260849 Fax: 00-972-3-6910045 E-mail: panama@netvision.net.il

Italy - Viale Regina Margherita No.239 Cuarto Piso, Interno 11 00198 Roma Tel: 00-39-6-44252173/44265436 Fax: 00-39-6-44265443

Japan - Rm. 902, No. 38 Kow Bldg.,12-24 ,Nishi- Azabu, 4-chome Minato-ku Tokyo (106) - Telephone: 0081-3-3499-3741 Tel: 00-81-3-5485-3548 Fax: 00-81-3-5485-3548 E-mail: panaemb@japan.co.jp

Jamaica - No.1 Braemar Ave. Suite B-4 Kingston Tel: 00-1-809-9781953 Fax: 00-1-809-9783980 E-mail: panama@oas.org

South Korea - No.1101, Garden Tower Bldg 98-78, Woomi-Dong Chongro-Ku, Seul C.P.O. BOX 3957 - Tel: 00-82-2-7650720 Fax: 00-82-2-27425874 E-mail: panaemba@nuri.net

Mexico - Schiller 326, Piso 8, ColoniaChapultepec-Morales, C.P. 11570, Mexico, D.F. Tel: 52-5--2504259 Fax: 52-5-2504674, E-mail: embpanmx@mail.internet,com.mx

Nicaragua - Del Hotel Colón una cuadra al lago y25 varas arriba, casaNo. 73, Managua. Tel: Fax: E-mail:cvergara@ibw.com.ni.

Paraguay - Calle Piribebuy # 765 C/O'leary, Tel: 00-596-21-443522, Fax:00-595-21-450936 E-mail: embapana@rieder.net.py.

Peru - Avenida Cornel Portillo No. 521, Lima 27 San isidro. Tel: 00-51-14-404874, Fax: 00-51-14404874 E-mail: linclark@amauta.rcp.net.pe

Philippines - Embassy of Panama in the Philippines - Rm.501 Victoria BLDG. 429 United Nations Ave., Ermita Manila 1054, Filipinas Central P.O. BOX 493, (MAIN OFFICE) Tel: 00-632-5212790 Fax: 00-632-5215755 E-mail: panemmnl@i-manila.com.ph

Portugal - Rua Pedro de Sintra No.15 1400, Lisboa Tel: 00-35-11-3642899 Fax: 00-35-11-3644589

Russia - Moskfilmosraya No.50 Tel: 00-7-095-1430361 Fax: 007-095-9560730 E-mail: empanrus@aha.ru

Singapore - 16 Raffles Quay No.41-06 Hong Leong Building Singapore 048581 - Tel: 00-65-2218677 Fax: 00-65-2240892 E-mail: pacosin@pacific.net.sg

Spain - Claudio Coello 86, 1 28006 Madrid Tel: 00-34-1-5765001 Fax: 00-34-1-5765001 Fax: 0034-1-5767161 E-mail: panaemba@teleline.es

Sweden - Ostermalmsgatan 34/2tr 114 32 Estocolmo P.O.BOX 26 146, S-100 41. Tel: 00-46-8-6626535 Fax: 046-8-6630407

Taiwan - 6 FL. No.111 Sung Chiang Rd. Taipei, Taiwan, R.O.C. Tel: 00-886-2-5099802 Fax: 00-96-25099801 E-mail: panachin@public3.bta.net.cn

Trinidad & Tobago - Highsquare Bldg, Suite No.6 Lst. Level 1-A Dere Street, Queen´s Park West Port of Spain Tel: 001-809-6233435 Fax: 001-809-6233440 E-mail: embapatt@wow.net

United Kingdom - Embassy of Panama in the United Kingdom - Panama House 40 Hertford Street London W1Y 7TG U.K Tel: 0207-409-2255   Fax: 0207-493-4499   E-mail: panama@panaconsul.co.uk

United States - 2862 Mc. Gill Terrace N.W. WASHINGTON, D.C. 2008. Tel: 001-202-4831407 Fax: 001-202-4838413 E-mail: EAA@PanaEmba-DC.CCMAIL.compuserve.com

Uruguay - Edificio Coimbra, Calle Jose Marti 3295 (Esq. Pedro Berro), Oficina 501 Apartado Postal 12071 Montevideo. Tel: 00-598-2-7080206 Fax: 00-598-2-780206

Venezuela - Calle La Guairita, Edificio los frailes Piso 6, oficina 6-A, Chuao, Apartado 1989 Caracas 1010A, Carmelitas, Tel: 00-58-2-929182 Fax: 00-58-2-928107.

Washington US - 2862 McGill Terrace, NW Washington DC 20008 (202) 483-1407 Fax- (202)483-8416

Texas - 24 Guenway Plaza, Ste. 1307 Houston, TX 77046 Tel: (713) 622-4451 Fax: (713) 622-4468

New York - 1212 Avenue of the Americas 10th Floor New York, NY 10036 Tel: (212)-840-2450 Fax: (212)-840-2469

New Orleans - 1324 World Trade Center No. 2 Canal Street New Orleans LA 70130 Tel: (504) 525-3458 Fax (504) 524-8960

Panama Trade Development Institute in Miami Regional Office 1477 South Miami Avenue Miami, FL 33130 Tel: (305) 374-8823 F ax: (305) 374-7822

Permanent Mission of Panama to the United Nations in New York - 866 United Nations Plaza, Suite 4030 New York, N.Y. 10017 USA - Tel: 001-212-421-5420 /5421 Fax: 001-212-421-2694 E-mail: panun@undp.org

Permanent Mission of Panama to the United Nations In Switzerland - 72 rue de Lausanne 1202 Ginebra, Suiza - Tel: 00-41-22-715-0450 Fax: 00-41-22-738-0363 E-mail: mission.panama@itu.int

Organization of American States - 201 Winsconsin Avenue N.W. Suite 240 Washington, D.C. 20007 Tel: 001-202-965-4819 /4826 Fax: 001-202-965-4836

Permanent Agricultural Mission of Panama to Rome - Viale Regina Margherita No. 239, 00198, Roma-Italia Tel: 0039-6-44265429 Fax: 0039-6-44252332 E-mail: faoprpan@tin.it

United Nations Organization for Science & Education - 1 rue Miollis, Oficina 501-503 75015 París Francia Tel: 00-33-1-45-683293 ó 00-33-1-45-683294 Fax: 00-33-1-43-060251 E-mail: dl.panama@unesco.org

UN Organization International - Elisabethstrasse 4/5/4/10, A-1010 Viena Austria - Tel: 0043-1-5872347 Fax: 0043-1-5863080

World Commerence Organization - 72 rue de Lausanne 1202 Ginebra, Suiza - Tel: 0041-22-715-0450 Fax: 0041-22-738-0363 E-mail: mission.panama-omc@itu.int

Embassies and Consulates
in Panamá City

Argentina - Calles 50 y 53 Urbanización Obarrio, Panamá Tel: (011-507)- 264-6989

Bolivia -Calle 50, 78 Panamá Tel: (011-507)- 269-0274

Brazil - Edificio El Dorado, Piso 1 Calle E Méndez, 24C Alegre Tel: (011-507) 263-5322/5 943/1390 140   Apartado Postal 4287 Zona 5 Fax: (011-507)-269-6316

Canada - Edificio Banco Central Hispano # 4   Avenida Samuel Lewis, Panamá Telephone: (011-507)- 264-9731/7115 Fax: (100-507)-263-8083

Colombia - Edificio Grobman, Piso 6 Calle Manuel M Icaza, 12 Panamá Tel: (011-507) 264-9266 Oficina   (011-507)-264-9644 Consejeria Militar Tel: (011-507) -223-6111 Fax: (011-507)-223-1134/223-4159

Costa Rica - Calle Gerardo Ortega, Panamá Tel: (011-507)- 264-2980

Cuba -Embajada de Cuba Avenidas Cuba y Ecuador, Panamá Tel: (011-507) 227-0359/5277 Fax: (011-507)-225-6681

Chile - Calle E Méndez y Vía España,Panamá Tel: (011-507)-223-9748

Ecuador - Calle Manuel Icaza, 12 Panamá Tel: (011-507)- 264-2654 Fax:(011-507)-223-0159 Oficina   Apartado 8380 Zona 7

El Salvador - Avenida Manuel Espinosa Batista, Panamá Tel: (011-507)-223-3020

France - Plaza de Francia, Panamá Tel: (011-507)-228-7824

Greece - Calle M Urbanizacion El Paical, Panamá Tel: (011-507)-260-2705

Japan - Edificio Sede Propia Calles 50 y 60- E Obarrio, Panamá Telephone: (011-507) 263-6155 Apartado Postal 1411-1 Telefax: (011-507)-263-6019

Libia - Avenida Balboa y Calle 32 Panamá Tel: (011-507)- 227-3342

Malta - Calle Elvira Méndez, Panamá Telephone: (011-507) 264-9538

Mexico - Edificio Bancomer, Piso 5 Calle 50 y 53, Panamá Tel: (011-507)-263-5021 Horario de Atención al Público 8:30 a.m. - 12:00
Nicaragua - Calle José de San Martín, 31 Panamá 223-0981

Peru - Embassy of Peru in Panamá City, Panamá - Calle Elvira Méndez y 52, Panamá Tel: (011-507)-223-1112

Poland - Torres del Pacífico Torre B, Piso 10 #10-A Calle Anastacio Ruíz Urbanización Marbella, Panamá Telephone: (011-507) 263-5097 Oficina del Consulado Comercial Tel: (011-507) 263-6254 Apartado 8782 Zona 5 Fax: (011-507)-223-3717.

Russia - Edificio Omega, Piso 7 Avenida Samuel Lewis, Panamá Tel: (011-507) 264-1408/1635 Fax: (011-507)- 264-1558

Spain - Frente al Parque Porras Avenida 6, 44 Panamá 227-5122/5472/5748 225-0549 Oficina Comercial Telephone: (011-507) 269-4018 Oficina de Cooperqación Técnica Tel: (011-507) - 264-2964 Fax: (011-507)- 227-6284 Apartado 1857 Zona 1

United States - Avenida Balboa Tel: (011-507)-227-1777 8:00-17:00 Monday-Friday Apartado Postal 6959 Zona 9 Fax: (011-507) 227-1964 Agencia Internacional para el desarrollo Tel: (011-507)-263-6011

Uruguay - Avenida Justo Arosemena y Calle 32, 4 Panamá Tel: (011-507)-225-9087.

Embassy of the Vatican in Panamá City - Punta Paitilla, Panamá Tel: (011-507)-269-212/3138

Venezuela - Torre Banco Union, Piso 5 Avenida Samuel Lewis, Panamá Tel: (011-507)-269-1244 Oficina Tel: (011-507)-269-1014/1194 Fax: (011-507)-269-1916

STAYING BUSY AND HAPPY IN PANAMA

Some Sound Advice

Retirement or just living in another country often presents new challenges for people because they are confronted with having a plethora of leisure time and the problem of what to do to with it. As you will see throughout this chapter, Panama is a wonderful place to live. In addition to being relatively inexpensive, there are many interesting activities from which to choose.

With coastlines on two oceans, jungles, rainforests, and mountain ranges, Panama offers a lot for people who are interested in the outdoors. There is some hobby or pastime for everyone regardless of age or interests. Even if you cannot pursue your favorite hobbies, you can get involved in something new and exciting. Best of all, by participating in some of the activities in this chapter, you will meet other people with common interests and cultivate new friendships in the process. You can even spend your time continuing your education or studying Spanish as we talk about in Chapter 7.

Most people you meet will also be expatriates, so you probably will not need that much Spanish to enjoy yourself. However, the happiest expatriates seem to be those who speak Spanish. They are able to enjoy the culture more fully, mix with the locals, and make new friends in the process.

Whatever you do, do not make the mistake of being idle. Over the years we have seen many fellow North Americans fail to use their time constructively, and destroy their lives by becoming alcoholics while living in Central America—a few even died prematurely. So, use the information we have provided in this chapter, and take advantage of the many activities Panama offers.

English Books, Magazines, and Newspapers

Books, newspapers, magazines and other printed matter in English are available at most leading bookstores, in souvenir shops of larger hotels, and at some newsstands.

Librería Argosy, located on Vía Argentina (Tel: 223-5344) has a selection of books in English. However, the best way to get your favorite book or magazine is to order it from the U.S. and have it sent to your via one of the private mail services.

El Hombre de la Mancha (Tel: 263-6218) www.books hombredelamancha.com, is a bookstore and café with some books in English.

A good way to stay informed about the local scene, is by reading the on-line version of *The Panama News* (Tel: 269-1456, Fax: 269-2035). The paper covers local news, business, cultural events, restaurants, and has a variety of ads. You may access it at: **www.thepanamanews.com**.

The Visitor/El Visitante (Tel: 225-6638) is published twice monthly in English and Spanish. It is more tourist oriented than

Why Did You Come Here?
What Do You Do?
By Martha Bennett

There are several species of extranjeros living in Panama for a variety of reasons and doing different things. They come to retire, for adventure, to invest or open a business, or to study with one thing in common: changing their lifestyle.

There are tourists. Some come to appreciate the flora and the fauna, volcanoes, beaches and mountains, and observe the Panamanian culture. Others flock for sports: deep sea fishing, diving, surfing, white water rafting, hiking or just hanging out. Everything is available except snow sports. Cultural events may be added on to either group's activities. Many people comes for the great restaurants.

The people who park here for six months to life do these things and more. Missionaries come for Latin language and culture. Others of all ages earn or supplement their income teaching languages, writing, renting rooms or acting as tour guides. There is a group, usually college educated, who ca not find, satisfactory jobs in North America. They are found in the tourist industry or working for international companies.

There are regulations, but in Latin countries, these are worked around. A slower pace of life and close family ties appeal to people in high stress jobs who have children. They come for a change of atmosphere. There is crime and substance abuse here, but the tightly knit community provides a healthier climate for raising children.

Retires participate in many things. Some renovate a dream house. Some persue the World Wide Web. The country club set plays golf, graces swimming pools, and dines elegantly. One can study yoga, painting, writing, language, pottery, gardening, holistic medicine and dance. Just about any indoor or outdoor activity can be found here.

Remember, living takes longer here. Time is spent finding things, fixing things, cutting red tape and avoiding long lines. But this pace allows more time for reading, observing, listening to music and just being. In Panama, we are more human beings than human doings.

the Panama News, is free and found in most hotels. The Visitor has country facts, lists current movies, sporting events, cabarets, concerts, restaurants, Spanish classes, and more.

Various business, bookstores, newsstands, some bookstores and shops in hotels around Panama sell the *Miami Herald International edition, New York Times Washington Post, Time Magazine, Newsweek, Barron's, International herald Tribune, Wall Street Journal* and more.

A large number of English magazines are sold at all of the branches of **Farmacia Arrocha** and **Gran Morrison** and in some supermarkets.

The **National University** bookstore has many good books in Spanish.

If you are fortunate and understand Spanish, or simply want to improve your language skills, you can read one of Panama's excellent Spanish language newspapers. It is not necessary to purchase them since most can be found online.

La Prensa (www.laprensa.com) is the most widely circulated daily newspaper in Panama. **El Siglo** (ww.elsiglo.com) is another popular Spanish language daily.

Panama has about 50 public libraries scattered around the country. It's most impressive library is **La Biblioteca Nacional** or National Library (Tel: 224-9466). Information can be found online at: www.binacional.ac.pa.

Television and Radio

You do not have to worry about missing your favorite TV show in Panama. Satellite cable television is available all over the country. You may view HBO, CNN, The Discovery Channel, CBS, NBC, ABC, FOX, ESPN, TNT and a whole lot more for around $40 monthly. A variety of American television channels provide viewing and entertainment at a low cost from **Direct TV** (Tel: 274-9200) www.directv.com.pa. Direct TV has offices

Opening an English Language Bookstore in Central America

By Mike Jones

My business partner and I are often asked how we decided to start a bookstore in Costa Rica. We began by listing all the businesses we thought might be interesting to operate and/or potentially profitable. The list we came up with included a pool hall, music store, bar, pharmacy, bagels shop, bookstore and laundromat. As we were mulling over the possibilities, we heard about a bar that was for sale. After talking to the owners of the bar and consulting with our lawyer, we decided to make an offer, contingent upon our being able to discuss with the building's landlord the changes we wanted to make to the bar. When the owners of the bar told us that it would not be possible to talk to their landlord prior to purchase, we balked at the deal, sensing bad faith. A few weeks later, some friends contacted us about an excellent retail location that was becoming available in downtown San José. Because the location is near to the Plaza de la Cultura, a point visited by nearly every tourist, we decided that an English language bookstore, whose main market would be tourists, might work. And so, within the space of two weeks we went from being bar owners to bookstore owners.

Our bookstore has now been opened nearly four years, and each year sales have nudged upward. There have been moments of despair, frustration and crisis, but the business appears to have finally left the crawling stage behind and is walking. I never owned a business before in the U.S. and do not think that only four years of business ownership prepares me to give general business advice. What I could instead offer is a handful of tips that relate specifically to expatriate business ownership.

The first relates to your decision about opening a business in Costa Rica. You must decide if you like the country! This is an obvious point, but I have seen many tourists arrive and decide to move here mainly on the basis of having enjoyed their vacation. The rhythm of day-to-day existence versus that of tourist life is entirely distinct. If you can pull it off financially, I would recommend first arriving for a six month visit to really test the idea that this is where you would like to live. Even then, you must keep in mind that there is a big difference between living here while not working and living here while running a business; all the things you enjoyed doing when you were free of work obligations, you will find little time for when you are starting up a business.

When you do decide to start a business, be prepared for a dual challenge, you will be facing all the standard problems of business ownership (managing cash, monitoring competition, attempting to increase sales, etc.) at the same time that you are learning a new culture and language.

As you go through the process of trying to decide what kind of business to open, it is common to make a list of kinds of businesses that exist in the home country but do not exist in Costa Rica. For several years we expatriates were clamoring for a bagelry and a micro brewery, and when they did finally arrive they met with considerable success. Nevertheless, it is important to keep in mind the significant cultural differences that exist between the home country and here, and that what works there will not always work here. The expatriate community is not so large that you can succeed simply by targeting that group. You need tico customers too, and disposable income is not too high here. Also, whatever business you choose, it is obviously important as an expatriate to respect the customs and moral standards of this country. One gentleman from Canada entered the store and told me he was planning on opening a topless car wash. I said, "I would suggest doing that in another country."

Expatriate business people need to resist the occasional pull toward paranoia, toward the notion that "they", the locals are all trying to take advantage of me. A more reasonable stance, I think, is to asume that in business everyone is trying to take advantage of everyone, regardless of national origin. So far, our only slightly significant encounters with less than honorable people have been two unfortunate business deals with other expatriate business people, who , because they had no strong family or financial ties to this country, were able to flee the country.

Despite a strong tendency on the part of U.S. media to represent Latin American governments as bureaucratic, inefficient mazes, we have found the opposite to be true in Costa Rica. Nearly all the legal and regulatory issues that we have been required to comply with have generally been handled swiftly and fairly inexpensively by our lawyer. Get a good lawyer whose practice focuses on expatriate clients. A related stereotype about Latin America is that it is rife with corruption. While there are great differences between countries, we have never had anyone approach us and insist that we pay a bribe as a condition for conducting business. True, we have had people offer us the option of a bribe in order to receive faster or better service. I've seen similar things happen in New York. A last word of advice...do not expect to get rich.

in there parts of the country: Bocas del Toro (Tel: 758-8913) and Chiriqui (Tel 775-0410). With this system you can receive up to 100 channels. DirectTV systems purchased in the U.S. will not work with the satellite systems in Latin America. NFL and NBA sports packages are now available. Members with Direct TV pay-per-view can see movies. Call 274-9200 to sign up for the special NFL package

Cable TV is available through **Cable Onda** (Tel: 264-7555) **Super Cable Panama** (260-5531) and **Astrovisión Cable TV** (Tel: 775-8288). There is a broad range of programs in English and Spanish available on cable TV.

Local Spanish television stations are: Channel 2, Channel 13, Channel 4 and Channel 5. Local programming may be found in the newspaper.

There are more than 50 radio stations on Panama. Radio stations play Latin music including *salsa, merengue* Latin jazz, classical, and even offer a few talk shows. However, some play rock in English, reggae and classical music. If you have a computer and are online, you may access a variety of radio stations from the U.S.

Video Rentals

Video buffs will be happy that there shops do business which rent videos like in the U.S. and Canada. Most movies you rent are in English with Spanish subtitles. The U.S. chain Blockbuster Video has twelve branches in the Panama City Area. Please see the phone book for the location nearest you.

Block Buster Video (main office) 270-3080
Video de las Américas 253-6545, 257-0303
(two locations)

Shopping

Shopping in Panama City is almost as good as in the U.S. Most anything can be found in Panama. One of the best things about living in Panama is that products are imported from around the world at reasonable prices. Thanks to low import duties and duty-free areas, shoppers will find unbelievable bargains on electronics, perfumes, fashionable clothing, and more. You can spend your free time doing some serious shopping, browsing or just window-shopping. Shopping is so good in Panama, that many Costa Ricans make special trips to Panama to buy goods that are not available in the own country.

Due to the large number of U.S. and Canadian citizens living in Panama, and a growing number of Costa Ricans exposed to U.S. culture by cable TV and visiting the States, there has been an influx of American products. If you live in Panama, you may have to substitute many local products for items you ordinarily use and do without some things. This is easy because of the variety of similar products available in Panama.

If you absolutely must have products from the States, you can go to the U.S. every few months—as many foreigners and wealthy Panamanians do— to stock up on canned goods and other non-perishable foods, clothing, sundries and cosmetics.

Everyday, more and more imported goods from the U.S. are available in Panama. Imported brand name cosmetics, stylish clothing, appliances, and some food, can now be found in many stores in most parts of the country.

In Panama City **Vía España** is an upscale shopping district within walking distance from many of the city's important hotels. Furthermore, many of the stores in the Colón Free Zone have outlets in the Panama City.

Bargain hunters will love the city's Avenida Central (20 blocks between Plaza Santa Ana and Plaza Cinco de mayo),.

which has a huge variety of shops where good deals can be found on jewelry, electronics, brand name clothes and digital cameras.

For you mall-rats or mall-crawler, there are also a number of local shopping centers that closely resemble U.S. style malls. **Los Pueblos** is a large shopping complex in Panama City area.

Multi Centro, presently under construction, promises to be a U.S.-style megamall and will have a large food court 280 stores, banks, casinos, a convention center nine movie theaters and a parking garage for over 3000 cars. It is located in the exclusive Paitilla area. The **Multiplaza** mega mall will soon be built by Grupo Roble. They have a couple of U.S. style malls by the same name in Costa Rica. Other malls and shopping centers are:

Centro Comercial Plaza Paitilla	Vía Italia
Centro Comercial El Dorado	Vía Ricardo J. Alfaro
Centro Comercial Plaza Edison	Vía Ricardo J. Alfaro
Centro Comercial Plaza Carolina	Vía España
Centro Comercial Plaza Concordia	Vía España
Centro Comercial Plaza Regency Vía	España
Cocois Department Store.	World Trade Center
Félix B. Maduro Dept. Store	Vía España
Figali Department Store	Vía España
Triángulo	Transitsmica

Most stores are open from 9:00 am to 6:00pm, Monday through Saturday. Some shopping centers on Central Avenue are open on Sunday.

Supermarkets, many of which are open 24 hours, are modern and well-stocked

For making large purchases, you can go to Panama's **Colón Free Zone**. It is the second largest free zone in the world and has 94 stores and warehouses. Almost every brand item in the world can be found there. The place has to be seen to be believed. You can find jewels, precious stones, embroidered tablecloths, oriental art, watches, perfumes, photography and electronic equipment, electric household products, fine glassware, and porcelain - all at reasonable prices.

Panama also offers an ample selection of native handicrafts. Panama's craftsmen are famous for their basketry, textiles, and wood carvings. Native crafts from all over Panama can be purchased in souvenir shops or either of Panama City's larger handicraft markets.

The newest shopping craze is the U.S. warehouse-style mega-stores like Wal-Mart and Target. They promise to change local shopping habits and pricing. **Price Smart**, is similar to the Costco chain in the U.S. The company is pioneering the "club" concept in Panama.

Central America's best shopping is found in Panama.

Since the store purchases large amounts of imported products it will pass its volume buying savings on to its club members. There is also a Price Smart in the city of David.

One thing you may need some time to get accustomed to is the way purchases are handled in some stores. One clerk will wait on you, another will ring up the purchase, and finally you will pick up your merchandise at another window. You find this system in most department stores, pharmacies, and older businesses. This system seems to create a lot of extra work for employees and delays for customers. The good news is that every day more and more stores are adopting the American style one-step self-service system. Panama City is a paradise for shoppers. Vía España and Avenida Central offer everything from the latest in fashion to the most complex computers and crafts at low prices. The craft stores offer a variety of straw and wood products, embroideries, and paintings, in addition to the famous *molas*, hand-made by the *Kuna Indians*.

Panamanian Pastimes

Panama has a wealth of indoor and outdoor activities designed for everyone regardless of sex, age, personal taste or budget. All of us—Panamanians, tourists and foreign residents—can participate in river rafting (some of the world's best), camping, world class diving, dancing, sea kayaking, weight lifting, tennis, baseball, soccer, swimming and surfing, bicycling, horseback riding, and sailing.

There are also plays, ceramic classes, movies, bird watching (some of the world's best), clubs, art galleries, nature tours, social clubs, museums, parks, zoos, and more.

There is something for everyone —so enjoy. Check the activities section of the *Panama News*, or *The Visitor/El Visitante*. If you speak Spanish there is a listing in the weekend section of one of the local Spanish language newspapers. You can find activities, cultural events and all sorts of entertainment listed there.

Bolera de Corundu (Tel: 232-8256) and Bolos El Dorado Tel: 260-2511) and **Bolorama** (Tel: 260-0971) are bowling alleys in the Panama City area.

Hiking is excellent in the mountains around Boquete and El Valle de Antón. Trails abound in both places and the scenery is excellent. Adventurous people can hike in the Darién and province of Panama. Bird watching is good in all of these areas.

Runners and joggers will like the four-mile seaside run along Balboa Avenue starting in Paitilla. The Amador Causeway or Calzada Amador is perfect place for jogging and biking. The causeway connects three islands and is far away form the hustle and bustle of the city.

Gyms and health clubs are good places to socialize and make new friends while working out. Some gyms even have spas, tennis courts, and swimming pools. Call around and visit those in your area to find out which club is right for you.

If you wish to join a private athletic club, country club or gym we suggest:

Gyms and more:
Gimnasio Hércules...260-2647
Steps 270-1349
Aerobics Drive...236-7062
Marina health Spa 269-4081
Balboa Yacht Club 228-5794
Club de Montaña (tennis)......................................225-6441
Panama Racquet Club 260-6884
Carrizal Country Club (tennis)...............................225-4797
* Check the phone book for more listings of gyms and private athletic clubs.

Baseball and Boxing
in Panama

Unlike the rest of Central America, baseball and boxing are more popular in Panama than soccer. Panama has had its share of luminaries in both sports.

Boxing has been popular since the early 1900's. Probably the most notable exponent of the sport is Roberto *"Mano de Piedra"* Durán. Known for his versatility and tenacity, Durán fought in several categories against some of the best fighters of all time and had an extraordinarily long career.

Many Panamanians have played in the major league baseball in the United States. Rod Carew was one of the best hitters of all time and was inducted into the baseball Hall of Fame. Another Panamanian, Mariano Rivera, is considered to be one of the best reliever in professional baseball. He currently plays for the New York Yankees. Every Panamanian boy dreams of following in the footsteps of these great players. Baseball is the number one sport played in Panama's schools.

Golf in Panama

Panama's beautiful scenery and good weather provide a perfect setting for playing golf. Panama has the best championship golf courses in all of Central America. Golf lovers will find an American-style golf course and sports club about 15-minutes from Panama City.

Most of Panama's golf courses have rental clubs and provide caddies. There is sometimes a difference in green fees if you are with a member as opposed to showing up at the course as a walk-on. Below is a description of some of the country's courses.

Nestled in the forests of the Panama Canal watershed lays **Summit Golf and Resort**. It is is a luxurious complex includes two courses, the first of which has a 18-hole, par 72 course, a 6 hole course for children. The new club also offers a restaurant with international cuisine; a swimming pool; an events hall and even day care for children. It is the only facility of its kind in Latin America equipped with GPS technology. This resort also caters to children by offering a family center, day care, and games for all ages. Sounds like it could not get any better? It does. The Summit Golf and Resort is just a short drive from downtown Panama.

Future plans include tennis courts, a basketball court, spa and gym. There are special packages available for guests of Panama's main hotels. To find out more contact this resort at: Tel: (507) 232-GOLF, Fax: (507) 232-4472, E-mail: summit@summitgolfpanama.com, or see www.summitgolfpaanama.com.

There is also another golf course at the **Coronado Hotel and Resort** (Tel: (507) 264-3164), E-mail: corogolf@sinfo.net. Coronado is an 18-hole, par 72 course offering 7,092 yards of professional play. This course is especially beautiful for its fruit trees, including the abundance of Mango trees, which surround the greens and fairways. To put it simply, the course is considered a "jewel" in all of Latin America.

The Panama Golf Club (Tel: 266-7777) welcomes non-members who are accompanied by members.

The Horoko Golf Club and Resort (Tel:211-3472) e-mail:horoko@sinfo.net is a 18-hole course located near Panama City.

There are also golf courses located in **Valle Escondido** near Boquete and on **Isla Taboga**.

Golfers may now keep on Panama's growing golf scene by subscribing to *Central America's Golf Magazine*, Tel: 011-(506) 231-6931, Fax: 011-(506) 232-1930, E-mail: golftennis@hotmail.com, www.golfmagazine.net.

For golf tours to Panama Costa Rica Golf Adventures at www.golfcr.com.

Museums and Art Galleries

Panama offers a variety of museums highlighting all aspects of its colorful past. Panama City boasts a variety of museums and art galleries. The country's newest and best museum is the **Museo del Canal Interoceánico**. Exhibits trace the history of the 8th wonder of this world, the canal.

Although not as impressive as museums in the States or Europe, there is still a lot to see. In general, Panama's museums provide a good perspective on the history and culture of the country. Here is a list of some of the best museums:

Museums:
Museum of Religious Colonial Art. 228-2897
Museum of Natural Science. 225-0645
Museo of Anthropology Reina Torres Araúz ...262-0415
Museum of History. 228-6231
Museum Afro-Antillano 262-5348
Museum of Contemporary Art........................262-8012
Museum Belisario Porras 994-6326
(Los Santos Province)
Museo de la nacionalidad...............................996-0077
 (Province of Herrera)
Manuel F. Zárate 994-5644
(Province of los Santos)
Museum of History and Culture 775-7839
(Chiriquí Province).

Art Galleries:

Artegama.. 264-1758
Galería de Arte Anonimos............................269-9714
Artecomsult Galería 269-1523
Bernheim Galería 223-0012
Imagen...226-2649
Habitante...264-6470
Legacy Fine Art...................................265-8141

Water Sports and Fishing

Panama's thousand miles of Caribbean and Pacific coastline, hundreds of islands, lakes and rivers, mountain streams, a combination of clear tropical water, reefs, and white sand beaches make it an outdoor lovers paradise.

Snorkeling and diving are very popular. Panama offers spectacular reefs on both the Pacific and Atlantic sides. The Bocas del Toro archipelago, Isla Contadora, and Isla Toboga are places to practice these water sports. Divers will find Panama's warm waters teeming with an unbelievable number of exotic fish. There are even several coral reefs worth exploring. There are several companies in Panama which provide lessons, equipment, and diving tours.

Costa Arriba is a stretch of coast east of Colón. María Chiquita, Langota, Bocas del Toro, and the Archipielago de Perlas are areas perfect for skin diving, diving and snorkeling.

Surfers of all ages will be pleased to know that Panama is quickly gaining popularity on the worldwide surf circuit due to its warm weather and, most importantly, great waves. Panama has some of the best surf spots in Central America. The country boasts close to forty prime areas for surfing on both the east and west coasts. The best surfing beaches in the country are Las Lajas, Isla Coiba, Isla Cebaco, Santa Catalina,

Punta Brava, Mariato, Cambutal, Playa Raga, Guanicos, Desfiladero, Madroño, Playa Venado, Río Mar, El Palmar, Teta, Serena, Malibú, Las Bóvedas, Panamá Viejo, Mojón Beach, and Jaque.

Wind surfing has also become popular in recent years. The country has several lakes including those in the canal where this sport may be practiced.

The rivers Chiriquí and Chiriquí Viejo, rated level 3 and 4 respectively, are excellent for whitewater adventure. There are several companies which offer river rafting. Kayaking is practiced in some areas of the country.

Panama lives up to its name, since Panama means "abundance of fish." The country is considered a year -round fisherman's paradise. It offers three world-class areas for deep-sea fishing.

Each area offers shipboard and beachfront lodging with either full or half-day trips. In addition, a number of the local hotels often organize deep-sea fishing expeditions. Outfitter can be found in Bocas del Toro on the Atlantic side, Panama City and Contadora on the Pacific side, and Lake Gatún inland. Many world fishing records have been set in the waters off and around the Pearl Islands. Angler reel in black and blue marlin, red snapper, mahi-mahi, sailfish from the Pacific, and tarpon and snook from the Atlantic. Lake Gatún is famous for bass fishing. There is also trout fishing in the rivers like Río Caldera which run down from the Barú Volcano near the town of Boquete in Chiriquí Province.

Boating is another activity you can enjoy in Panama. Boaters can find several places to dock while they enjoy the country. You can easily travel by yacht through the Canal, sail the Pacific Ocean or explore the San Blas, Bocas del Toro or Las Perlas Archipelagos. "Yachties" will find all they need at **Panama Canal Yacht Club** located at Cristóbal (Tel: 441-5882), **Balboa Yacht Club** (Tel: 228-5794), **Club de Yates y Pesca** (Tel:

I found My Water World in Panama

By Paul Karns

I used to live in West Palm Beach, Florida. I was working an administrator for a large company for almost 20 years. I experienced a combination of job burn out with no hope of vertical movement because of my age. I became very tired of the treadmill existence and wanted something different.

A friend lent me Christopher Howard's bestselling book about Costa Rica. I read it from cover to cover and became sold on the country. I packed my bags and moved to Costa Rica. I ended up renting an apartment in a building where a friend of my mother's son had settled. I used the lovely town of Heredia as a home base and began to explore the country.

After seeing much of Costa Rica, on a whim I decided to visit Panama. A lot of people had told me about the area of Bocas del Toro, so I decided to check it out. As it turned out, I did not have to go much farther.

Right away Bocas reminded me of Key West, Florida. I liked the fact that the area was not that developed, the laid back locals, and, above all, the warm tropical weather.

Despite the small town feel of the place, I found a lot to do. There is an internet café, good eateries, some night life, an ATM machine, and even a Spanish school. Crime is almost nonexistent and I feel much safer living here than in the U.S.

There are numerous beach- related activities to stay busy. The diving is excellent. You can sail, surf, and fish everyday. IN Bocas you can birdwatch, beach comb or just experience a magnificent sunset.

Within a week I found a small house to rent on Isla Bastimientos, which is a 10-minute boat ride from Bocas del Toro.

I've really fallen in love with the area and have just purchased 3/4 of an acre of land about a hundred yards from the beach. I plan to build a small home with a cement slab floor and wooden walls. I will not have A.C. since ceiling fans will do the job. I plan to install Direct TV, so I will be able to see movies. The world news does not really interest me since one tends to lose all sense of time and forget about the craziness of the outside world in this tropical paradise.

I even found love in Bocas in the form of a beautiful, young Panamanian woman. Last week we wanted to do something adventurous, so we flew to Panama City to see a Latin rock concert.

Not a bad life for a guy in his fifties.

227-0145) and the new **Flamenco Yacht Club** (Tel: 314-0665) at the end off the beautiful Amador Causeway. If you do not know how to sail, you can learn at one of these yacht clubs or marinas.

Parks for Nature Lover

Many people consider Panama one of the best ecotourism destinations in the world. Because of its unique geographical location, as a narrow land bridge between two continents, Panama has a greater diversity of wildlife than any country in Mesoamerica. Panama is the home to an amazing diversity of wildlife. Around 1,000 birds migrate through or inhabit Panama. The country is also home to over 200 species of mammals, 350 kinds of amphibian and reptiles over 1,000 species of butterflies, 56 types of freshwater fish, over 100 animal species found nowhere else in the world and thousands of species of orchids.

Presently, about 29% of Panama's territory is protected in 14 national parks, more than a dozen reserves, and 10 wildlife refuges. In fact, the Smithsonian Institute has installed an ecological research station where scientists from around the world study the country's unique biodiversity.

Volcán Barú National Park is one of the most beautiful regions of the country. The surrounding area is so magnificently beautiful that it is frequently called the "Switzerland of the Americas." On a clear day, both the Pacific and Atlantic Oceans can be seen from the top of the volcano.

Bastimentos National Park in Bocas del Toro is a great place to observe marine in its protected coral reef. A variety of sea turtles use this area for nesting. The park also serves as a refuge for birds, mammals, reptiles and other animals. Some of the country's other important national parks are **Isla Barro Colorado**, **Parque Nacional Chagres**, **Parque Nacional**

Sarigua, Parque Nacional de la Amistad and **Parque Nacional de Darién**, which has one of the most vast jungles in America.

You really do not have to venture far from Panama City to find a tropical forest. It is the only park in Latin America with a tropical forest within a metropolitan capital. **Parque Nacional Metropolitano** is located at the edge of the city and about a 15 minute taxi ride from most hotels. The park is a home to more than 200 species of birds, monkeys, reptiles, and other animals.

Where to Make New Friends

You should have no problem making new friends of either sex in Panama, but might have some difficulty meeting Panamanians if you speak little or no Spanish. However, some Panamanians speak a little English and are dying for the chance to perfect their English language skills while you work on your Spanish. Perhaps you can find someone to exchange language lessons. This is a good way to make new acquaintances and learn how Spanish is really spoken.

You most certainly will find it easier to meet fellow Americans in Panama than in the U.S., because Americans living abroad tend to gravitate toward each other. Newcomers only have to find an enclave of fellow countrymen and they can make new friends. You cannot help bumping into other Americans since Panama is such a small country. There are many English-speaking people working in Panama City. In areas like Boquete and Bocas del Toro, you will also find people who speak English. Another good way of making contact with other foreign residents is by participating in some of the activities listed in the weekly editions of the The Panama News and The Visitor. English publications serve as a vital link in the foreign community, or "Gringo Grapevine"and help to put you in touch with a whole network of expatriates and the services they offer.

You have no excuse for being lonely unless you want to be. Just be yourself and you will find Panama is just the place for you. If you cannot find the club your looking for, then try starting one. There are clubs for almost any interest in Panama. Church groups are another good place to meet people.

CLUBS:
Canadian Club of Panama
City Club of Panama (expensive).....................210-1366
Club de Golf 266-7777
Club de Montaña 230-1158
Lions Club...225-0721
Rotary Club...226-2684
Kiwanis Club 232-6286

Love and Permanent Companionship

If you are looking for romance, Panama might just be the right place for you.

Men will have no problem meeting Panamanian women. Panama's women seem to like older, more experienced men. Many Latin women actually seek out relationships with older men who are financially more secure. It is not unusual to see a wife who is ten to twenty years younger than her spouse. This practice may be frowned upon in some countries but is accepted in Central America. Many retires we know claim to feel rejuvenated and to have a new lease on life after becoming involved with younger women.

This may seem a case of simply greed to an outsider or an inexperienced bystander, and perhaps it is. However, with proper love and care the situation can easily be turned into a loving and lasting relationship. And when that happens, that is a Latin woman is truly in love with you, she will be all the things you have always wanted — caring, understanding, devoted, and forgiving.

In general, Latin women are more warm-hearted and devoted than their North American counterparts. They consider you a joy. One retiree we know boasts, "The women here really know how to treat you like a king!"

A man does not even have to be rich to meet women—a $1,500 Social Security check translates to a millionaire's pay in Panama.

No wonder Latin women are highly sought by foreign men. However, before becoming involved with a Central American woman, you should realize the many cultural differences that can lead to all sorts of problems, especially if you do not speak Spanish fluently.

Latin women are know for their beauty

One of the more outward differences between Latin women and North American women is the way they dress. Latin women are conscious of the way they dress and look, and like to be very feminine and fashionable.

Most cannot afford it but will spend every last cent to look good and make sure you notice her. Latin women, in general, like to show their sensuality.

Usually, Latin women are more jealous and possessive than American women, and tend not to understand our ways unless they have lived in the United States. Also, be aware that because of their comparative wealth, most Americans, especially the elderly, are considered prime targets for some unscrupulous Latin females.

We advise you to give any relationship time and make sure a woman is sincerely interested in you and not just your money—you will save yourself a lot of grief and heartache in the long run. Since prostitution is legal and available to men of all ages, be careful of the ladies of ill repute.

Many foreigners after inviting one of these females to spend the night, wake up the next day without the woman and minus wallets and other valuables.

Most single men can avoid getting involved with gold digger, prostitutes, or other troublesome women if they know where to look for good women.

One American we know ran an ad in a local Spanish newspapers and ended up screening hundreds of women before finding his ideal mate. As far as we know he is still happily married. Taking classes at the university is another way to meet quality women. Universities are usually full of beautiful well-educated females. Cafés, restaurants, bars and other places around the university are good places to meet women. If you have Panamanian friends, they will usually be able introduce you to someone worthwhile.

The key is finding a nice, traditional Central American woman and avoiding getting involved with "bad" Latin women. Every country in Central America has plenty of working girls and hustler. They hang out at the popular bars and discos specifically to pick up guys. They also go shopping in the malls, ride buses, and go to grocery stores. So just because you have met a nice girl in a typical working girl hang out, does not mean you have met a quality person. If you know what to look for, they are easy to spot.

Many men have knowingly and unknowingly married bad women. Some girls are honest and will directly ask you for money. The hustler are more dangerous because their agenda is to really take you to the cleaners and they do not rule out marrying you to achieve this objective. Some men say that have lost everything from airline tickets that are cashed instead of used, large sums of money the girls claim they need to get visas, houses, and more. These are the women who contribute to the bad stories you may hear about some Latin women. So falling in love with a bad girl will typically lead to a lot of heartache and problems. Unfortunately, they are the easiest girls to meet in many instances and a good number of men fall into this trap.

A very small number of these women will become good wives. They are often women who have been sexually or otherwise abused at a very young age so the problem is very deeply rooted. So, your chances of converting them are very slim. No matter how gorgeous the girl is, it is just not worth it.

The best way to spot a bad girl is her profile. They never have a job, never live with their parents, never have phone numbers, and never invite you to their home or introduce you to their friends or family. They do not want to leave any trail for you to track them down later. They typically come from very poor backgrounds and have very little education, rarely completing high school.

They are quite aggressive and target older Americans. Often they speak a little English and will start up a conversation with you or smile at you, until you make the first move. They will appear friendly and sincerely interested in you. They are always attractive or very young. They will always ask for your phone number.

The best way to politely get rid of one of these women is to ask them to loan you a little money. You will immediately see their interest disappear. Actually, a nice Latin woman might just loan you the money.

Women you see working in stores are usually poorly educated and from poor families. Some may show an interest in an older American who is friendly with them, but the relationship is likely to be overly influenced by a poor woman looking for a rich American husband.

Foreign men should beware of the so-called "Latin set-up." We have heard countless stories where women get pregnant as a ploy to get a foreigner to marry them. We believe it is our duty to alert men about this underhanded and self-centered method of ensnaring them into an unwanted relationship.

In general, a nice Latin woman typically lives with her parents until she gets married. Single daughters are not encouraged to get jobs, unless the parents are very poor. Instead they are expected to help with taking care of the house or study.

Quality Latin women from traditional family backgrounds are raised to take care of their man. They can be quite possessive and jealous at times. But this is only because they are very emotional and deeply in love with their man. They tend to seek out long term relationships, starting at a very young age. It is quite rare for a Panamanian women to have any interest in casually dating many different guys.

When approached by strangers, they are friendly and helpful by nature. All Latin women value making new friends. Americans often misread this friendliness and think the woman has a romantic interest in them. In order for the women to develop any romantic interest in you at all, they have to first know from a trusted third party that you are looking for a long-term relationship. After a brief encounter, a decent woman will never ask for your phone number. If you ask for her number, she will always give you the wrong number in order to avoid appearing rude. Nice women live with their parents and would never want to have strange guys calling their house. From a romantic interest point of view, quality Latin women are very difficult to meet.

If the woman is convinced you are seriously looking for a long-term relationship, she will then start to show an interest in getting to know you better. Her initial physical attraction to you will usually be of very minor importance to her. Her main interest will be focused on your personality: Are you are a kind person? Can you offer minimum security to raise a family? Do you sincerely care about her family? Would you make a good father?

Over the years we have encountered a lot of foreigners who end up not using common sense and end up getting involved with people with whom they would probably never associate back home. This brings us to the story of "Dumb and Dumber."

Dumb came to Central America about twelve years ago from the U.S., where he was a successful businessman. Almost upon arriving here he became romantically involved with a woman of ill- repute. He was basically too lazy and busy getting drunk to find a quality mate. Over the course of his relationship he lost about $300,000 because he entrusted his business dealings to his girlfriend. After splitting up with her and having to give her half of everything he owned because of their common law situation, he goes and gets involved with another women who will probably "take him to the cleaners" someday.

Dumber came to Central America as a millionaire. The first thing he did was get romantically involved with a woman of the night. Dumber also spent most of his time in bars like Dumb. Consequently, when he broke up with his lady friend, after a few years together, he had to pay her around $50,000. He is now with another woman and most likely supporting her whole family. He will probably end up broke like Dumb. Neither Dumb nor Dumber speak Spanish nor have made any effort to understand the locals and constantly refer to them in derogatory terms.

The majority of foreign men who come to Central America do not share Dumb and Dumber's fate. Nevertheless, you should learn a lesson from this story.

A Walk on Panama's Wild Side

The author of this guidebook feels it is his responsibility to paint a realistic picture of all of the aspects of living in Panama. He would not be doing a service to our readers if he did not cover the subject of prostitution. However, let it be known that in no way does he condone the sexual exploitation of minors. In this section he only provides information about sexual relationships between consenting adults.

As in the rest of Latin America, many males have their first sexual experience with prostitutes. In order to control the propagation of venereal disease and AIDS, prostitutes are required by the government to undergo regular health checkups by the Ministry of Health or *Ministerio de Salud* in order to practice their trade legally. Most upscale brothels make sure their employees have their health papers and tests up to date.

Unlike the United States, Canada, and many parts of the world and despite the fact that it is a Catholic country, prostitution is openly practiced. Most of the women take great care to hide their work from their families and friends. However, these women work to support their families. Many of these women can make more money providing sex for hire than by doing other work. The average wage say for a secretary is about $200 a month, more if she speaks English. Some of the more successful upper end sex workers can make a couple of thousand dollars a month.

Like most cities in Latin America, Panama City has its share of strip clubs, Cabarets, massage parlous, and brothels.

Elite (Tel: 263-6890) is located in the heart of the banking district. **The Josephine's** (Tel:223-0035) and **Josephine's Gold** (Tel: 263-6890) are the sister nightclubs. Both establishments offer shows featuring beautiful women.

If you are looking for a relaxing massage and steam bath, there are a number of massage parlors to cater to your needs. **Caribbean Center** (Tel: 236-6151), **Royal Elegance Center** (Tel: 264-3313 or 264-7991) and **Golden Time** (Tel:266-0329) are to top massage parlors. **Oasis** (264-4785), **Erotic Massage** (623-2581 or 614-1722), **Girl's Fantasy** (227-4608 or 603-8652), **Paraiso del Placer** (Tel: 225-9768), **Sensual Girls** (235-8067 or 674-7331), **Secrets Massages** (315-1377 or 649-9047), **Extreme Night Girls** (227-4608 or 603-8652), **Exclusive's Girls** (614-1722), **Lips Nice Company** (690-0306), **Candy's** (600-1922), **Satin Babes** (226-4001 or 617-1345), **Seductores Masajes** (623-2581 or 694-8002) and **Magic Massage** (Tel: 261-9803 or 617-1345) all offer massage services at their place or yours.

There are brothels scattered around Panama City, Colón, and some other areas of the country. A few of these establishments are in seedy areas so you exercise extreme caution before frequenting any of them.

One, interesting phenomenon are Central America's famous "love motels." Several dozen are found around the Panama City area and do a brisk business. Many foreigners do not know the difference between a 'hotel' and 'motel'. In Panama and the rest of Central America motels are for making love and serve no other purpose.

These establishments exist for discrete liaisons between adults. Bosses and their secretaries, men with prostitutes, young lovers who still live at home, and others enjoy these convenient establishments. Patrons can hide their car as well as their lovers in one of these places. Rooms may be rented for several hours. Fresh towels, sheets, food drink and even a condom are provided. Each room also has a small waist-level little window for you to pay and for staff to hand you alcoholic beverages, soft drinks, food, towels, and more. Clients and staff of the motel never see each others' faces.

Most rooms also have a TV, some with pornographic movies, and music. There is a big curtain or door which is closed immediately to hide the identity of the couple and their vehicle. On weekend nights and during lunch Panama city's motels fill up quickly. It is very easy to find one of these motels once you have lived in Panama for a while. Just ask a taxi driver or one of your friends.

Nightlife and Entertainment

Panama City probably has the best nightlife in Central America. Panamanians will party almost any night of the week. There are countless bars, dance halls, pool halls, small neighborhood bars and discotheque all over Panama City and in most other parts of the country. Panamanians love to dance.

Most of these nightspots will appeal to anyone from- 16 to 50, give or take a little for the young at heart.

No doubt when you have lived in the country for a while, the dance bug will bite you. There are numerous dance academies that offer classes for all levels of experience in various styles of Latin American dance.

Once you have mastered the basic dance steps and can dance to the rhythms of *salsa, merengue, cumbia,* and other Latin dances, put on your best pair of dancing shoes and go to one of the country's numerous dance halls.

Panama City's many discotheque and dance halls play music for all tastes until the wee hours of the morning; admission is inexpensive or free. International liquors and cocktails, as well as all local beers and beverages, are served. Some establishments offer a happy hour in the late afternoon. Also, keep in mind that many of these clubs serve food and the traditional heaping plates of delicious local appetizer or hôrs d'oeuvres, called *bocas.*

Here are few places to go:
Rock Cafe 264-5364
Bacchus Discotheque(Calle Elvira Méndez).....263-9005
Patatus (Urbanización Marbella)......................264-8467
Dreams (Villa España).....................................263-4248
Capo's Bar (Boulevard El Dorado)...................260-1123
Pavo Real (English style pub) 269-0504
Las Bóvedas (live jazz)...................................228-8068

Gambling

Gamblers can even find a bit of Las Vegas in Panama. In Panama, casinos and other games of chance are operated both under the government and privately. Panamanians play slots and tables (blackjack, craps, roulette, poker). Bingo is also very popular in Panama.

There are a number of popular gambling houses that can be found in downtown Panama. The three most attractive casinos are located in the **Hotel Caesar Park**, the **Miramar Inter-Continental**, and the **Hotel el Panama**.

The most popular form of gambling in Panama is the national lottery or *lotería*. It is truly a national pastime. Lottery is played twice weekly on Wednesdays and Sundays. Profits from the national lottery go to support hospitals and local charities. The lottery is operated by the government-owned *Lotería Nacional de Beneficiencia*. Tickets are sold all over the country. Tickets are sold by vendors who can be found hawking them in every city and town in the country.

One of Panama's casinos

If you are lucky enough to win the huge, annual Christmas Lottery, or *Gordo Navideño*, you will become very rich and will probably be set up for life.

To find the results of the lottery, look in the local newspaper. Bingo is also available. In Panama, no earnings from games of chance are subject to taxation.

There is horse racing at **Presidente Remon Racetrack** every Thursday, Saturday, Sunday, and holidays.

Here is a list of casinos in Panama City:

Bambit Resort ....Tel: 714265
Caesar Park Panama Hotel ....Tel: 226-4077
Caribe Hotel (Av. Peru & Calle 28 Este) ....Tel: 272-5251
Coronado Club Suites Resort.....................Tel: 240-4444
El Panama Hotel (Via España) ....Tel: 695-000
Europa Hotel (33 Via España and Calle 42). ....Tel: 636-911
Gran Hotel Soloy(Av. Peru & Calle 30) ....Tel: 271-133
Hotel El Panama (España111) ....Tel: 695-000
Hotel Internacional (Plaza 5 de Mayo). ....el: 621-0000
Hotel Plaza Paitilla Inn (Via Italia)................Tel: 269-1122
Riande Continental Airport Hotel ....Tel: 203-333
RiandeContinental Hotel (Via Espana)...........Tel: 639-999
Riande Granada Hotel................................Tel: 644-900

Movies and Theaters in Panama

Movie theaters are found all over the Panama City area and in other large cities. Most of these theaters show first-run movies usually a month or two after they first are released in the United States.

Fortunately, the majority of movies are shown in English with Spanish subtitles. The cost of a movie is under $4.00.

Just like in the U.S. to see what's playing look in the Spanish newspapers under *cartelera*.

Film buffs will be pleased to know that classic and foreign films may be seen at the National University.

Movies (*Cines*) in Panama City and Other Areas

CineMark.	314-6001/02
Cines Brasil, España y Obarrio	264-8411
Cine Plaza	269-4928
Cineplex Dorado Mall	236-7847
Cine Alhambra Chanis (Chanis)	235-9671
Cine Alhambra Plus (Vía Transístmica)	229-6847
Cine Alhambra Vía España	264-3217
Cines Aries	269-1632
Cine Extreme Planet (Ave. Balboa)	214-7022
Cine Los Pueblos (Vía Tocumen)	217-7123
Cine Conquistador(Vía Tocumen)	217-6008
Cine Universitario (International and old movies)	264-2737
Cine Galeria (Santiago, Veraguas)	958-5266
Cine Nacional (David, Chiriquí)	774-7887
Multicines Espinar (Colón)	470-0215

Theaters (*Teatros*) In And Around Panama City

Panama City has its share of theaters. Most live plays are in Spanish. Current plays and musical events are also listed in the activities section of local newspapers like **La Prensa**. If you have the chance check out The National Theater with it's beautiful interior.

Teatro del Círculo de Panamá............................261-5375
Teatro de La Cúpula.......................................223-7516
Teatro Infantil Tía Dora..................................264-7239
Teatros Nacional..262-3682
Teatro Anayansi y Teatro La Huaca.................226-7000
Teatro Museo Reina Torres de Araúz...............262-0415
Teatro Balboa..272-0372
Teatro La Huasca...262-3682
Ancon Theater Guild (Ancón)........................252-6786

Recently released movies in English are shown here.

(OMMUNI(ATION)

Telephone and Internet Service

Keeping in touch with family friends is not a problem in Panama. Panama has an excellent privatized telephone system, with around 400,000 phone lines. **Cable & Wireless** provides telecommunication coverage nation wide. Presently they offer international telephone, fax, telegraph, and some e-mail services. They also offer provide such innovative services as answering, voice messages and beeper services. In 1997, they became the first private company to take over the previously inefficiently run government phone system. Now they have a virtual monopoly when it comes to residential and business service.

Obtaining a phone line and to open an account in Panama costs around $50 for Panamanian citizens and $100 for non-citizens. It usually takes about a week to have a regular phone connected.

Calls within the country are a bargain. You can call any place in the country for only a few cents. If your house or apartment does not have a phone, do not worry. Public telephones are just about everywhere in Panama and use $.05,

$.10, and $.25 cent coins. Both Panamanian and U.S. coins are the same size and interchangeable. Coin -operated pay phones cost $.15 for three minutes. Phones accepting pre-paid phone cards are slowly replacing coin-operated phones.

You can also make international calls from most hotels, private phones in homes or offices. The procedure is just like in the U. S. by direct dialing or first talking to the operator (*operadora*). The access numbers for calling Panama from abroad are 011-507 plus the seven-digit number. Panama has no city codes. To call or fax the U.S. from Panama dial 001 + area code + the number.

AT&T, MCI and **Sprint** offer direct dial service from any phone in Panama. Dial 109 for AT&T, 108 for MCI or 115 for Sprint to reach an English-speaking operator. You may dial 106 to reach an international long -distance operator. Most operators speak English.

International calls cost a little over $1.00 Monday to Saturday, 7am to 5pm; 5pm to 12 am around $.75, 12am to 7am around $.50 per minute.

Cellular phone service is available in Panama and they have become a "status symbol. "Almost everyone including middle and all upper-class *panameños* and foreign businessmen seem to have a cell phone. **Cable Wireless** (Tel: 161 or www.cwmobile.com) and **Bell South** (Tel: 265-0111) are the main players in the cellular phone market. Panama's cellular phones are digital. Nokia, Motorola, Ericson, and other major brand name cell phones are available in Panama. It usually takes a few hours to get a cell line in Panama. **Rent de Panama** (226-7302 or 613-7890), Centel (Tel:226-3233) and Rental Express (Tel:236-6710) provide daily, weekly and monthly cell phone rentals.

Helpful phone numbers in Panama City

National Operator	101
Directory Assistance Operator	102
Fire	103
Police	104
International Long Distance	106
International Airport	238-4160
Customs	232-6277
Centro Médico Paitilla	265-8888
Hospital Nacional	207-8110
Hospital Santo Tomás (Emergency)	225-1536
Hospital San Fernando(Emergency)	229-2004
Traffic Police (In case of an accident)	232-5614

Computer buffs will be pleased to know Internet services are available throughout Panama. Internet services in Panama are completely privatized, thus there are a host of companies offering a range of services for those interested in connecting to the Internet. Most ISP's, or Internet Service Providers, work on a "flat fee" basis, meaning there is a monthly charge for unlimited time on the web. The cost associated with this service varies from company to company, however, the price tends to hover between $24.00 and $40.00 per month. Some companies provide much more in the way of customer support than others, which is often reflected in their price. Cable modems and DSL lines are also available. To get hooked up to the Internet in Panama, contact **Cable & Wireless** at 882-2229 or e-mail them at: Internet.ventas@cwpanama.net. Other internet providers are: **Broadband** (Tel: 264-4134 or ventas@broadbandwc.com) and **internet** (Tel: 206-3600 or ventas@pa.inter.net)

For those interested in connecting to the web in a "*Cybercafe* or *Internet Cafe*" you are in luck. Panama City has numerous of these shops, many of them are located around the university area or near El Panama Hotel. Prices vary from one Cafe to another, but the average price is between $0.75-$2.00 per hour, depending on the quality of the connection and computers. Most cafe's have Window's-based computers and offer printing services; some actually have scanners and internet phone set-ups.

Although the sound quality is not too good, Internet users can now make long distance telephone calls with their computers. Net calls are dirt-cheap. All you need is a headset and to hook up with a company like **www.dialpad.com** and you are in business.

Mail Service

Panama's postal system offers postal services comparable to that in many countries abroad. **Correos y Telégrafos** offers a wide range of services.

Just as in the United States, mail may be received and sent from the post office (*correo* or *casa de correos*). Other small cities and towns in rural areas have their own centrally located post offices. An airmail letter from Panama to the U.S. costs $.35; an airmail letter to Europe is $.45. Airmail between the United States or Europe and Panama usually takes about five to ten days. A postcard to North America is around $25.

Curbside boxes for mail pick up and door-to-door-delivery are almost nonexistent in Panama. You will have to mail your letters from the post office or from a hotel if you are a guest. Since there is no home delivery, you will need a post office box. Getting a post office box is a straightforward process, but vacant boxes can sometimes be hard to come by as they are in great demand. Boxes by sharing with friends, neighbors, extended family or a business associate. In theory, said practice is not permitted, but many people do it and nobody seems to check closely. To apply for a post office box, go to the post office nearest your office or home.

Rental rates for P.O. boxes are $20 yearly for a personal box and around $40 for a business box. You have to pay your fee for a P.O. box between January 15 and March 15th

You may also receive mail in the general delivery section (*entrega general*) of your local post office. This is especially useful in isolated regions of the country. All letters must have your name, the phrase *entrega general* and the name of the nearest post office. Be sure the sender writes the country's name as 'República de Panama' rather than 'Panama,' or the mail may be returned to the sender. You will need an ID to pick up your mail.

You should avoid having anything larger than a letter or a magazine sent to you in Panama through the regular mail. Therefore, it is better to have friends bring you large items, pick them up when you are visiting the States, or use one of the private mail companies mentioned in this section.

Receiving Money from Abroad

Do you plan on having money sent to you in Panama? The fastest and safest way to receive money while visiting or residing in Panama is to have an international money order or any other type of important merchandise or document shipped to you by one of the worldwide courier services, such as DHL or UPS. Letters and small packages usually take about two working days (Mon.–Fri.) to reach Panama from the United States or Canada.

Many worldwide air couriers have offices in Panama City, such as **DHL** (800-DHL1 or 271-3400), **Federal Express** (271-3838 or 800-1122), **UPS** (Tel: 269-9222) **Jetex** (Tel: 269-1755).

U. S. banks can wire money to banks in Panama. This method is safe, but can be slow at times, as many bureaucratic delays can develop while waiting for checks to clear. You are also charged a fee for the transfer.

Western Union (800-2274) in Panama is another way to make money transfers in the country.

You can always have a trustworthy friend or relative bring you up to $10,000 when they come to Panama.

Automatic Teller Machines (ATMs) are found all over the country. You cannot transfer money directly but can get cash advances from one of your credit or debit cards. Use of ATMs along with cashing a personal check are perhaps the fastest way to get money.

Another safe way of having checks sent to you is through the private mail service we list in the next section.

Once you have established a permanent residence in Panama you can have Social Security and Veteran's benefits mailed to you directly through the U.S. Embassy. However, these checks usually do not arrive until sometime after the tenth of each month.

Private Mail Service

The U.S. based company **Mail Boxes Etc**. has six braches in the Panama City: Paitilla (Tel: 264-7038), Albrook (Tel: 314-06010 El Dorado (360-2070), San Francisco (270-13270) El Cangrejo Via Argentina (Tel: 214-4620) and Vía España (264-3325). They are mail forwarding services that provide clients with a mail drop and P.O. Box in Miami, and a physical address there. This enables customers living in Panama to have their mail sent to the Miami address where the companies forward the mail to Panama. They also do packaging, have fax and internet services, and offer photocopying.

Airbox Express (Aerocasillas) (Tel:269-9774 Fax: 269-9396) in Panama City and (Tel: 775-4512, Fax:774-7496 E-mail: info@airbox.com) www.airbox.ws) in David is another company offering a mail drop in Miami.

The companies above provides much faster service than the regular Panamanian mail system to access mail order products from the U.S., to enable clients to subscribe to magazines and newspapers at U.S. domestic rates, to help obtain replacement parts from abroad, and to order directly from mail order catalogs like Land's End, J.C. Penny and L.L.

Bean. Large automobile parts may also be ordered from the U.S.

Rates at any of this private mail services vary monthly depending on the amount of mail you receive and whether you have a business or personal account.

We have used one of Aeropost's' sister companies in Costa Rica for over four years and in general their service has been good. Due to the nature of our book business, we have an unusually high volume of incoming and outgoing mail. Our letters, books, packages, monies and other mail, reach their U.S. destinations almost as fast as if there were mailed from another city in the States. This reliable service makes doing business from Central America very easy.

Other services offered include Certified Mail, Registered Mail, Express Mail and FEDEX, UPS, DHL or other courier services.

Rates at any of these private mail services run from about $15.00 to $60.00 or more per month depending on the amount of mail you receive whether you have a business or personal account, and where they can send or receive packages.

Mail Boxes Etcetera has several outlets in Panama City

Necessity Begets An International Mail Service
By Chuck Swett

Back in the good old days, the early sixties Jimn Fendell had been here 10-plus years (arrived with parents in 1951), and I was just getting over the caravan like, Pan-American Airways milk-run through Central America, things were a lot different here. The nearest beach, Puntarenas, was four hours away, via Cambronero, with fog so thick you had to ride on the hood of the car and guide the driver. You could go to the movies for a few cents, and fill up a VW for almost nothing. The train ride to Puntarenas was one big long party. And you could walk down any street in San José at any hour without ever considering yourself to be in danger.

But the one thing you would not even consider doing , unless you really felt generous toward the customs officer population, was subscribe to National Geographic, The Saturday Evening Post, or Life Magazine. Playboy would probably not even make it off the plane, much less through the postal system. The custom was to find out who was traveling and ask them to bring that car part or special shampoo or the latest Beatles album, when they came back.

As the country and the expatriate colony grew, communications media began to introduce new goodies and remind the foreigners of things they were accustomed to at home but could not easily get on the local market.

Our innovative friend Jim began to recognize the need for an alternative means of establishing and regaining that "link to home" that was missing. A reliable way to get people's important mail safely to its destination, and to allow them to enjoy a "taste of home" in their adopted country. That need finally took shape in Aerocasillas, twelve years ago.

Envisioned as becoming "The best personalized network for receiving and sending documents and merchandise between the rest of the world and our country," this way both national and international markets were opened to our clients.

Pioneering the field of private international mail service in this country, Aerocasillas has built a growing user base of 25,000 satisfied customers, with over 3,000 active accounts. This is the result of over twelve years of constant dedication to fulfilling the needs of our clients and seeking ways to improve on the service we provide.

Aerocasillas is based in Costa Rica but has a sister company in Panama.

EDUCATION

How to Learn Spanish

Although many of Panama's well-educated people speak English (and many English-speaking foreigners live permanently in Panama), Spanish is the official language. Anyone who seriously plans to live or retire in Panama should know Spanish. Frankly, you will be disadvantaged, handicapped, and be considered a foreigner to some degree, without Spanish. Part of the fun of living in another country is communicating with the local people, making new friends, and enjoying the culture. Speaking Spanish will enable you to achieve these ends, have a more rewarding life, and open the door for many new, interesting experiences. Knowing some Spanish also saves you money when you're shopping and, in some cases, keeps people from taking advantage of you.

If you take our advice and choose to study Spanish, for a modest fee you can enroll at one of Panama's intensive conversational language schools. In addition to language instruction, most of these schools offer exciting field trips, interesting activities and room and board with local families—all of which are optional. Living with a family that speaks little—or preferably no—English is a wonderful way to improve your language skills, make new friends, and learn about Panamanian culture at the same time.

Spanish is not a difficult language to learn. With a little self-discipline and motivation, anyone can acquire a basic Spanish survival vocabulary of between 200 and 3000 words in a relatively short time. Many Spanish words are similar enough to English, so you can guess their meanings by just looking at them. The Spanish alphabet is almost like the English one, with a few minor exceptions. Pronunciation is easier than in English because you say words as they look like they should be said. Spanish grammar is somewhat complicated, but can be made easier if you are familiar with English grammar and find a good Spanish teacher. Practicing with native speakers improves your Spanish because you can hear how Spanish is spoken in everyday conversation. You will learn many new words and expressions not ordinarily found in your standard dictionary.

Watching Spanish television and listening to the radio and language cassettes can also improve your Spanish. We suggest that if you have little or no knowledge of spoken Spanish, you purchase the one-of-a-kind Spanish Survival book and accompanying cassette advertised in this book. Although it was written for learning Costa Rican style Spanish, most of the material is applicable to Panama. It is designed especially for people planning to retire or live in any Central America country. It makes learning easy because the student learns the natural way, by listening and repeating as a child does—without the complications of grammar. If you are interested in a deeper study of Spanish, we are including a list of language schools at the end of this section. Please check first with the school of your choice for current prices.

Super Tips for Learning Spanish
by Christopher Howard M.A.

1) Build your vocabulary. Try to learn a minimum of five new words daily.

2) Watch Spanish TV programs. Keep a note pad by your side and jot down new words and expressions. Later use the dictionary to look up any words and expressions you don't understand.

(3) Pay attention to the way the locals speak the language.

(4) Listen to Spanish music.

(5) Talk with as many different Spanish speakers as you can. You will learn something from everyone. Carry a small notebook and write down new words when you hear them.

(6) Read aloud in Spanish for five minutes a day to improve your accent.

(7) Try to imitate native speakers when you talk.

(8) Don't be afraid of making mistakes.

(9) Practice using your new vocabulary words in complete sentences.

10) When you learn something new, form a mental picture to go along with it—visualize the action.

11) Try to talk in simple sentences. Remember, your Spanish is not at the same level as your English, so simplify what you are trying to say.

12) If you get stuck or tongue-tied, try using nouns instead of complete sentences.

13) Remember Spanish and English are more similar than different. There are many cognate (words that are the same of almost the same in both languages).

14) Learn all of the basic verb tenses and memorize the important regular and irregular verbs in each tense.

15) Study Spanish grammar, but don't get bogged down in it.

16) Read the newspaper. The comic strips are great because they have a lot of dialog.

17) It takes time to learn another language. Don't be impatient. Most English speakers are in a hurry to learn foreign languages and get frustrated easily because the process is slow. Study a little bit everyday, be dedicated, persist and most of all enjoy the learning process.

¡Buena suerte! Good luck!

Getting a Head Start
by Christopher Howard M.A.

If you are seriously considering moving to a Latin American country, you should begin to study Spanish as soon as possible.

Here are a few suggestions that will give you a head start in learning the language. Look for some type of Spanish course that emphasizes conversation as well as grammar and enroll as soon as possible. University extension, junior colleges, and night schools usually offer a wide range of Spanish classes.

You should also consider studying at a private language school like Berlitz if there is one near where you reside. Many of these schools allow the students to work at their own pace.

Another excellent way to learn Spanish, if you can afford it, is to hire a private language tutor. Like private schools this type of instruction can be expensive, but is very worthwhile. The student has the opportunity of working one-on-one with a teacher and usually progresses much faster than in a large group situation.

If you happen to reside in an area where there are no schools that offer Spanish classes, you should go to your local bookstore and purchase some type of language cassette. This way, at least you will have a chance to learn correct pronunciation and train your ear by listening to how the language is spoken.

Listening to radio programs in Spanish and watching Spanish television are other ways to learn the language if you are fortunate enough to live in an area where there are some of these stations.

You can also spend your summer or work vacations studying Spanish in Mexico or Costa Rica. This way you will experience language in real life situations. These language vacations can be enjoyable and rewarding experiences.

Finally, try befriending as many native Spanish speakers as you can who live in the area where you reside. Besides making new friends, you will have someone to practice with and ask questions about the language.

By following the advice above and making an effort to learn the language, you should be able to acquire enough basic language skills to prepare you for living in a Spanish speaking country. Best of all, you will acquire the life-long hobby of learning a new language in the process.

Excellent Books for Learning Spanish

Costa Rica Spanish Phrasebook, by Thomas B. Kohnstamm.Lonely Planet. A handy pocket-size book for Costa Rica.

Costa Rica Spanish Survival Course, and 90 minute cassette by Christopher Howard. Costa Rica Books. A books of basic survival Spanish with a sections on Costa Rican idioms. A 90 minute cassette is included for pronunciation purposes.

Madrigal's Magic Key to Spanish, by Margarita Madrigal. Dell Publishing Group , 666 Fifth Ave, New York, NY 10103. Provides an easy method of learning Spanish based on the many similarities between Spanish and English. This book is a "must" for the beginner.

Open Door to Spanish - A Conversation Course for Beginners by Margarita Madrigal. Regent Publishing Company. (books 1 and 2). Two other great books for the beginner.

Spanish for Gringos, by William C. Harvey. Barron's Press. This is an amusing book that will help you improve your Spanish.

Breaking Out of Beginning Spanish, by Joseph J. Keenan. University of Texas Press. This helpful book is written by a native English speaker who learned Spanish the hard way. It contains hundreds of practical tips.

Barron's Spanish Idioms, by Eugene Savaia and Lynn W. Winget. This book has more than 2,000 idiomatic words and expressions. It is a helpful handbook for students of Spanish, tourists, and business people who want to increase their general comprehension of the language.

Guide to Spanish Idioms, by Raymond H. Pierson. Passport Books, 4255 West Touchy Ave, Chicago, Illinois, 60646. Contains over 2,500 expressions to help you speak like a native.

Barron's Basic Spanish Grammar, by Christopher Kendris. An in-depth study of Spanish grammar.

Nice n' Easy Spanish Grammar, by Sandra Truscott. Passport Books. Basic grammar.

A New Reference Grammar of Modern Spanish, by John Butt and Carmen Benjamin. NTC Publishing Group. This one of the best reference books ever written in Spanish grammar. It is very easy to use and understand.

Talk Spanish Today, 2470 Impala Dr., Carsbad, CA 92008. Call 800-748-54804.

Barron's 1001 Pitfalls in Spanish, by Julianne Dueber. This guide points to the most common errors students make and shows how to correct them.

Barron's Spanish Vocabulary, also by Julianne Dueber. A good book for building vocabulary.

Household Spanish, by William C. Harvey. Barron's Press. A user-friendly book especially for English-speakers who need to communicate with Spanish-speaking employees.

Useful Reference Books

Dictionary of Spoken Spanish Words, Phrases and Sentences. Dover Publications Inc., New York, NY. ISBN 0-486-20495-2. This is the best of all phrase dictionaries. We recommend it highly.

Cassell's Spanish Dictionary -New World Edition by Anthony Gooch and Angelica García de Paredes. Macmillan Publishing Company., Inc. An excellent Spanish dictionary.

Webster's New World Spanish Dictionary, by Mike Gonzalez. Prentice Hall. Also covers Latin American usage.

The New World English/Spanish Dictionary, by Salvatore Ramondino. A Signet Book. Another excellent dictionary of Latin American Spanish.

Latin-American Spanish Dictionary, by David Gold. Ballantine Books. A good dictionary of Spanish used in Latin America.

The type of Spanish spoken in Panama is basically standard Castilian Spanish except for one big difference which confuses beginning students.

You will notice that Panamanians frequently use local expressions called *panameñismos* (See the list in this chapter) that are not used in other Latin American countries. You will be shocked hearing this expression used so frequently in everyday conversation.

A trait of the Panamanians is the common use of *don* (for a man) and *doña* (for a woman) when addressing a middle age or older person formally. These forms are used with the first name — as in the case of the famous *"Don Juan."* However, you will usually hear the more traditional *señor* or *señora* used instead of *don* or *doña*.

Language Schools

IIERI has an excellent conversational program offering total immersion Spanish, flexible schedules, small classes, technical Spanish for business people, and more. Altos del Chase, El Dorado, Vía Amistad, Casa 42-G, Tel/Fax: (507) 260-4424.

Spanish Learning Center of Panama offer Spanish for Academic Purposes, Spanish for Business Purposes, Spanish for Medical Purposes, Spanish Immersion Spanish Exam Preparation, Small Classes (5 or less per class), One-to-One / Private Lessons and home stays with friendly Panamanian families. Tel: (507) 213-3121 or 697-3863 E-mail: spanishlearning@hotmail.com info@spanishpanama.com or see www.spanishpanama.com

Berlitz Language Center Anastasio Ruiz-Edificio Plaza Balboa Bay Local 3, Panama City Panama Tel: (507) 265.4800

AmeriSpan Unlimited located in Altos de Chases, an upper- middle class residential section that is peaceful and safe.

Frequently Used Panameñismos
(Panamanian Expressions)

Amachinarse - Sad, discouraged
Arrecostarse - To sponge off another person
Babosada - Stupid thing
Bocinche -Gossip
Cacharpa - An old beat-up car
Confianzudo - Abusive person
Cuentear - To lie
Cupo - Available space in a bus
Chanchada - an evil act
Chicha - an alcoholic drink made of fermented corn
Chirola - Slang for jail
Desplatado - Without money
Embolatar - To party
Emparrandarse - Also to party
Encomienda - A postal package
Enganche - A job, work
Engomado - To have a hangover
Escachalandrado - Poorly dressed
Ficha - A person with a dubious background
Fondeado - Someone who has money
Fregar - To bother someone
Fregón - Someone who bothers a lot
Fulo - A person who has red hair
Gallina - A coward person
Gallo - An intelligent man
Garrotera - A beating
Guacho - type of rice-based dish
Guaracha - a type of dance
Guarapo -Sugar Cane juice
Habladera - A lot of conversation
Hartón - A person who eats a lot
Huesear - To be lazy, loaf

Hueso - A job, work
Jabonada - A verbal attack
Jardín - A kind of bar and dancehall
Joder - To bother someone
Jopo - Someone's butt
Juega de vivo - Brag or act cool
Jumado - Drunk
Lambisconería - Praise
Lavada - Insult
Leche - Lucky
Lechudo - A lucky person
Loquear - To act crazy or do something crazy
Loro - A person who talks a lot
Marcareal - A jail cell
Machetear - Criticize
Malgeniado - In a bad mood
Mangajo - A person who doesn't dress well
Manilla - A type of baseball mitt
Matasano - A funny name for doctor
Menjurje - A type of brew or mixture
Mergolla - Money
Mieditis - Fear
Molote - A big uproar or scandal
Mordida - A type of bribe
Moquilloso - A person with a runny nose
Muérgano - A good for nothing person
Negrear- To treat a person disparagingly
Pachuco - A wide type of pants
Paparruchada - Something stupid
Parqueadero - A parking lot
Pava - a cigarette butt
Vaina - is a commonly used word for everything. The closet translation in English is 'thing."
Wachiman or *Guachiman* - A watchman or guard

* Courtesy of *La Prensa* newspaper

Only a few minutes away is Centro Comercial El Dorado, an area with good shopping and an active night-life. 4 hours daily instruction (20 hrs/week), small group instruction (max 4), private room with host family P.O. Box 40007 Philadelphia, PA 19106-0007 United States Tel: 800-879-6640

See the Yellow Pages for more schools under Idiomas.

Panama's Universities

If you wish to continue your education, university level courses are available to foreigners in subjects such as business, art, history, political science, biology, psychology, literature, and Spanish, as well as all other major academic areas.

Panama has four main universities. The **University de Panamá** is the largest university in the country and official university of the Republic. Its main campus is located in Panama City's El Cangrejo section. It also operates six smaller campuses in other provinces of the country. The **Technological University** (Tel: 236-0444), also know as *La Tecnología*, has its main campus in Panama City and several smaller regional campuses in Chiriquí (Tel:775-4563), Bocas del Toro (758-8373), Azuero (966-8448), Coclé (997-9623), Colón (473-0337), La Chorrera (244-0377) and Veraguas (999-3991).

The **Universidad Santa María** la Antigua (Tel: 230-4011) is a private catholic university with campuses in Panama City and Colón. **La Universidad Latina de Panamá** (Tel: 230-8600, E-mail mercadeo@ns.ulat.ac.pa or see www.ulst.ac.pa) offers excellent MBA and doctorate programs in marketing, banking, finance, human resources, and business administration. There are regional campuses in David (Tel: 774-3737), Santiago (Tel: 998-5412) and Chitré (Tel: 996-1179). They even offer group and individual Spanish classes for foreigners. Their classes emphasize conversation, vocabulary and grammar. Five levels are offered and the duration of each class is six weeks.

Other private universities offering a broad range of studies are: **ULACIT** (Tel:2245377, E-mail: admision@ulacit.ac.pa), Universidad **INTER AMERICANA** (Tel: 263-7787, Fax: 263-3688) and **Interamericana de Educación a Distancia de Panamá** or **UNIEDPA** (Tel: 227-2902.). The latter offers extension classes in Chiriquí, Herrera, Veraguas, Darien, Colón, Penonome, and Tonosi.

Fort Clayton is a former U.S. military base located near the Panama Canal's Miraflores Locks.

Today Fort Clayton has been transformed into the **City of Knowledge** or *Ciudad de Saber.*

Panama has many outstanding universities.

The campus is located on 120 hectares and includes 300 buildings with classrooms, conference centers, housing for hundreds of students, a restaurant, day-care center, and a pool and gym.

The former base is now becoming an international center for technology and research. Many university programs—especially in the sciences—have their eye on this new campus as a place to study abroad since the infrastructure and facilities are already in place. Foreign students may study ecology, biology, environmental studies, and sustainable development. Ciudad de Saber offers classes in Spanish and English so local students may have access to a high-quality education without leaving their home country.

Florida State University offers an international program. For more than forty years, the Panama Campus of the university has provided study toward associate and bachelor's degrees for thousands of U.S. and international students. One of Central America's safest and most hospitable countries with Panama City the region's major international trade center-Panama abounds with opportunities for international learning and research. Students earn an American degree in a Latin American, bilingual/bicultural environment that combines the study of science, business, language, and history. The beautiful campus of Florida State University-Panama borders the Pacific end of the Panama Canal. For more information phone 850-644-3272.

Private Schooling

For those of you with children, Panama has many public schools, numerous private bilingual schools, and an English-language, or American schools.

Public schools tend to be crowded and even have two sessions per day to accommodate the large number of students.

Legal foreign residents are entitled to attend public schools. All public schools and most private schools operate on the Panamanian school year which is from March to December. All students from pre-kinder to twelfth grade are required to wear uniforms in both public or private school. However, since all instruction is in Spanish, you should not even think of enrolling your children in a public school unless they speak, read, and write Spanish fluently. If your children are not Spanish speakers you may have to enroll them in a private school.

The **International School of Panama** was founded in 1982 by a group of interested parents from the Panamanian and International community. It is a non-profit private Junior-Kinder-through-12th grade school offering innovative English-language based education. Panama's private English-language school is exceptional, has high academic standards, and is accredited in the U.S. by the Southern Association of Colleges and Schools.

This school is academically oriented and prepares students for admittance to colleges in the U.S. as well as in Panama. English is taught as a primary language and Spanish is offered as both a primary and second language.

In some ways this school is better than similar institutions in the U.S.A. because not as many harmful distractions or bad influences exist in Panama. Children also have the opportunity to learn a new language, which is great value to them.

The International School of Panama is located in the eastern suburbs of Panama City. All classrooms are spacious and air-conditioned. The school has a library/media center and high speed Internet connection. The academic year runs from early August, ends in early June, and is divided into two semesters. For additional information: Tel: (507) 266-7862, Fax: (507) 266-7808, E-mail: isp@isp.edu.pa or see www.isp@edu.pa.

It is a good idea to visit any school before deciding if it is right for your child. You should ask to visit a couple of classrooms as well as see all of the facilities. This way you may view the school's infrastructure. Make a list of the pros and cons of each school before making your final decision. Find out about the teacher-student ratio. Be sure to see what percentage of the students graduate and go on to universities in Panama and the U.S. Finally, try to talk to other foreigners who have children enrolled in private schools to see if they are satisfied with the quality of education their children are receiving.

We talked with one couple from the U.S. who did not have the resources to afford a private school so they opted for home schooling.

A Panamanian private school

They recommended several programs which you can find on the Internet: **www.calvertschool.edu**, **www.unl.edu** and **www.keystonehighschool.com**.

Other private schools are:

Academia Interamericana
Tel: (507) 271-0012

Balboa Academy
Tel: (507) 211-0035
www.balboaacadeyweb.com

British International School
Tel: (507) 316-4085

Colegio Episcopal de Panamá
Tel: (507) 223-4836

Colegio Internacional SEK
Tel: (507) 220-2046

Colegio Nuestra Señora de Lourdes
Tel: (507) 231-0389

Colegio María Inmaculada
Tel: (507) 260-4616

Colegio San Agustín
Tel: (507) 271-4590

Escuela Franco Panameña
Tel: (507) 226-8356

Escuela Montessori de Panamá
(507) 226-1596

Instituto Episcopal San Cristóbal
Tel: (507) 224-4665

Instituto Italiano Enrico Fermi
Tel: (507) 226-2002

Instituto Tecnológico Barú
Tel: (507) 221-3221

Oxford International
Tel: (507) 265-6422

Panamerican Bilingual School
Tel: (507) 266-6513

Saint George de Panama
Tel: (507) 220-4585

St. Mary's School
Tel: (507) 315-0725

The King's School
Tel: (507) 265-6565

The Lincoln Academy
Tel: (507) 223-4666

The Oxford School
(507) 321-0061

To find more private schools look in the local yellow pages under *Escuelas*.

GETTING AROUND

Travel to, in, and around Panama

Most direct flights through Miami cost less, however there are flights from your home to Panama City by way of Los Angeles, New York, Washington, DC, Houston, New Orleans or Costa Rica. The airlines currently offering service from the United States to Panama City are **Aviateca** (800-327-9832), **Continental** (800-231-0856), **Delta** (800-221-1212), **Mexicana** (800-531-7921), **Grupo Taca** (800-535-8780), **American** (800-433-7300) and **United** (800-241-6522) . **Lacsa's** toll-free number is 800-225-2272 in the U.S.A. and 800-663-2444 in Canada.

Copa 800-359-2672 or www.copaair.com is the country's international airline and has flights to over 30 cities in 20 countries. They now offer direct flights to Los Angeles, Miami (2 1/2 hours), Orlando, and Newark.

Panama has two international airports: one in Panama City and the other in David. Tucumen International Airport, near Panama City, is where most international flights arrive. David's Enrique Malek Airport handles flights to and from San José, Costa Rica.

Some airline tickets are good for a year but you need permission from the **Panamanian Immigration Department** to stay in the country longer than 90 days, as a tourist or under a tourist visa. If you are planning to travel to or from Panama during December you may have to buy a ticket months in advance due to the Christmas holidays.

If you plan to travel or explore the Caribbean or South America from Panama, you can usually save money by buying a round-trip ticket to your destination. Many of the airlines mentioned above provide flights between Panama and the rest of the region. When leaving the country you have to pay a $20 departure tax. Retires pay $10.

Tico Travel (800-493-8426) specializes in tickets to Panama from the US. We highly recommend this agency for booking your trip to Panama

International Airlines Located In Panama City

Aeroflot	225-0497
Air France	223-0204
Airitalia	269-2161
American Airlines	269-6022
Aviateca	238-4015
Avianca	223-5225
British Airways	236-8335
Continental	263-9177
COPA	227-5000
Cubana	227-2122
Grupo Taca	269-6066
Iberia	227-2966
KLM	264-6395

Lacsa	265-7814
Lan Chile	226-0133
Lufthansa	269-1549
Mexicana	264-9855
TACA	257-9444
United	269-8555

Domestic Airlines

Smaller domestic airlines or charters, called air taxis are used for flights to more than 20 major large cities and towns within the country. The most you will pay is $120 for a round-trip ticket. Flights depart from Marcos A. Gelbert (Patilla) Airport in Panama City. **Aeroperlas** (Tel:269-4555) www.tacaregional.com/aeroperlas flies to David, Changuinola-Bocas del Toro, Santiago, Isla Contadora, La Palma-El Real, Darien and other destinations. Other domestic airlines are:

Aero Taxi	264-8644
Ansa	226-7891
Aviatur	270-1748

Traveling by Bus in Panama

Bus fares in Panama City and to surrounding suburbs are very cheap. To get the bus driver to stop yell *parada*.

Depending on the distance, the cost is around $.15 to $.25 per trip. It is very easy to get around the city using public transportation. Throughout the country local buses usually run from 5am to 10pm daily. However, since taxis are so affordable, we recommend you take one if you are in a hurry.

Since there is no rail road, the majority of Panamanians travel by bus to the interior of the country. For a very low cost

($2– $6, or about $1 per hour of driving time) you can take a bus to almost anywhere in the country.

Many Panamanians do not own cars, so they depend on buses for traveling to other parts of the country. Riding a bus provides the perfect opportunity to get to know people on a personal basis, see the lovely countryside, and learn something about the country and the culture. Most buses used for these longer trips are modern and very comfortable. Buses are crowded on weekends and holidays, so buy your tickets in advance or get to the station early. Be sure to check for schedule changes. Bus information may be obtained by calling 232-5803.

Bus Travel to and from Panama

If you want to travel to Costa Rica or other Central American countries, you can use the bus services listed. Buses are air-conditioned and include bathrooms for your comfort and fairly luxurious by Latin American standards.

Panama has excellent bus service.

Tica Bus (Tel: 262-2084) operates daily direct buses between Panama City and San José, Costa Rica, Nicaragua, and on to San Salvador. **Panaline** (Tel: 262-1618) also provides a similar service.

Panama's Taxis

Panama's taxis do not have meters as in to her countries. So remember to discuss the price first to avoid problems. Nevertheless, taxis are affordable. In Panama City, taxi drivers charge by zones. The official rate is $1.00 per zone plus $.25 for each additional person. Tipping the driver is not required. If you have a lot of places to visit, it is better to hire a taxi by the hour for about $7.00.

Taxies are plentiful and can be found around every public square and park, outside discotheque, on most busy streets, and in front of government buildings and most hotels. Be careful since many taxis parked in front of hotels may overcharge. It is better to stop one on the street. Some of the drivers claim they work exclusively for the hotel and will overcharge you.

Taxis may be found all over Panama City

They will try to double the fare to account for driving back to the hotel.

Many times the explanation is fair and the driver is honest. If you have a complaint and the driver works for the hotel, you have immediate recourse, the hotel's management.

There are also Tourist Taxis or *taxi de turismo*. They are air-conditioned and generally cost $5 within the city. If you rent them by the hour, the charge is around $10.

Taxis are almost always available except during the rainy season, especially in the afternoon when it usually rains. You may also have trouble getting a cab on weekdays during rush hour between 7 a.m. and 9 a.m. and 4:30 p.m. to 6:30 p.m.— as in most cities. It is also sometimes very difficult to find a taxi late at night or during the Christmas holiday season.

To hail a taxi just yell, "Taxi!" If a taxi is parked just say *libre* (free) to the driver to see if a cab is available. If the taxi is available, he will usually nod or say, *sí* (yes). If you want to stay on a taxi driver's good side, NEVER slam the taxi's doors.

If you call a taxi, be able to give your exact location in Spanish so the taxi driver knows where to pick you up. Be sure to give your exact location and mention cross streets and important landmarks. If your command of Spanish is limited, have a Spanish speaker write down directions to your destination. We know one old grouchy gringo who has never made an effort to learn a word of Spanish. He has all the directions of the places he has to go written in Spanish for taxi drivers.

Listings for taxis in Panama City can be found in the phone book. Here is a list of some of the taxi companies:

America	221-1865
El Parador	223-7694
Latino	226-7313

San Cristóbal...221-8704
Setsa...221-8594
Union Servicio Unico...221-4074
Radio Taxi Omega..229-0101
El Dorado..260-4505

Automobile Rentals

Major international car rental agencies and private car rentals are conveniently located all over Panama City. Most rental agencies operate like those in the United States. The cost of renting a vehicle depends on the year, model, and make of car. Rental rates are higher than the US. Expect to pay up to $100 for a four-wheel drive vehicle. It is a highly advisable to purchase full coverage auto insurance, which covers accidents and car theft.

Always phone or make arrangements for car rentals well in advance. For a list of car rental agencies, see the yellow pages.

Avis...264-0722
Budget..263-8777
Dollar...270-0355
Hertz..264-1111
National..264-8277
Thrifty..264-2613
Toyota..223-6085

Driving in Panama

You may use your current driver's license for up to 90 days if you are a tourist. After 90 days you must get a Panamanian driver's license. At present foreigners can obtain a Panamanian license if they possess a valid U.S. license. All permanent residents and retires must have a Panamanian license to drive in Panama.

It is relatively easy to obtain a license if you meet the requirements. In order to obtain a license you will have to have an immigration visa, a passport, valid license from your home country, and pay a fee. You will then have to take a short blood test and take the results to the **Ministerio de Gobierno**. Your license will be good for the duration of your visa.

Whether you are renting a car or using your own automobile, always keep the proper documents in your car. Every vehicle should have a copy of the official Panama driving manual, a flashlight, and first-aid kit. If a policeman should stop you, above all be polite, stay calm, and do not be verbally abusive. Most traffic police are courteous and helpful. However, if you commit a traffic violation, some policemen will try to have you pay for your ticket on the spot. Be advised this is not the standard procedure. If this happens to you, there are two offices where you can complain. Finally, if you are involved in a traffic accident, **do not move your car** and be sure to contact the local traffic police. This is important for insurance purposes. Also call the **Policía de Tránsito** to report an accident at tel: 232-5614.

Always remember to use your seat belt since driving without it may get you a ticket.

Be very careful when driving in Panama City or any other city. Many streets in Panama are narrow, one-way, and very crowded due to heavy traffic. Most streets' names are on small blue signs on the sides of buildings. Some streets do not even have signs. Also be forewarned that Panamanians often do not come to a complete stop at stop signs.

There is some car theft in Panama. To discourage thieves you should always park your car in your garage or public parking lots. If you park on the street make sure there is someone like a guard who can watch your car. Always lock your car and set the alarm system.

When driving in the countryside, drive only during the day, watch out for livestock, and be sure to use some kind of map. Do not get off the main paved road unless absolutely necessary during the rainy season if your car does not have four-wheel drive. You may end up getting stuck in the mud.

While driving in the countryside watch out for motorcycle policeman with radar. They are on the look out for speeders.

If you're thinking of driving from the US, see Chapter 4 for all of the details.

Driving Times from Panama City

LOCATION	DISTANCE (miles)	TIME
Colón	17	30 minutes
Portobello	65	1 hour 40 minutes
Chorrea	20	40 minutes
Chame	48	1 hour 15 minutes
San Carlos	58	1hour 35 minutes
El Valle	78	2 hours 5 minutes
Santa Clara	73	1 hour 55 minutes
Antón	84	2 hours 10 minutes
Penonomé	94	2 hours 25 minutes
Natá	115	2 hours 53 minutes
Aguadulce	122	3 hours 1 minute
Divisa	133	3 hours 16 minutes
Santa María	136	3 hours 20 minutes
Parita	149	4 hours 10 minutes
Pesé	166	4 hours 10 minutes
Chitré	157	3 hours 50 minutes
Los Santos	159	3 hours 55 minutes
Guararé	172	4 hours 15 minutes
Las Tablas	175	4 hours 20 minutes
Pocrí	190	4 hours 50 minutes
Pedasí	203	5 hours 20 minutes
Ocú	152	3 hours 46 minutes
Atalaya	156	3 hours 51 minutes
Santiago	155	4 hours 25 minutes
Soná	184	5 hours 15 minutes

Tolé	218	5 hours 40 minutes
Remedios	243	6 hours 25 minutes
San Félix	231	4 hours 55 minutes
San Lorenzo	248	5 hours 20 minutes
David	274	6 hours
Boquete	299	6 hours 45 minutes
Concepción	284	6 hours 5 minutes
Volcán	309	6 hours 55 minutes
Cerro Punta	319	7 hours 15 minutes
Puerto Armuelles	330	7 hours 7 minutes
Costa Rican Border	307	6 hours 32 minutes

Keeping Your Bearings Straight

Panama City extends about 6 miles along the Pacific coast, with Panama Bay to the south, The Panama canal to the west, Forest to the north, and the ruins of Panama Vieja on the east. In Panama City the avenues run parallel to the coast, with streets running perpendicularly. The city has three almost parallel streets which run east to west. Avenida Balboa runs along the Pacific Ocean and eventually turns inland at the ruins of Panama Viejo. Vía Transístmica leads out of the city to Colón. Vía España is located between Avenida Balboa and Vía Transístmica and is lined with shopping malls, restaurants, and more. The city is divided into dozens of neighborhoods. Be aware that some streets change names all of a sudden.

Be careful when trying to find your way around since many of the streets have several names. Therefore, it is easier to refer to landmarks like a church or specific building to get your bearings. The locals use known landmarks to get around, to locate addresses, and give directions. For example, in finding a house someone might say, "From Saint Paul's Church, 200 meters west and 300 meters south." If you are unfamiliar with this system, it is almost impossible to find your way around, and easy to get lost. Do not worry, after you have lived in Panama City awhile, you will get used to this system. In the event you get lost, you can always ask Panamanians for directions—provided you understand a little Spanish or they

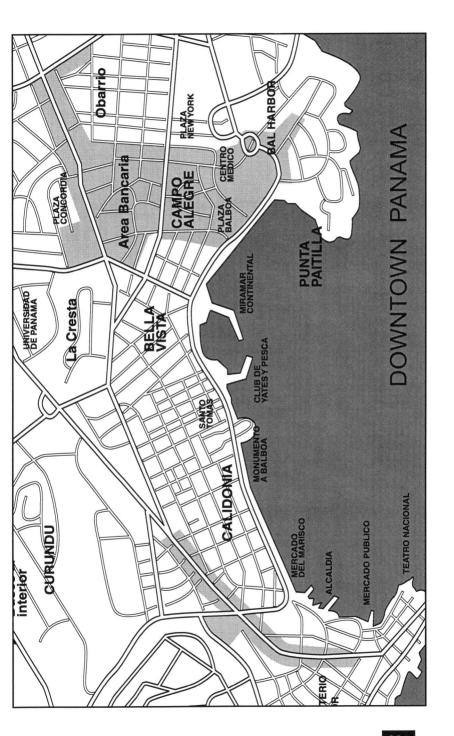

DOWNTOWN PANAMA

speak some English.As you know, Panamanians are generally very friendly and are usually happy to help you find the address you are looking for. However, it is always a good idea to ask a second person, because most Panameños are embarrassed to admit they do not know an address and will sometimes give you directions whether they know where you want to go or not.

Boat Travel

In the Bocas del Toro, San Blas Islands, and Archipelago de las Perlas, boat travel is the main means of transportation. Many ferry trips are offered from Panama City to isla Taboga and Isla Contadora. Boat tour of the canal may even be arranged. The **Balboa Yacht Club** Tel: 228-5794 or 228-5196 is the in-place for propel interested in boating. However, the new **Flamenco Yacht Club** Tel: 314-0665 marina@fuerteamador.com or see www. fuerteamador.com at the end of the Amador Causeway really puts it to shame. The place is in a absolutely beautiful setting with a view of Panama City's skyline in the distance. The facilities are first-class. There is a duty-free shop, a small shopping center and a night club located in an old U.S. bunker nearby. The drive to the marina along the causeway is really breathtaking.

The Amador Marina with Panama City in the background

MORE USEFUL INFORMATION

Where to find Affordable Foods

A wide variety of delicious tropical fruits and vegetables grow in Panama. It is amazing that every fruit and vegetable you can think of besides some exotic native varieties flourish here. Do not be surprised if you see some fruits and vegetables with which you are unfamiliar. More common tropical fruits such as pineapples, *mangos* and *papayas* cost about a third of what they do in the United States. *Bananas* can be purchased at any local fruit stand or street market for about five cents each.

Once you have lived in Panama, you can do as the locals do and eat a few slices of mouth-watering fruit for breakfast at one of the many sidewalk *fruterías* or fruit stands all over the country.

Besides fruits and vegetables, many other bargain foods are available in Panama. Bakeries sell fresh homemade breads and pastries. Supermarkets are much like markets in the U.S.; everything is under one roof, but the selection of products is smaller. There are even 24-hour mini-markets in gas stations like the 7-Eleven or Circle-K types found in the U.S.

Some imported packaged products can be found in supermarkets. Since most foods are so affordable in Panama, you will be better off changing your eating habits and buying more local products to keep your food bill low. The major supermarkets, replete with products are found all over Panama. **Super Xtra, Super 99** and **Supermercados Rey** are the largest supermarket chains in Panama. **Pricesmart** (Tel: 265-2311) has four locations in Panama and offers warehouse-style shopping like Costco in the U.S. Just as in the U.S., some stores are open 24 hours a day.

A few words about Panama's excellent seafood. With oceans on both sides, the country has a huge variety of fresh seafood. Tuna, dorado, *corvina* (sea bass) abound as well as lobster, shrimp of all sizes and some crab. Rainbow trout from the country's mountain streams are also available. Ceviche is a type of raw marinated fish dish which is widely consumed.

Panama has many U.S. style supermarkets

Ceviche de Corvina
(Marinated White Seabass)

1 lb. seabass, cut in small pieces
3 tablespoons onion, finely chopped
1 tablespoon celery, finely chopped
2 tablespoons fresh coriander, chopped
2 cups lemon juice
Salt, pepper and Tabasco Sauce
1/2 teaspoon Worcester Sauce

Combine all ingredients in a glass bowl. Let it stand for at least four hours in the refrigerator.
Serve chilled in small bowls topped with catsup and soda crackers on the side. Serves 8.

TRES LECHES
(Three Milk Cake)

Cake Base
5 eggs
1 teaspoon baking powder
1 cup sugar
1/2 teaspoon vanilla
1 1/2 cups of flower
Preheat oven at 350 F. Sift baking powder. Set aside. Cream butter and sugar until fluffy. Add eggs and vanilla and beat well. Add flour to the butter mixture 2 tablespoons at a time, until well blended. Pour into greased rectangular Pyrex dish and bake at 350 F for 30 minutes. Let cool. Pierce with a fork and cover. For the filling combine 2 cups of milk, 1 can of condensed milk and one can of evaporated milk. Pour this mixture over the cool cake. To make the topping, mix 1 1/2 cups of half & half, 1 teaspoon vanilla and a cup of sugar. Whip together until thick. Spread over the top of the cake. Keep refrigerated. Serves 12.

Panama has a large selection of delicious typical dishes from which to choose. *Gallo Pinto* is a breakfast dish consisting of rice and beans. *Carimañolas* is a delicious pastry made with yucca, flour, and filled with chopped meat and deep-fried. *Empanadas* are pastries made from yellow corn meal, and stuffed with meat. *Hojaldres* are puffy tortillas made with wheat flour and come in a variety of shapes. *Tasajo* is smoked, dried beef. *Patacones* are fried green slices of plantain. *Ropa Vieja* is one of Panama's most popular meat dishes. *Sancocho* is a type of stew made with vegetables and spices. *Tamales* are made with corn with chicken or pork and wrapped in banana leaves. *Casado* is a standard dish usually consisting of rice, black beans, fried plantain and cabbage.

Bocas are side dishes, usually served free in bars with each drink you order.

Natural fruit juice drinks are very popular in Panama. *Chicheme* is a local drink made from corn and milk. *Guarapo* is a sugar cane juice based drink. Another popular beverage is a *resbaladera*, which is made from oatmeal and milk.

Beer as well as other alcoholic beverages are very popular in Panama. Some of the best beers are Balboa, Cristal, and Atlas.

Restaurants

Panama's diverse culture is reflected in its wide variety of cuisine. Throughout Panama's history it has welcomed immigrants from all over the world. Those who came to build the canal brought their own rich culinary traditions. Today Panama City offers a variety of restaurants with different dishes to satisfy the most sophisticated gourmet tastes and pocket book.

In all there are over 200 restaurants in Panama City. You can find authentic Spanish, Columbian, Mexican, Greek, Korean, Japanese, Chinese, Indian, French, Swiss Italian food,

American food, as well as Panama's traditional dishes mentioned above.

Panama's dinning scene is dominated by a large number of seafood restaurants.

The international fast food chains have a strong presence in the Panama City area. Dairy Queen, Pizza Hut, McDonald's, KFC, Burger King, Subway, Popyes Chicken, Wendy's, and others can be found in several locations. Unlike the States, most of these fast food places offer home delivery.

Health conscious people will be pleased to know that Panama has a couple of vegetarian restaurants.

Fast food restaurants are all over Panama City

Here is a partial list of Panama City's better restaurants:

Angel (Spanish and seafood)..............................263-6411
Bar/Restaurant 1985 ((French seafood).............263-8541
Benihana (Japanese)..263-9817
Café du Liban (Lebanese) 212-158
Churrasceria (Brazilian and International) 213-1554
Crostini (Italian) 270-0477
El Casco Viejo (French).....................................223-3306
El Meson del Prado (Spanish)...........................260-9227
El Patio Mexicano (Mexican)............................236-4878
El Pavo Real (European) 269-0504
El Trapiche (Panamanian food) 269-4353
Evergarden (China)...270-7552
Fiesta Mexicana(Mexican) 260-2317
Korea House (Japanese and Korean) 223-0176
La Cascada (Seafood and meats)......................262-1297
La Cocotte (French)...213-8250

Friday's is a favorite with the locals.

La Fonda Antioqueña (Columbian). 221-1268
Las Bovedas (Seafood/French) 228-8068
Las Tinajas (Panamanian) 269-3840
La Toja (Seafood). 269-3004
Madame Chang (Chinese and Tai) 269-1313
Mangos Bar & Grill (American) 264-6484
Marbella (Seafood) 225-9065
Mexico Colonial (Mexican) 226-1093
Monsoon (Southeast Asian) 270-0477
Ozone Café (International) 214-9616
Portobello Room (French and Panamanian) 269-5000
Portofino (Italian) 264-7006
Rincon Suizo (Swiss and Seafood) 263-8541
Sushi-Itto (Japanese) 265-1222
Steinbocck (German). 270-2784
The Wine Bar (Good wine, food and live music)

Religion

Although 90% of Panamanians are Roman Catholic, there is freedom of religion and other religious views are permitted. Episcopal, Baptist, Greek Orthodox, 7th Day Adventist, Methodist, Mormon, Pentecostal, Hundu, and Jewish people all have their respective houses of worship in the Panama City area. Look in the "Yellow Pages" to find the house of worship of your choice.

Panama's Holidays

Panamanians are very nationalistic and proudly celebrate their official holidays, called *feriados*. Plan your activities around these holidays and do not count on getting business of any kind done since most government and private offices will be closed. Like other countries in Central America, the whole country shuts down and everyone takes off work during *Semana Santa* (the week before Easter) and the week between Christmas and New Year's Day. It's important to know these dates so you can plan around them.

January 1	New Year's Day
January 9	Martyr's Day
February/March	Carnival Tuesday
March /April	Holy Week, Holy Thursday, Good Friday and Easter Sunday
May 1	Worker's Day
August 15	Founding of Old Panama
October 12	Columbus Day - Discovery of America
November 1	National Anthem Day
November 2	All Saints' Day
November 3	Independence Day -Separation of Panama from Colombia in 1903
November 4	Flag Day (Government holiday only)
November 10	First Call for Independence
November 28	Independence from Spain, 1824
December 8	Mother's Day
December 25	Christmas Day

Bringing Your Pet to Panama

We did not forget those of you who have pets. There are procedures for bringing your pets into the country that require very little except patience, some paperwork, and some fees.

List of requirements:

(1) Rabies vaccination

(2) Health certificate which has to be authenticated by a Panamanian Consulate. A registered veterinarian from your hometown must certify that your pets are free of internal and external parasites. It is necessary that your pet has up-to-date

vaccinations against rabies (The rabies vaccination must NOT be older than one year). It is also good idea to have the vet provide certificates stating your animal has been vaccinated against distemper, leptospirosis, hepatitis, and parvovirus within the last three years.

(3) One week before your pet's arrival you must arrange permission for a "home quarantine." A letter has to written to the Ministry of Health with the age and type of animal, the owners complete name, where the animal will live, and the owner's passport number.

(4) In order to avoid quarantine, a vet at the airport in Panama should confirm that the pet is in good health. You will need to have a vet meet your flight.

(5) Fees for this service are $130.00, payable to "Banco Nacional de Panama" at the airport in Panama.

For more information you may contact the airport in Panama at 011-507-262-2132 or any Panamanian Consulate in your home country.

If you are bringing an exotic animal to Panama —parakeet, macaw or other—you will need special permits .

If the animal is traveling with you as part of your luggage, the average rate is $50 U.S. from one destination to the next (i.e. Los Angeles—Miami—Panama City). If your pet travels alone, depending on size and weight, the average rate is between $100 to $200 U.S. Please consult your airline for the actual price. Call the 800 toll-free cargo section of American Airlines and they will tell you the cost.

Whether your pet is traveling with you or separately, be aware that the weather can delay your animals arrival in Panama. If the temperature is above 85 degrees or below 40 degrees at either your point of departure or a layover, your animal will not be able to travel. We know of several people who have arrived at the airport only to find out their animals could not travel due to a change in the weather. Call your airline the day you intend to ship your animal and again an hour or two before departure to see if your animal will be allowed to travel. This way you can avoid unpleasant surprise Also make sure your dog or cat has an airline approved portable kennel. These rules are very strict and the kennel must be the appropriate size for your animal or it will not be allowed to travel. Some airlines rent kennels. Make sure your kennel has a small tray so your pet can have food and water during the journey. Two to eight hours is a long time to go without food or water.

If there is a layover in Miami, the baggage handlers will give water to your pet. The operator at American Airlines told us about a special service which will walk your dog for an extra charge at some airports. Some people suggest tranquilizing dogs and cats when shipping them by plane. We talked to our vet when we were going to ship our large Siberian husky, and he did not seem to think it was a good idea. We also asked a friend who ships show dogs all over the U.S. and he said to use our own judgment since tranquilizers can make an animal ill.

If you want to take your pet out of Panama you will need a special permit, a certificate from a local veterinarian and proof that all vaccinations are up-to-date. When you obtain these documents, take them to the Ministry of Health and your pet is free to leave the country. You will need to include the following information in for the pet's exit papers: The name of the owner, pet's name, breed, weight a certificate from the vet, and your passport number. The day you leave, plan on being at the airport at least two and a half hours early, since all your pet's papers must be stamped before departure.

By the way, there are many veterinarians in Panama. A visit ranges between $15 and $25 depending on what type of services are provided. Most vets will make house calls. To find a veterinarian, look under *veterinaria* in the yellow pages or talk to friends who have pets. They also offer laboratories, a pharmacy and more. Some vets offer boarding services if you have to go on a trip and have nobody to take care of your animals. Prices run around $10 per day.

Here is a partial list of veterinarians

Clínica Veterinaria Brazil	221-6910
Clínica Veterinaria Los Andes	237-6860
Clínica Veterinaria"Benji"	261-4170
Veterinaria K-NINO	236-7131
Clínica Veterinaria Mundo Animal	261-7995
Clínca Veterinaria San Antón	223-0784
Clínica Veterinaria Sao Paulo	277-6377
Clínica Veterinaria Tocana	221-6443
Super Pet	226-5766
Clínica Veterinaria Pet Saloon	229-9233
Pet Fashion	315-1910
Hospital Vterinaria	226-1454
Clínica Veterinaria Melo (David)	777-1009

Understanding the Metric System

If you plan to live in Panama, it is in your best interest to understand the metric system. You will soon notice those automobile speedometers, road mileage signs, the contents of bottles, and rulers are in metric measurements. Since you probably did not study this system when you were in school and it is almost never used in the U.S., you could become confused.

To Convert:	To:	Multiply by:
Centigrade	Fahrenheit	1.8 then add 32
Square km	Square miles	0.3861
Square km	Acres	247.1
Meters	Yards	1.094
Meters	Feet	3.281
Liters	Pints	2.113
Liters	Gallons	0.2642
Kilometers	Miles	0.6214
Kilograms	Pounds	2.205
Hectares	Acres	2.471
Grams	Ounce	0.03527
Centimeter	Inches	0.3937

* Courtesy of *Central America Weekly*.

FINAL THOUGHTS AND ADVICE

Personal Safety in Panama

Panama is the safest place in Central and South America and the Pinkerton Global Intelligence Agency recently gave Panama the highest rating for tourist safety. In fact, living in Panama is much safer than residing in most large cities in the United States or Latin American countries, but you should take some precautions and use common sense to ensure your own safety. Remember you should be careful in any third world country.

In Panama, the rate of violent crimes is very low, but there is a problem with theft, especially in the larger cities. Thieves tend to look for easy targets, especially foreigners, so you cannot be too cautious. Make sure your house or apartment has steel bars on both the windows and garage. The best bars are narrowly spaced, because some thieves use small children as accomplices as they can squeeze through the bars to burglarize your residence.

Make sure your neighborhood has a night watchman if you live in the city. Some male domestic employees are patient and often watch a residence for a long time to observe your comings and going. They can and will strike at the most opportune moment.

You should take added precautions if you live in a neighborhood where there are many foreigners. Thieves associate foreigners with wealth and look for areas where they cluster together. One possible deterrent, in addition to a night watchman, is to organize a neighborhood watch group in your area.

If you leave town, get a friend or other trustworthy person to house-sit.

Mountain areas offer some spectacular views and tranquility but are less populated and usually more isolated. This makes them prime targets for burglars and other thieves. We have a friend who moved to a beautiful home in the hills, but was burglarized a couple of times. Out of desperation he had to hire a watchman and buy guard dogs. Unfortunately, a few weeks later he was robbed while doing an errand in town. This is the down side to living off-the-beaten-path.

If you are really concerned about protecting your valuables, you will be better off living in a condominium complex or an apartment. Both are less susceptible to burglary due to their design and the fact that, as the saying goes, there is safety in numbers.

Private home security patrols can provide an alarm system and patrol your area for a monthly fee. There are a few companies which specialize in security systems for the home and office. Some even offer very sophisticated monitored surveillance systems.

If you own an automobile, you should be especially careful. Thieves can pop open a locked trunk and clean it out in a few minutes. Make sure your house or apartment has a garage with iron bars so your car is off the street.

When parking away from your house, always park in parking lots or where there is a watchman. He will look after your car for a few cents an hour when you park it on the street. It is not difficult to find watchmen since they usually approach and offer their services as soon as you park your car.

Never park your vehicle or walk in a poorly lit area. Avoid walking alone at night, and during the day stay alert for pickpockets. Pickpockets like to hang around bus stops, parks, and crowded marketplace.

Panama City is safer than most capital cities. Use common sense and stick to well traveled areas and keep alert for pickpockets. The city of Colón has a crime problem, so it is wise to use a taxi to get around the city. You should never flaunt your wealth by wearing expensive jewelry or carrying cameras loosely around your neck since they make you an easy mark on the street. Keep a good watch on any valuable items you may be carrying. It is advisable to find a good way to conceal your money and never carry it in your back pocket. It is best to carry money in front pockets. It is also a good idea to always carry small amounts of money in several places, rather than all your money in one place. If you carry large amounts of money, use travelers checks. Be very discrete with your money. Do not flash large amounts of money in public. Every time you finish a transaction in a bank or store, put away all money in your purse or wallet before going out into the street.

Be aware of who is around you and what they are doing. Thieves often work in teams. One will distract you while the other makes off with your valuables. Never accept help from strangers and ignore and never accept business propositions or other offers from people you encounter on the street. Never pick up hitchhikers.

Men should also watch out for prostitutes, who are often expert pickpockets and can relieve the unsuspecting of their valuables before they realize it.

If you are a single woman living by yourself, never walk alone at night. If you do go out at night, be sure to take a taxi or have a friend go along.

White-collar crime exists in Panama and a few dishonest individuals—Americans, Canadians, and Panamanians included—are always waiting to take your money. Over the years many unscrupulous individuals have set up shop here. We have heard of naive foreigners losing their hard-earned savings to ingenious scams. Con men prey on newcomers. One crook bilked countless people out of their money by selling a series of non-existent gold mines here and abroad. He is still walking the streets today and dreaming up new ways to make money.

One "dangerous breed of animal" you may encounter are some foreigners between 30 and 60 years of age who are in business but do not have pensions. Most of them are struggling to survive and have to really hustle to make a living in Panama. In general they are desperate and will go to almost any means to make money. They may even have a legitimate business but most certainly will try to take advantage of you to make a few extra dollars. The majority of the complaints we hear about people being "ripped off" are caused by individuals who fit this category.

On your first trip to Panama be overly cautious. Be wary of blue ribbon business deals that seem too good to be true, or any other get-rich-quick schemes—non-existent land, fantastic sounding real estate projects, phony high-interest bank investments, or property not belonging to the person selling it. If potential profit sounds too good to be true, it probably is.

Always do your homework and talk to other expats before you make any type of investment. There seems to be something about the ambience here that causes one to trust total strangers. The secret is to be cautious without being afraid to invest. Before jumping into what seems to be a once-in-a-lifetime investment opportunity, ask yourself this question: Would I make the same investment in my hometown? Do not do anything with your money in Panama that you wouldn't do at home. A friend and long-time resident here always says jokingly when referring to the business logic of foreigners who come to Central American countries, "When they step off the plane they seem to go brain dead."

Most people in Panama are honest, hard-working individuals. But don't assume people are honest just because they are nice. Remember it does not hurt to be overly cautious.

If you are robbed or swindled under any circumstances, contact the police.

Life As An Expatriate

Throughout this book we have provided the most up-to-date information available on living and retirement in Panama. We have also provided many useful suggestions to make your life in Panama more enjoyable and help you avoid inconveniences. Adjusting to a new culture can be difficult for some people. Our aim is to make this transition easier so you can enjoy all the marvelous things Panama offers.

Before moving permanently to Panama or any other country, we highly recommend spending some time there on a trial basis to see if it is the place for you. We are talking about a couple of months or longer, so you can experience Panamanian life as it is. Remember visiting Panama as a tourist is quite another thing from living there on a permanent basis. It is also good to visit for extended periods during both the wet and dry seasons, so you have an idea of what the country is like at all times of the year. During your visits, talk to many retires and gather as much information as possible before making your final decision. Get involved in as many activities as you can during your time in the country. This will help give you an idea of what the country is really like.

The final step in deciding if you want to make Panama your home, is to try living there for at least a year. This should be sufficient time to get an idea of what living in Panama is really like and what problems may confront you while trying to adapt to living in a new culture. It may also let you adjust to the climate and new foods. You can learn all the do's and don'ts, ins and outs, and places to go or places to avoid before making your final decision.

You may decide to try seasonal living for a few months a year. Many people spend the summer in the U.S. or Canada and the winter in Panama (which is its summer), so they can enjoy the best of both worlds—the endless summer.

Whether you choose to reside in Panama on a full or part-time basis, keep in mind the cultural differences and new customs. First, life in Panama is very different. If you expect all things to be exactly as they are in the United States, you are deceiving yourself. The concept of time and punctuality are not important in Latin America. It is not unusual and not considered in bad taste for a person to arrive late for a business appointment or a dinner engagement. This custom can be incomprehensible and infuriating to North Americans, but will not change since it is a deeply rooted tradition.

As we previously mentioned, bureaucracy often moves at a snail's pace in Latin America, which can be equally maddening to a foreigner. In addition, the Latin mentality, machismo, apparent illogical reasoning, traditions, different laws, and ways of doing business, seem incomprehensible to a newcomer.

Getting Past Culture Shock

Unlike twenty years ago, the majority of people (especially travelers) know the term Culture Shock. However, there still exists an "it won't happen to me" attitude in many who move overseas. The symptoms can be severe, including difficulty sleeping, loss of appetite, paranoia, and depression. Denial of the possibility of Culture Shock and ignorance of its symptoms can result in increased difficulty in adjustment to a new life overseas. A basic understanding of the reasons why it happens and what you can do about it are essential when making an international transition.

Culture shock occurs when people find that their ways of doing things just don't work in the new culture. It is a struggle to communicate, to fulfill the most basic needs, and many find that they are not as effective or efficient as before in their jobs and in their personal lives. All this loss of competence threatens a person's sense of identity. The abilities and relationships that we relied on to tell us who we are, are absent and we find ourselves a little lost in our new homes. To reestablish our selves in a new context requires proactive planning in a number of different areas of life.

There are four basic areas of Culture Shock, like four legs to a chair. They are the physical, intellectual, emotional, and social. To have the smoothest possible transition, one needs to employ a balanced approach in each of the areas.

After a transition such as an overseas move, the rhythms of everyday life are interrupted, including our exercise and eating habits. Often people neglect their exercise regiment because they don't know where to find a gym or they don't feel safe running or exercising in public places. Similarly, diets are neglected or some begin drinking too much alcohol. The way that our bodies feel physically directly affects our emotional health. A healthy diet and consistent exercise can help balance our emotional lives when confronting the difficulties of an international move.

The second area of concern is the intellectual dimension. When we step into a new culture we often find that we understand very little about the local customs and history. Due to our lack of understanding we sometimes assume that people think like us and value the same things we do. Reading and inquiring about the history and the culture of Panama can help one to see things from a Panamanian's perspective and develop greater empathy for their culture and ways of thinking.

Tending to emotional needs when moving overseas will help us to weather the ups and downs of the adjustment period. Finding people that are in similar positions that you can talk to and confide in helps to alleviate some of the loneliness that one feels. Also, when a person begins to feel down, sometimes they are listening to negative "tapes" in their head. One's "tapes" consist of the things we tell ourselves or the conversations that we have in our own mind. The negative tapes need to be consciously changed to positive hopeful messages. From "I am a failure and I hate this place" to "things are getting better every day." It may seem somewhat Pollyanna, but it really works.

Finding a group of friends, learning the language, and getting involved in clubs or activities helps to fill the social needs that we have when changing our latitude. This requires time and dedication, especially if one wants to meet locals. Meeting locals is essential for long-term happiness overseas, but it can take a long period of time and a great deal of proactive planning. It may sound harsh, but it's important to remember that the locals don't really need you. They have their families and friends from their whole lives. You need to insert yourself in their lives.

In my time working with people in international transition I have seen may cases of fabulous success, but I have also seen many spectacular failures. If a person develops a plan and proactively carries it out, it is very probably that you will find success and happiness in your new Latin home.

Eric Liljenstolpe is President and founder of the GLOBALSOLUTIONS GROUP (GSG), an organization based in San José, Costa Rica, committed to enhancing intercultural understanding. GSG offer seminars and workshops to help people during the cultural adjustment process. You can check out upcoming events and learn more about what GSG offers at www.gsgintercultural.com.

You will notice countless other different customs and cultural idiosyncrasies after living in Panama for a while. No matter how psychologically secure you are, some culture shock in the new living situation will confront you. The best thing to do is respect the different cultural values, be understanding and patient, and go with the flow. Learning Spanish will ease your way.

The fastest way to fit in with the locals is to speak the native language. You don't have to be fluent in Spanish. The locals will recognize your interest; doors will open and friendships will blossom.

Whatever you do try to avoid being the Ugly American. We know cases where Americans have caused themselves a lot of problems by their obnoxious behavior and by trying to impose their American ways on the locals.

You should also read *Survival Kit for Overseas* **Living** by L. Robert Kohls, Intercultural Press, P.O. Box 700, Yarmouth, Maine 04096. This guide is filled with useful information about adjusting to life abroad.

Panama is an exciting place to live, but poses many obstacles for the newcomer. Don't expect everything to go smoothly, or be perfect at first. By taking the advice we offer throughout this book, and adjusting to the many challenges, you should be able to enjoy all of the country's wonders.

Our recommendation is don't burn your bridges or sever your ties with your home country, you may want to return home.

Finally, try taking the adaptability test on page 245 to see if you are suited for living abroad.

STEPS FOR IMPORTING ARMS/HANDGUNS

We have received numerous requests from people wanting to relocate about Panama's handgun laws. First check with your airline about their policy on packing guns in your luggage.

1) Power of attorney and request document submitted through a lawyer, with fiscal/legal stamps in the amount of $4.00 indicating in detail what it is that you are importing, what is the exact use of your weapon, and why it is needed.

2) You will only be authorized to import a maximum of three weapons every five years.

(3) A legal decree No. 2 dated January 2, 1991 Article 19.

(4) A copy of your personal I.D. with a picture authenticated by the Civil Registry.

(5) A bill of sale for your arm or handgun.

(6) A brochure about the arm/handgun (Translated into Spanish).

(7) A copy of a gun permit issued by the PTJ (Judicial Technical Police).

(8) Your police record

Time

Panama is on Eastern Standard Time and an hour ahead of the rest of Central America.

M.R.T.A. Overseas Living Adaptability Test

Using the figures 1 (below average), 2 (average) or 3 (above average), ask yourself the following questions and rate your answer accordingly. Couples should take the test separately. As you take the test, write your selected numbers down, then add them together. When completed, refer to the Score Comments Box at the bottom of this page.

1) Open to new adventures
    select one: 1 2 3
2) Flexible in your lifestyle
    select one: 1 2 3
3) Enthusiastic to new things in a new and different culture
    select one: 1 2 3
4) Able to make and enjoy new friends:
    select one: 1 2 3
5) Willing to learn at least basic phrases in a new language
    select one: 1 2 3
6) Healthy enough mentally and physically not to see family, friends and favorite doctor for occasional visits
    select one: 1 2 3
7) Confident enough to be in a "minority" position as a foreigner in a different culture
    select one: 1 2 3
8) Independent and self-confident enough not to be influenced by negative and often ignorant comments against a possible move to a foreign country
    select one: 1 2 3
9) Patient with a slower pace of life
    select one: 1 2 3
10) Usually optimistic
    select one: 1 2 3
11) Eager to travel to a new country
    select one: 1 2 3
12) Open mind to dealing with a different type of bureaucracy
    select one: 1 2 3
13) Understand enough to look at things in a different light without being critical and accepting the differences
    select one: 1 2 3
14) Financially stable without needing to work
    select one: 1 2 3

Score Comments:	
Your Score	Evaluation
37-45	Great move abroad
30--36	Will have a few problems
22-32	Some problems but possible
Less than 22	Forget it, stay home!

Courtesy of Opportunities Abroad. This test taken from the book "Mexico Retirement Travel Assistance." To order write M.R.T.A., 6301 S. Squaw Valley Rd., Suite 23, Pahrump, NV 89648-7949

23 Things Every Prospective Expatriate Should Know

by Shannon Roxborough

When moving to a foreign country, making adequate pre-departure preparations is essential. Here are some tips to make your international move easier.

1) Be sure to undergo a complete medical check-up before leaving to avoid dealing with a major health issue overseas.

2) Take one or more advance trips to your destination to familiarize yourself. It's worth the investment.

3) Take the appropriate documents on the advance trip to start the immigration paperwork. Consulate personnel in the country can secure the visa and residency permit more efficiently than those working thousands of miles away.

4) If you have dependent children, in your pre-departure research, be thorough in seeking the availability of education in your host country.

5) Make sure you and your family understand the country's culture so that they know what will be accepted in terms of volunteer and leisure activities at your new home.

6) In case of health emergencies, make sure you know good health-care providers and how to contact them.

7) Use a travel agency for booking en-route travel so you may search for low-cost fares.

8) Check into purchasing round-trip tickets for en-route travel. They may be less expensive than one-way. And the return ticket may be used for other travel.

9) Remember the sale of your Stateside home increases year-end tax costs due to lost interest deduction.

10) Cancel regular services and utilities. Pay the closing bill for garbage collecting, telephone, electricity, water, gas, cable TV, newspapers, magazines (or send them a change of address), memberships such as library and clubs, store accounts (or notify them that your account is inactive), and credit or check - cashing cards that will not be used.

11) Leave forwarding address with the Post Office or arrange for a mail forwarding service to handle all your U.S. mail.

12) Give notice to your landlord or make applicable arrangements for the sale of your home.

13) Have jewelry, art, or valuables properly appraised, especially if they will be taken abroad. Register cameras, jewelry and other similar items with customs so that there will be no problem when reentering the U.S.

14) Make sure a detailed shipping inventory of household and personal effects (including serial numbers) is in the carry-on luggage and a copy is at home with a designated representative.

15) Obtain extra prescriptions in generic terms and include a sufficient supply of essential medicine with the luggage.

16) Obtain an international driver's license for all family members who drive. Some countries do not recognize an international driver's license but they issue one of their own, provided you have a valid home country license. Bring a supply of photographs as they may be required in the overseas location for driver's licenses and other identification cards.

17) Bring a notarized copy of your marriage certificate.

18) Arrange for someone to have power of attorney in case of an emergency.

19) Close your safety deposit box or leave your key with someone authorized to open it if necessary.

20) Notify Social Security Administration or corporate accounting department (for pensions) where to deposit any U.S. income. Make sure the bank account a d routing numbers are correct.

21) Bring copies of the children's school transcripts. If they are to take correspondence courses, make arrangements prior to departure and hand-carry the course material.

22) At least learn the Language basics prior to going to a foreign country. Trying to integrate with the new culture without the ability to communicate can be frustrating if not impossible.

23) Learn about the country's people and way of life before moving there. Go to your library, call your intended destination's tourism board and read all of the travel publications (magazines and travel guidebooks) you can to educate yourself.

Though this short article only provides a brief overview of the essentials, use it as a guide to prepare yourself for a smooth transition abroad.

Useful Resources:
Transitions Abroad Magazine 800 293-9373
A Guide to Living Abroad 609-924-9302

INDISPENSABLE SOURCES OF INFORMATION ABOUT LIVING IN PANAMA

LIVE IN PANAMA is a time-proven company offering well-organized introductory trips from the U.S. for those people interested in moving to Panama, Nicaragua or Costa Rica. For more information contact them toll-free at: 800-365-2342 E-mail:crbooks@racsa.co.cr or see www.liveinpanama.com. All trips are organized by Christopher Howard, the author of this best-selling guidebook and renowned expert on living and doing business in Central America. He has had many years experience conducting relocation tours in Costa Rica and Nicaragua. See Chapter 1 for a sample itinerary.

RELOCATION AND RETIREMENT CONSULTANTS have helped newcomers find success and happiness in Costa Rica, Nicaragua, Panama and other Central American countries for over 15 years. They offer an extensive network of contacts and insider information for potential residents and investors. See www.liveincostarica.com or contact them at: SJO 981, P.O. Box 025216, Miami, FL 33102-5126, E-mail: crbooks@racsa.co.cr or costaricaconsultants@hotmail.com.

PANAMA RELOCATION SERVICES will assist you with everything you need to know for your move to Panama. You can find information about them at: Tel: 507-269-3431, Fax: 507-270-0687, E-mail: info@panamarelocation.com or see www.panamarelocation.com.

LIVING IN PANAMA YAHOO NEWS GROUPS - http://groups.yahoo.com/group/viviendo en panama. By joining one of these groups you can stay up with all the major news about living in Panama and different views about living in the country.

WHOSE NEW CLUB is a godsend for the newly arrived resident. A monthly newsletter is published. For information write to Apdo. 0832-3356, World Trade center, Panama R.P. or call 269-5005 or 223-4146.

USEFUL INTERNET RESOURCES

www.liveinpanama.com - Living in Panama
www.panamaretirementproperties.com - Real estate
www.amso.org - Organizations for foreigners
www.panamain-fo.com- Good source of information
www.panacham.com - More useful information
www.internationalliving.com - Investments
www.eascapeartist.com - Everything
www.ipat.gob.pa - Tourism and more
www.registro-publico.gob.pa - Property titles
www.panamarelocation.com - For expatriates
www.orcag.com - Roberto Guardia R.—Good lawyer
www.panamacham.com - Good business site
www.amsoc.org - Living in panama
www.panamainfo.com/english - general information
www.usembassy.state.gov/panama - U.S. embassy
www.businesspanama.com - Business
www.us-panama.org - Business
www.ascotadvisory.com - Investment information
www.elsiglo.com - Spanish news
www.copaair.com - Airline
www.panamatravel.com - Travel
www.explorepanama.com - Travel
www.lonelyplanet.com - General Information
www.panamainfo.com - Information
www.presidencia.gob.pa/- Government information
www.panabolsa.com - Local stock market
www.panamacity-fl.worldweb.com -Panama City
www.centralamerica.com - Good information
www.hotels4travellers.com - Hotels
www.pancanal.com - The canal

SUGGESTED READING

BOOKS

Path Between The Seas: The Creation of the Panama Canal, 1870-1914 by David McCullough The story of the Panama Canal is complex, full of heroes, villains, and victims. McCullough's long, richly detailed, and eminently literate book pays homage to an immense undertaking.

Lonely Planet Panama (Panama, 2nd Ed) by Scott Doggett. An excellent guide for tourists or future residents who want to explore the country.

Panama Now, the new edition of Panama's yearbook Focus Publications e-mail: focusint@sinfo.net. Lavishly illustrated with 28 chapters giving a vivid portrait of the country. Look for it at newsstands, in hotels and any bookstore in Panama.

Living in Panama, by Sandra T. Snyder. This guide is the perfect ccompliment to "Living and Investing in the New Panama. You should have both if you plan to make the move. To order see www.pananarelocation.com.

Getting to Know Panama by Michele Labrut. It contains a lot of information about the country. Available from Focus Publications Tel: (507) 225-6638 E-mailfocusint@sinfo.net.

Ulysses Travel Guide Panama (Ulysses Travel Guides) by Marc Rigole, Claude-Victor Langlois. This is the only other travel guidebook besides Lonely Planet's version.

Operation Just Cause: The Storming of Panama by Thomas Donnelly, et al . The authors visited each major battle site to write this authoritative and vivid account of Operation Just Cause--and offer a firsthand account of the planning, execution, and aftermath of the U.S. invasion of Panama, and the fall of General Noriega, in December, 1989

A Guide to the Birds of Panama by Robert S. Ridgely, John A. Gwynne. A bible for bird watchers.

^The Panama hat Trail by Tom Miller andTony Hillerman. The real history of the Panama hat.

How Wall Street Created a Nation: J.P. Morgan, Teddy Roosevelt, and the Panama Canal by Ovidio Diaz Espino, Ovidio Diaz Espino. With the drama of detective fiction, How Wall Street Created a Nation illustrates how a combination of financial gain and arrogant American imperialism culminated in the building of the Panama Canal.

The Building of the Panama Canal in Historic Photographs by Ulrich Keller. A good photographic account of the construction of the canal.

The Tailor of Panama by John Le Carre. The greatest spy novelist of the Cold War era, continues his post-Cold War quest to define the genre he helped perfect. The Tailor of Panama is something else entirely: a spy novel with no spies in which the bad guys reap most of the rewards.

America's Prisoner: The Memoirs of Manuel Noriega by Manuel Noriega, Peter Eisner. Noriega has a unique perspective on U.S. involvement in Latin America, and he has a heap of dirty laundry he's more than willing to air.

Ruben Blades: Salsa Singer and Social Activist (Hispanic Biographies) by Barbara C. Cruz. A thoughtful biography of the three-time Grammy-winning singer, actor, and activist.

Escape from America, by Roger Gallo. Available from: http://www.escapeartist.com. This book is a must read for anyone who wants to relocate overseas. It has the answers to all of your questions plus profiles of the best countries in which to live. We recommend this book highly.

The World's Retirement Havens, by Margret J. Goldsmith. This guide briefly covers the top retirement havens in the world. Most of the material is still current since it was published in 1999. You may obtain this guide from John Muir Publications, P.O. Box 613, Santa Fe, New Mexico 87504.

How I Found Freedom in An Unfree World, by Harry Browne, Liam Works — Dept. FB, P.O. Box 2165, Great Falls, MT 59403-2165 or toll-free 1-888-377-0417. This book will revolutionize your life.

Driving the Pan-American Highway to Mexico and Central America, by Raymond & Audrey Pritchard, $18.95. This is the only book available if you are planning to drive from the U.S. to Costa Rica via the Pan-American Highway. It is available from Costa Rica Books.

Costa Rican Spanish Survival Course, by Christopher Howard. This one-of-a-kind book comes with a 90-minute cassette to accelerate the learning process. Also good for Panama since the Spanish is similar in both countries. Also a vailable from Costa Rica Books.

A Travelers Guide to Latin American Customs and Manners, by Elizabeth Devine. Published by St. Martin's Press. This book helps the newcomer understand the Latin way of life.

PERIODICALS

The Visitor/El Visitante newspaper is published is published twice monthly and packed with entertainment information to keep you busy.

Focus on Panama published twice a year and very helpful

MOVIES

The Tailor of Panama is the recent movie version of the book.

℘ All of the titles above with an asterisk **, are also available through Costa Rica Books' mail order catalog: Suite 1 SJO 981, P.O. Box 025216, Miami FL 33102-5216. To order directly, include $3.00 postage for the first book in the U.S. (Canada $4.00, Europe $5.00) and $1.00 for each additional book. Write for more details and a complete list of our other products and prices. You may call toll-free 800-365-2342 for more information. <u>You may also order our products through</u> **www.costaricabooks.com** .

IMPORTANT SPANISH PHRASES AND VOCABULARY

You should know all of the vocabulary below if you plan to live in Panama.

What's your name?	¿ Cómo se llama usted?
Hello!	¡Hola!
Good Morning	Buenos días
Good Afternoon	Buenas tardes
Good night	Buenas noches
How much is it?	¿Cuánto es?
How much is it worth?	¿Cuánto vale?
I like	Me gusta
You like	Le gusta
Where is...?	¿Dónde está...?
Help!	¡Socorro!
What's the rate of exchange	¿Cuál es el tipo de cambio?

I'm sick	Estoy enfermo	day after	
		tomorrow	pasado mañana
where	dónde	week	la semana
what	qué	Sunday	domingo
when	cuándo	Monday	lunes
how much	cuánto	Tuesday	martes
how	cómo	Wednesday	miércoles
which	cuál or cuáles	Thursday	jueves
why	por qué	Friday	vienes
		Saturday	sábado
now	ahora		
later	más tarde	month	mes
tomorrow	mañana	January	enero
tonight	esta noche	February	febrero
yesterday	ayer	March	marzo
day before		April	abril
yesterday	anteayer	May	mayo

June	*junio*	tall	*alto*
July	*julio*	tired	*cansado*
August	*agosto*	bored	*aburrido*
September	*septiembre*	happy	*contento*
October	*octubre*	sad	*triste*
November	*noviembre*		
December	*diciembre*	expensive	*caro*
		cheap	*barato*
spring	*primavera*	more	*más*
summer	*verano*	less	*menos*
fall	*otoño*	inside	*adentro*
winter	*invierno*	outside	*afuera*
		good	*bueno*
north	*norte*	bad	*malo*
south	*sur*	slow	*lento*
east	*este*	fast	*rápido*
west	*oeste*	right	*correcto*
		wrong	*equivocado*
left	*izquierda*	full	*lleno*
right	*derecha*	empty	*vacío*
easy	*fácil*	early	*temprano*
difficult	*difícil*	late	*tarde*
big	*grande*	best	*el mejor*
small	*pequeño, chiquito*	worst	*el peor*
a lot	*mucho*	I understand	*comprendo*
a little	*poco*	I don't	
there	*allí*	understand	*no comprendo*
here	*aquí*	Do you speak	
nice, pretty	*bonito*	English?	*¿Habla usted inglés?*
ugly	*feo*		
old	*viejo*	hurry up!	*¡apúrese!*
young	*joven*	O.K.	*está bien*
fat	*gordo*	excuse me!	*¡perdón!*
thin	*delgado*	Watch out!	*¡cuidado!*

open	*abierto*	bill	*la cuenta*
closed	*cerrado*		
occupied		blue	*azul*
(in use)	*ocupado*	green	*verde*
free (no cost)	*gratis*	black	*negro*
against the		white	*blanco*
rules or law	*prohibido*	red	*rojo*
exit	*la salida*	yellow	*amarillo*
entrance	*la entrada*	pink	*rosado*
stop	*alto*	orange	*anaranjado*
		brown	*café, castaño*
breakfast	*el desayuno*	purple	*morado,*
lunch	*el almuerzo*		*púrpura*
dinner	*la cena*		
cabin	*la cabina*	0	*cero*
bag	*la bolsa*	1	*uno*
sugar	*el azúcar*	2	*dos*
water	*el agua*	3	*trés*
coffee	*el café*	4	*cuatro*
street	*la calle*	5	*cinco*
avenue	*la avenida*	6	*seis*
beer	*la cerveza*	7	*siete*
market	*el mercado*	8	*ocho*
ranch	*la finca*	9	*nueve*
doctor	*el médico*	10	*diez*
egg	*el huevo*	11	*once*
bread	*el pan*	12	*doce*
meat	*el carne*	13	*trece*
milk	*la leche*	14	*catorce*
fish	*el pescado*	15	*quince*
ice cream	*el helado*	16	*diez y seis*
salt	*la sal*	17	*diez y siete*
pepper	*la pimienta*	18	*diez y ocho*
post office	*el correo*	19	*diez y nueve*
passport	*pasaporte*	20	*veinte*
waiter	*el salonero*	30	*treinta*

40	*cuarenta*	400	*cuatrocientos*
50	*cincuenta*	500	*quinientos*
60	*sesenta*	600	*seiscientos*
70	*setenta*	700	*setecientos*
80	*ochenta*	800	*ochocientos*
90	*noventa*	900	*novecientos*
100	*cien*	1000	*mil*
200	*doscientos*	1,000,000	*un millón*
300	*trescientos*		

* If you want to perfect your Spanish, we suggest you purchase our best-selling Spanish book, "*The Costa Rican Spanish Survival Course*", and 90-minute cassette mentioned in Chapter 7. It is a one-of-a-kind pocket-sized course designed for people who want to learn to speak Spanish the Central American style Spanish.

IMPORTANT TELEPHONE NUMBERS

LONG DISTANCE WITHIN PANAMA..101
INFORMATION 102
FIRE DEPARTMENT 103
POLICE 104
TIME OF DAY..105
LONG DISTANCE INTERNATIONAL....................................106
MCI...108
AT&T (INTERNATIONAL CALLS)..109
SPRINT 115
CUSTOMER SERVICE TELEPHONE COMPANY 123
CUSTOMER SERVICE (CELL PHONES)..................................161
PHONE REPAIR..888
RED CROSS (AMBULANCE) 228-2187
PRIVATE AMBULANCE SERVICE 263-4522
PANAMANIAN SOCIAL SECURITY 229-1133
MEDICAL EMERGENCIES ....264-1739 OR 227-4122
ELECTRIC COMPANY ....800-0111 OR 315-7222
WATER COMPANY 229-3477
TOCUMEN AIRPORT..238-4322
HOSPITALS
Centro Médico Patilla 265-8800
Clínica Bella Vista. 227-1266
Hospital Pediátrico (Children's Hospital) San Fernando....229-3800
Clínica Hospital América...............................229-2221/229/1627
Clínica San Fernando 229-3800
Hospital Santo Tomás. 227-4122
Hospital Centro Médico Mae Lewis (DAVID). 775-4616
IMMIGRATION 227-1448
CHAMBER OF COMMERCE 227-1233
TOURISM INSTITUTE (IPAT) 226-7000
NATIONAL PARKS 232-7228
EMBASSIES
U.S. EMBASSY 227-1777
CANADA..264-9731
UK 269-0866
COSTA RICA 264-2937
COLOMBIA 223-3535
NICARAGUA..223-0981

Panamanian Corporation Law

CHAPTER I: Incorporation

ARTICLE 1. Two or more persons of lawful age, of any nationality even though not residing in the Republic of Panama, may, in accordance with the formalities hereinafter provided, form a corporation for any lawful purpose or purposes.

ARTICLE 2. Such persons desiring to form such a corporation shall sign articles of incorporation which shall set forth:

1. The names and domiciles of each of the subscribers of the articles;

2. The name of the corporation which will not be the same as or similar to that of another, already existing corporation so as to cause confusion. The name shall include a word, phrase or abbreviation indicating that it is a corporation, as distinguished from a person or an association of another type. The name of the corporation may be expressed in any language.

3. The general purpose or purposes of the corporation;

4. The amount of the capital stock and the number and par value of the shares into which it is to be divided; and, if the corporation is to issue shares without par value, the statements required by Article 22 of this law;

The capital stock and par value of shares of any corporation may be expressed in the legal currency of the Republic or in gold units of the legal currency of any other country, or in both;

5. If there are to be shares of different classes, the number of shares to be included in each class and the designations, preferences, privileges and voting rights or restrictions or other qualifications of the shares of each class; or a statement that such designations, preferences, privileges and voting powers or restrictions or other qualifications can be determined by resolution of the majority in interest of the Stockholders or of the majority of the Directors;

6. The number of shares of stock that each subscriber of the articles of incorporation agrees to take;

7. The domicile of the corporation and the name and domicile of its resident agent in the Republic, who may be a person or corporation;

8. Its duration;

9. The number, names and addresses of its Directors, of which shall not be less than three;

10. Any other lawful provisions which the subscribers of the articles of incorporation may desire to include.

ARTICLE 3. The articles of incorporation may be executed in any place, within or outside this Republic, and in any language.

ARTICLE 4. The articles of incorporation may be in the form of a public deed, or in any other form, provided that said articles be acknowledged by a Notary Public or by any other official authorized to make acknowledgements at the place of execution.

ARTICLE 5. If the articles of incorporation are not in the form of a public deed, they must be protocolized in the office of a Notary of the Republic.

If said document should be executed outside of the Republic of Panama, it must be authenticated by a Panamanian Consul before it is protocolized, or if there should be no Panamanian Consul, by the Consul of a country friendly to Panama. If the Articles of Incorporation are drafted in a language other than Spanish they must be protocolized with an authorized translation executed by an official or public interpreter of the Republic of Panama.

ARTICLE 6. The public deed or the protocolized document containing the articles of incorporation must be presented for registration in the Mercantile Registry.

The incorporation of the corporation shall not have effect as to third parties until articles of incorporation have been registered.

ARTICLE 7. Any corporation formed under this law may amend its articles of incorporation in any respect provided such amendments conform to the provisions of this law.

Therefore, the corporation may, by such amendment: change the number of its shares of stock or of any class of its stock outstanding at the time of such amendment; change the par value of the outstanding shares of any class having such a value; change the outstanding shares of any class having par value into the same or different number of shares of the same or a different class without par value; change the outstanding shares of a class without par value into the same or different number of shares of the same or different class having par value; increase the amount of the number of shares of its authorized stock; divide its authorized capital into classes; increase the number of classes of its authorized capital; or change the designations, rights, privileges, preferences, voting powers, restrictions or qualifications of stock. But the capital stock of a corporation shall not be reduced except in accordance with the provisions of articles 14 et seq. of this law.

ARTICLE 8. The amendments shall be made by the persons designated hereinafter and in the manner provided in this law with respect to the execution of the articles of incorporation.

ARTICLE 9. Amendments to the Articles of Incorporation made before stock has been issued shall be signed by every subscriber of the articles of incorporation and by every subscriber to the stock of the corporation.

ARTICLE 10. In case stock has been issued, such amendments to the articles of incorporation shall be signed:

(a) By the holders of all the outstanding shares of the corporation entitled to vote thereon, in person or by proxy, and shall be accompanied by a certificate of the Secretary or an Assistant Secretary of the corporation stating that the persons who have executed said amendments, in person or by proxy, constitute the holders of all the outstanding shares of the corporation entitled to vote thereon; or

(b) By the President or a Vice-President and the Secretary or an Assistant Secretary of the corporation, who shall sign and annex thereto a certificate stating that they have been authorized to execute said amendments by resolution adopted by the owners or their proxy of a majority of such shares and that such resolution was adopted at a stockholders meeting held on the date specified in the notice or waiver of notice.

ARTICLE 11. In case the amendments to the Articles of Incorporation alter the preferences of outstanding shares of any class or authorized shares having preferences which are in any respect superior to those of outstanding shares of any class, such certificate mentioned in

Article 10 (b) shall state that the officers signing the same document have also been authorized to execute such amendments to the Articles of Incorporation by resolution, adopted in person or by proxy of the holders of a majority of the outstanding shares of each class entitled to vote thereon, adopted at a stockholders' meeting held on a date specified upon notice or waiver of notice.

ARTICLE 12. If the articles of incorporation require more than a majority of the outstanding shares of any class or classes in order to effect any amendment of any provision of the articles of incorporation, the certificate referred to in paragraph (b) of article 10 shall state that such amendment has been authorized in that manner.

ARTICLE 13. Unless the articles of incorporation or any amendment thereof otherwise provide, in the event of an increase of stock, each stockholder shall have a pre-emptive right to subscribe, in proportion to the number of shares then held by him, the shares of stock issued pursuant to such increase.

ARTICLE 14. Any corporation may reduce its authorized capital stock by an amendment of its articles of incorporation; but no distribution of assets may be made pursuant to any such reduction, which will reduce the actual value of its remaining assets to an amount less than the total amount of its debts and liabilities plus the amount, as reduced, of its issued capital stock.

There shall be annexed to the amendment to the articles of incorporation a certificate, issued under oath by the President or a Vice-President and of the Treasurer or an Assistant Treasurer, stating that no distribution of assets made or to be made pursuant thereto will violate the provisions contained in this article.

In the absence of fraud, the judgment of the Directors as to the value of the assets, and their determination of debts and liabilities, shall be conclusive.

ARTICLE 15. Any corporation, unless its articles of incorporation otherwise provide, may acquire shares of its own stock by purchase or otherwise. If such acquisition or purchase is made out of funds or properties other than the surplus or the net profits of the corporation, the shares of stock so purchased or acquired shall be canceled and the amount of issued stock of the corporation shall be reduced accordingly; but such shares may be reissued if the authorized capital stock s have been reduced by such retirement.

ARTICLE 16. Shares of its own stock acquired by any corporation out of its surplus or net profits may be held by such corporation, or sold or otherwise disposed of from time to time for its corporate purposes and may be retired or reissued by the Board of Directors.

ARTICLE 17. No corporation shall directly or indirectly vote any shares of its own stock.

ARTICLE 18. No corporation shall purchase or otherwise acquire its own stock out of fund or property other than its surplus or net profits, if such purchase or acquisition will reduce the actual value of its assets to an amount less than the total amount of its debts and liabilities plus the amount of its issued capital stock so purchased or acquired. In the absence of fraud, the judgment of the Directors as to the value of the assets, and their determination of the debts and liabilities, shall be conclusive.

CHAPTER II: Corporate Powers

ARTICLE 19. Every corporation organized in accordance with this law shall have, in addition to other powers specified in this law, the following powers:

1. To sue and be sued in any court;

2. To adopt and use a corporate seal and alter the same at its convenience;

3. To acquire, purchase, hold, use and convey real and personal property of all kinds and make and accept pledges, leases, mortgages, liens and encumbrances of all kinds;

4. To appoint officers and agents;

5. To make contracts of all kinds;

6. To make by-laws not inconsistent with any existing laws of the Republic or its articles of incorporation, for the management, regulation and government of its affairs and property, the transfer of its stock and the calling and holding of meetings of its stockholders and directors, and for all other lawful matters;

7. To carry on business and to exercise its powers in the Republic and foreign countries;

8. To dissolve itself or to be dissolved in accordance with the law;

9. To borrow money and contract debts in connection with its business or for any lawful purpose; to issue bonds, notes, bills of exchange, debentures and other obligations and evidences of indebtedness (which may or may not be convertible into stock of the corporation) payable at a specified time or times or payable upon the happening of a specified event or events whether secured by mortgage, pledge or otherwise or unsecured for money borrowed or in payment for property purchased or acquired or for any other lawful objects;

10. To guarantee, acquire, purchase, hold, sell, assign, transfer, mortgage, pledge or otherwise dispose of or deal in shares of the capital stock or bonds, securities or other evidences of indebtedness created by other corporations, or of any municipality, province, state or government.

11. To do all things necessary for the accomplishment of the objects enumerated in its articles of incorporation or any amendment thereof or necessary or incidental to the protection and benefit of the corporation, and in general to carry on any lawful business whether or not such business is similar in nature to the objects set forth in its articles of incorporation or any amendment thereof.

CHAPTER III: Stock

ARTICLE 20. Every corporation shall have power to create and issue one or more classes of shares of stock with such designations, preferences, privileges, voting powers or restrictions or qualifications thereof and other rights as its articles of incorporation provide and subject to such rights of redemption as shall have been reserved to the corporation in such articles of incorporation.

The articles of incorporation may provide that shares of stock shall be convertible into the shares of other classes.

ARTICLE 21. Shares of stock may have a nominal or par value. Such shares may be issued as fully paid and non-assessable, as partly paid or without any payment having been made thereon. Unless the articles of incorporation otherwise provide, fully paid and non-assessable shares having a par value, or securities or shares convertible into such shares, shall not be issued for a consideration which, in the judgment of the Board of Directors, is less in value than the par value of such shares or of the shares into which such securities or shares are convertible. Nor shall certificates for partly paid shares state that there has been paid thereon an amount greater than the value, in the judgment of the Board of Directors, of the consideration actually paid thereon. Such consideration may be money, labor, services, or property of any kind.

In the absence of fraud, the judgment of the Board of Directors as to the value of any such consideration shall be conclusive.

ARTICLE 22. Shares of stock may be created and issued without par value provided the articles of incorporation include the following statements:

1. The total number of shares that may be issued by the corporation;

2. The number of shares, if any, with par value and the par value of each;

3. The number of shares without par value;

4. Either one of the following statements:

(a) The stated capital of the corporation shall be at least equal to the sum of the aggregate par value of all issued shares having par value plus a certain determined amount in respect to every issued share without par value plus such amounts as from time to time by resolution of the Board of Directors may be transferred thereto; or

(b) The stated capital of the corporation shall be at least equal to the sum of the aggregate par value of all issued shares having par value plus the aggregate amount of consideration received by the corporation for the issuance of shares without par value, plus such amounts as from time to time by resolution of the Board of Directors may be transferred thereto.

There may also be included in such articles of incorporation an additional statement that the stated capital shall not be less than the amount therein specified.

ARTICLE 23. Subject to the designations, preferences, privileges and voting powers or restrictions or qualifications granted or imposed in respect to any class of shares, each share with or without par value shall be equal to every other share of the same class.

ARTICLE 24. A corporation may issue and may sell its authorized shares without par value for such consideration as may be prescribed in its articles of incorporation; or for such consideration which, in the judgment of the Board of Directors, shall be the fair value of such shares; or for such consideration as from time to time may be fixed by the Board of Directors, pursuant to authority conferred in such articles of incorporation; as shall be consented to or approved by the holders of at least a majority of the shares entitled to vote.

ARTICLE 25. Any and all shares referred to in Articles 22, 23 and 24 of this law shall be deemed fully paid and non-assessable. The holders of such shares shall not be liable to the corporation or its creditors in respect thereto.

ARTICLE 26. The shares of a corporation shall be paid at such time and in such a manner as the Board of Directors may determine. In case of default in the payment, the Board of Directors may either proceed against the defaulting stockholder to enforce payment of the amounts due and unpaid and to collect such damages as the corporation may have suffered, or rescind the subscription contract in respect to the stockholder in default, having the right in this last alternative to retain for the corporation such amounts as the defaulting stockholder may be entitled to receive from the funds of the corporation.

In the event that the corporation should proceed to rescind the subscription contract in respect to the stockholder in default and to retain for the corporation the amounts to which the stockholder may be entitled, the Board of Directors shall give at least sixty days advance notice to such stockholder. Shares acquired by the corporation by virtue of the provisions of this article may be reissued or re-offered for subscription.

ARTICLE 27. Every certificate of stock shall contain the following statements:

1. The reference to the registration of the corporation in the Mercantile Registry;

2. The amount of its capital stock;

3. The number of shares owned by the stockholder or bearer;

4. The class of share, if there is more than one class, and if the stock is classified, a summary statement of the special conditions, designations, preferences, privileges, voting powers, restrictions or

qualifications that one of the classes of the shares has over the others.

5. If the shares, which it represents, are fully paid and non-assessable, the certificate of stock shall so state; and if such shares are not fully paid and non-assessable, the certificate shall state the amount or amounts which have been paid thereon;

6. If the shares are represented by certificate issued in the name of the owner, it should contain the name of said owner.

ARTICLE 28. Shares may be issued to bearer only if fully paid and non-assessable.

ARTICLE 29. Shares represented by certificates issued in the name of the owner shall be transferable on the books of the corporation in such manner and under such regulations as may be provided in the articles of incorporation or in the by-laws. But in no case shall the transfer of stock be binding on the corporation unless it shall have been registered in the corporation books.

If the stockholder shall be indebted to the corporation, the corporation may refuse to permit the transfer of his stock until such indebtedness is paid. But, in all cases, the transferor and the transferee shall be jointly liable for the payment of the amounts owed to the corporation by virtue of the shares so transferred.

ARTICLE 30. Shares issued to bearer shall be transferable by delivery of the certificate or certificates representing title.

ARTICLE 31. If so provided in the articles of incorporation, any holder of a certificate for shares issued to bearer may exchange such certificate for a certificate or certificates for a like number of shares of the same class issued in his name; and the holder of a certificate for shares issued in the name of the owner may exchange it for a certificate for a like number of shares issued to bearer.

ARTICLE 32. The articles of incorporation may provide that in case a stockholder desires to sell, transfer, or otherwise dispose of his shares of stock, the corporation or some stockholder or stockholders thereof shall have a preferential right to purchase such shares.

Any other restrictions upon the transfer or transferability of the shares may also be imposed; but any restriction absolutely preventing a stockholder from selling, transferring, or disposing of his shares of stock shall be invalid.

ARTICLE 33. A corporation may issue a new stock certificate in place of any certificate previously issued by it alleged to have been destroyed, lost or stolen. The Board of Directors may, in such cases, require the owner of the destroyed, lost, or stolen certificate to post security against any claim that may be made against the corporation or damage suffered by it.

ARTICLE 34. The articles of incorporation may provide that the holders of any designated class or classes of stock shall not be given voting rights; or they may otherwise limit or define the respective voting powers of the several classes of stock.

Such provisions of the articles of incorporation shall be controlling in all elections and in all proceedings in which the law requires the vote or the written consent of the holders of all of the shares or of a specified proportion of the shares of the corporation.

The articles of incorporation may also provide that for specified purposes the vote of more than a majority of the holders of any class of stock shall be required.

ARTICLE 35. One or more stockholders by agreement in writing may transfer stock to a voting trustee or trustees for the purpose of conferring upon it or them the right to vote thereon in the name and in place of the owner for the period and upon the terms and conditions therein stated. Other stockholders may transfer their stock to the same trustee or trustees and thereupon shall be a party to such agreement. The certificates of stock so transferred shall be surrendered and canceled and new certificates therefore issued to such trustee or trustees, in which it shall appear that they are issued pursuant to such agreement, and in the entry of such ownership in the proper books of the corporation that fact shall also be noted. In order for the provisions contained in this article be carried into effect, it will be necessary that a certified copy of such agreement be filed with the corporation.

ARTICLE 36. Every corporation organized under this law shall keep at its office in the Republic, or at such other place or places as the articles of incorporation or the by-laws may provide, a book to be known as the Stock Register, containing (except in the case of shares issued to bearer) the names alphabetically arranged of all persons who are stockholders of the corporation, showing their places of domicile, the number of shares held by each one respectively, the date of acquisition thereof, and the amount paid thereon or that they are fully paid and non-assessable. In the case of shares issued to bearer, such Stock Register shall state the number of shares so issued and the date of issue and that such shares are fully paid and non-assessable.

ARTICLE 37. Dividends may be paid to the stockholders from the net earnings of the corporation or from the surplus of its assets over its liabilities and capital stock, but not otherwise. The corporation may declare and may pay dividends upon the basis of the amount actually paid upon partly paid shares of stock.

ARTICLE 38. When the directors shall so determine, dividends may be paid in stock of the corporation, provided the stock issued for such purpose shall be duly authorized and provided, if such stock has not heretofore been issued, there shall be transferred from surplus to the capital of the corporation an amount at least equal to that for which such stock could be lawfully issued.

ARTICLE 39. Every stockholder shall be personally liable to the creditors of the corporation only to an amount equal to the amount not paid on his stock; but no action shall be brought against a stockholder for any debt of the corporation until judgment therefore has been rendered against the corporation and execution thereon has been returned unsatisfied in whole or in part.

CHAPTER IV: Stockholders' Meetings

ARTICLE 40. Whenever under the provisions of this law the approval or authorization of the stockholders is required, the notice of such stockholders' meeting shall be in writing and in the name of the President, Vice-President, Secretary or an Assistant Secretary or of such other person or persons so authorized by the articles of incorporation or the by-laws.

Such notice shall state the purpose or purposes for which the meeting is called and the time and place at which it is to be held.

ARTICLE 41. All meetings of stockholders shall be held within the Republic, unless otherwise provided in the articles of incorporation or by-laws.

ARTICLE 42. Such notice shall be given at such time prior to any such meeting and in such manner as the articles of incorporation or by-laws of the corporation provide; but unless they otherwise provide, such notice shall be given personally or by mail upon each stockholder of record entitled to vote at such meeting not less than ten and no more than sixty days before such meeting.

If the corporation has issued shares to the bearer, notice of stockholders' meetings shall be published in such manner as the articles of incorporation or by-laws provide.

ARTICLE 43. Any stockholder may waive notice of any meeting by document signed by him or his representative either before or after the meeting.

ARTICLE 44. The resolutions approved in any meeting at which all stockholders are present, in person or by proxy, shall be valid for all purposes and the resolutions approved in any meeting at which a quorum is present, notice of which shall have been waived by all absent stockholders, shall be valid for all purposes stated in such waiver, even though in either of the above-mentioned cases the notice required by this law, the articles of incorporation or the by-laws has not been given.

ARTICLE 45. Unless otherwise provided in the articles of incorporation, every stockholder of a corporation shall be entitled at each meeting of stockholders thereof to one vote for each share of stock registered in his name on the books of the corporation regardless of the class of said stock and whether it has a nominal or par value. It is hereby understood, however, that unless contrary provision should be made in the articles of incorporation, the directors may prescribe a period not exceeding forty (40) days prior to any meeting of the stockholders during which time no transfer of stock on the books of the corporation may be made, or may fix a day not more than forty (40) days prior to the holding of any such meeting as the day as of which all stockholders (other than the holders of shares issued to bearer) entitled to notice of and with the right to vote at such meeting shall be determined, in which case, only stockholders of record on such day shall be entitled to notice of or to vote at such meeting.

ARTICLE 46. In the case of shares issued to bearer, the bearer of a certificate or certificates representing such shares shall be entitled to one vote at any meeting of the stockholders for each share of stock entitled to vote at such meeting, represented by such certificate, upon presentation at such meeting of such certificate or certificates, or upon presentation of such other evidence of ownership as may be prescribed by the articles of incorporation or by-laws.

ARTICLE 47. At any meeting of the stockholders any stockholder may be represented and vote by proxy or proxies (who need not be stockholder(s)) appointed by an instrument in writing, public, or private, with or without power of substitution.

ARTICLE 48. The articles of incorporation of any corporation may provide that at all elections of directors of such corporation each holder of stock possessing the right to vote for directors shall be entitled to as many votes as shall equal the number of his shares of stock multiplied by the number of directors to be elected, and that he may cast all of such votes for a single director or may distribute them among the number to be voted for any two or more of them as he may see fit.

CHAPTER V: Board of Directors

ARTICLE 49. The business of every corporation shall be managed by a Board of Directors composed of not less than three directors, all of whom shall be male or female persons of legal age.

ARTICLE 50. Subject to the provisions of this law and of the articles of incorporation, the Board of Directors of every corporation shall have absolute control over and full direction of the affairs of the corporation.

ARTICLE 51. The Board of Directors may exercise all of the powers of the corporation except such powers that are by law, the articles of incorporation or by the by-laws, conferred upon or reserved to the stockholders.

ARTICLE 52. Subject to the provisions of this law and the articles of incorporation, the number of Directors shall be fixed by the by-laws of the corporation.

ARTICLE 53. A majority of the Board of Directors of a corporation at a meeting duly assembled shall be necessary to constitute a quorum for the transaction of business. However, the articles of incorporation may provide that a certain number of the directors, whether more or less than a majority, shall be sufficient to constitute a quorum.

ARTICLE 54. The act of a majority of the directors present at a meeting at which a quorum is present shall be the act of the Board of Directors.

ARTICLE 55. Unless otherwise provided in the articles of incorporation, no director need be a stockholder.

ARTICLE 56. The directors may make, alter, amen, and repeal the by-laws of the corporation, unless otherwise provided by the articles of incorporation, or in the by-laws adopted by the stockholders.

ARTICLE 57. The directors of every corporation shall be chosen at the time and place and in the manner provided for by the articles of incorporation or by-laws.

ARTICLE 58. Vacancies in the Board of Directors shall be filled in the manner prescribed by the articles of incorporation or by-laws.

ARTICLE 59. Subject to the provisions contained in the two foregoing articles, vacancies, whether resulting from an increase in the authorized number of directors or otherwise, may be filled by the vote of a majority of the directors then in office.

ARTICLE 60. If the directors are not elected by the specific day designated for that purpose, the directors then in office shall continue to hold their offices and discharge their duties until their respective successors shall have been elected.

ARTICLE 61. Unless otherwise provided in the articles of incorporation or in the by-laws, the Board of Directors may appoint two or more of their members to constitute a committee or committees, who shall have and exercise the powers of the Board of Directors in the management of the business affairs of the corporation to the extent and subject to the restrictions expressed in the articles of incorporation, the by-laws, or the resolutions appointing such committees.

ARTICLE 62. If the articles of incorporation so provide, at any meeting of the directors, any director may be represented and vote by proxy or proxies (who need not be directors), appointed by an instrument in writing, public, or private, with or without power of substitution.

ARTICLE 63. Directors may be removed at any time by the vote of holders of a majority of the outstanding shares entitled to vote for directors. Officers, agents, and employees may be removed at any time by resolution adopted by a majority of the directors, or in such a manner as the articles of incorporation or by-laws provide.

ARTICLE 64. If any dividend or distribution of assets be declared or paid which reduces the value of the assets of the corporation remaining after the payment of such dividend or such distribution, as the case may be, to less than the aggregate amount of its debts and liabilities, including capital stock, or if a reduction of capital stock be made, except in accordance with the provisions of this law, or if any report or statements be made which shall be false in any material representation, the directors of the corporation who assent thereto with knowledge of the impairment of the capital stock or of such falsity, as the case may be, shall be jointly liable to the creditors of the corporation for any loss or damage arising therefrom.

CHAPTER VI: Officers

ARTICLE 65. Every corporation shall have a President, a Secretary, and a Treasurer, who shall be chosen by the Board of Directors and may also have such other officers, agents, and representatives as the Board of Directors or the by-laws or the articles of incorporation may determine and who shall be chosen in the manner provided thereby.

ARTICLE 66. Any person may hold two or more offices, if so provided by the articles of incorporation or by the by-laws.

ARTICLE 67. No officer need be a director of the corporation unless the articles of incorporation or by-laws so require.

CHAPTER VII: Sale of Assets and Franchises

ARTICLE 68. Every corporation may, by action taken at any meeting of its Board of Directors, sell, lease, exchange, or otherwise dispose of all or substantially all of its property and assets, including its goodwill and its corporate franchise, upon such terms and conditions as its Board of Directors deems expedient, provided it is authorized by the affirmative vote of stockholders holding a majority of the shares entitled to voting power and given at a stockholders' meeting called for that purpose in the manner provided in Articles 40 through 44 of this law or authorized by the written consent of such stockholders.

ARTICLE 69. Notwithstanding the provisions contained in the preceding article, the articles of incorporation may require that the consent of the stockholders be expressed in a special manner in order to grant the authority referred to in said article.

ARTICLE 70. Unless the articles of incorporation provide otherwise, the vote or assent of stockholders shall not be necessary for a transfer of assets in trust, or to encumber them by pledge or mortgage to secure indebtedness of the corporation.

CHAPTER VIII: Mergers

ARTICLE 71. Subject to the provisions of their articles of incorporation, any two or more corporations organized under this law may merge into a single corporation. The Directors, or a majority of them of each of such corporations desiring to merge, may enter into an agreement signed by them, describing the terms and conditions of the merger, the mode of carrying the same into effect, and stating such other facts as are necessary to be stated in articles of incorporation and in accordance with this law, as well as the manner of converting the shares of each of the constituent corporations into shares of the new corporation, with such other details and provisions as are deemed necessary or desirable.

ARTICLE 72. The agreement may provide for the distribution of cash, notes, or bonds in whole or in part, in lieu of stock, provided, however, that upon such distribution the liabilities of the new corporation, including those derived by it from the constituent corporations and including the amount of capital to be issued by the new corporation pursuant to the terms of merger agreement, shall not exceed the value of its assets.

ARTICLE 73. Said agreement shall be submitted to the stockholders of each of the constituent corporations at a meeting thereof called separately for the purpose of considering the same, of which meeting notice shall be given in the manner required by articles 40 to 43 of this law. At said meeting said agreement shall be considered and a vote taken for the adoption or rejection of the same.

ARTICLE 74. Unless the articles of incorporation otherwise provide, if the votes of stockholders of each corporation representing a majority of the shares entitled to vote thereon shall be for the adoption of said agreement, then that fact shall be certified on said agreement by the Secretary or Assistant Secretary of each corporation; and the agreements so adopted and certified shall be signed by the President or Vice-President and Secretary or Assistant Secretary of each of said corporations in the manner and in accordance with the requirements specified in Article 2 of this law with reference to the execution of articles of incorporation.

ARTICLE 75. The agreement of merger so executed shall be filed for registration in the Mercantile Registry as required in the case of articles of incorporation and when so filed shall be the agreement and act of consolidation of said corporations.

ARTICLE 76. When such agreement of consolidation is executed and filed as required by the two preceding articles, the separate existence of each constituent corporation shall cease and the merged corporations shall become a single corporation in accordance with said agreement possessing all the properties, rights, privileges, powers, and franchises, and subject to the restrictions, obligations and duties of each of the constituent corporations; provided that all rights of creditors and all liens upon the property of either of the constituent corporations shall be preserved unimpaired, but such liens shall be limited to the property affected thereby at the time of the merger. All debts, liabilities, and duties of the constituent corporations shall appertain to the consolidated corporation and may be enforced against it to the same extent as if they had been incurred by it.

ARTICLE 77. The articles of incorporation of any corporation may provide and determine conditions, in addition to the requirements of this law, upon which such corporation may merge with any other corporation.

ARTICLE 78. Any action or proceeding pending by or against the extinguished corporations or any one of them, the consolidated corporation shall continue as a party to the action.

ARTICLE 79. The liability of corporations or the stockholders, directors, or officers thereof, or the rights and remedies of the creditors thereof or of persons doing or transacting business with such corporations shall not in any way be lessened or impaired by the merger of two or more corporations under the provisions hereof.

CHAPTER IX: Dissolution

ARTICLE 80. If the Board of Directors deems it advisable that any corporation organized under this law should be dissolved, the Board may, by a majority of the whole Board, approve an agreement of dissolution and, within the ten ensuing days, shall call or cause to be called, in the manner provided in articles 40 through 43 hereof, a meeting of the stockholders having voting power to take such action to approve or reject the resolution adopted by the Board of Directors.

ARTICLE 81. If, at such meeting of the holders of a majority of the shares entitled to vote such stockholders by resolution consent to the dissolution, copy of such resolution together with a list of the names and residences of the Directors and Officers, certified by the President or a Vice-President and the Secretary or an Assistant Secretary, and the Treasurer or an Assistant Treasurer, shall be made and executed and filed for recording in the Mercantile Registry as required in Article 2.

ARTICLE 82. Upon such filing at the Registry Office, a copy thereof shall be published in one issue of a newspaper published in the place where the office of the dissolved corporation was situated in this Republic, or if there be no such newspaper then in the Official Gazette of the Republic.

ARTICLE 83. Whenever all the stockholders with voting power consent in writing to a dissolution, no meeting of the Board of Directors or of the Stockholders shall be necessary for that purpose.

ARTICLE 84. The document setting forth such consent of the stockholders shall be protocolized and filed for record in the Mercantile Registry and published in the manner provided in Article 82 hereof. Once these formalities have been complied with, such corporation shall be deemed to be dissolved.

ARTICLE 85. All corporations, whether they expire by their own limitation or are otherwise dissolved, shall nevertheless continue to exist for the term of three years from such expiration or dissolution for the purpose of prosecuting or defending suits by or against them or enabling them to settle their business and dispose of and convey their property and to divide their capital stock, but under no circumstance may it continue the business for which said corporation was established.

ARTICLE 86. When any corporation expires by its own limitation or is otherwise dissolved, the Directors shall act as trustees of such corporation with full power to settle the affairs, collect the outstanding debts, sell and convey the property of all kinds, and divide the monies and property among the stockholders, after paying the debts of the corporation, and they shall have authority, in the name of the corporation, to sue for the recovery of its debts and property and to defend it when sued for debts owing by such corporation.

ARTICLE 87. In the case of the foregoing article, the Directors shall be jointly responsible for the debts of the corporation, but only up to the amount of the moneys and properties which have come into their control.

ARTICLE 88. The Directors shall have the power to apply monies and property of the corporation to the payment of a reasonable compensation for their services and to fill any vacancies which may occur in their number.

ARTICLE 89. The Directors, acting as trustees pursuant to the provisions of Articles 86, 87 and 88, shall act by majority vote.

CHAPTER X: Foreign Corporations

ARTICLE 90. A foreign corporation may maintain offices or agencies and carry on business in the Republic, provided it files in the Mercantile Registry the following documents for recording:

1. Deed of protocolization of its Articles of Incorporation;

2. Copy of its last balance sheet accompanied by a declaration of the amount of its capital engaged or to be engaged in business in the Republic;

3. A certificate setting forth that it is incorporated and organized under the laws of the country of its domicile authenticated by a Consular Representative of the Republic in said country, or if there be none, then by that of a friendly nation.

ARTICLE 91. A foreign corporation maintaining an office or carrying on business in the Republic of Panama which has not complied with the requirements of this law may not sue in any court of the Republic, but may be sued therein. Any such corporation shall furthermore be liable to a fine of up to FIVE THOUSAND BALBOAS (B/.5,000.00) to be imposed by the Secretary of Finance and the Treasury.

ARTICLE 92. A foreign corporation carrying on business in the Republic which has recorded its articles of incorporation in the Mercantile Registry according to this law, shall be required to record in such Registry all amendments of such articles of incorporation and the instruments of consolidation or dissolution affecting it.

CHAPTER XI: Sundry Provisions

ARTICLE 93. National or foreign corporations established or having agencies or branches in the Republic at the time that this law comes into effect shall be governed insofar as refers to the contracting parties by their articles of incorporation, their by-laws, and the laws in force at the time of their organization or of their establishment in the Republic, as the case may be.

ARTICLE 94. National corporations organized before this law comes into effect may, at any time, be governed by the provisions of this law; this fact must be set forth in a resolution adopted by the stockholders, which must be recorded in the Registry Office.

The stockholders of national corporations actually dissolved but not yet liquidated may, for the purpose of the liquidation, be governed by the provisions of this article, provided that it is so resolved by a number of stockholders not less than that required by the by-laws to provide for the dissolution of the corporation before the expiration of the term fixed for such corporation.

ARTICLE 95. All the provisions heretofore in force relative to corporations are hereby repealed.

ARTICLE 96. This law shall come into effect on the first day of April, 1927.

INDEX

NOTES

NOTES